D1453320

The Strategist

The Life and Times of Thomas Schelling

How a Game Theorist
Understood the Cold War
and Won the Nobel Prize
in Economics

by ROBERT DODGE

with a foreword by Richard Zeckhauser

ISBN-13: 978-1-884186-37-0
ISBN-10: 1-884186-37-8

Printed in the United States of America.

Hollis Publishing
95 Runnells Bridge Road
Hollis, NH 03049
t: 603.889.4500 • f: 603.889.6551
books@hollispublishing .com

For Jane and Anne

Table of Contents

THOMAS SCHELLING, RICOCHET THINKER

By Richard Zeckhauser

Ramsey Professor of Political Economy, Harvard University

Thomas Schelling, in his presence as well as his work, demonstrates how readily mental models can lead you astray. This preeminent nuclear strategist—or more accurately a prevent-nuclear-war strategist—often arrives at unconventional recommendations on critical policy issues. One might expect someone broody or quirky or dark.

In fact, Schelling exudes a down-home appeal, taking delight in discussions of family and friends, hikes and trips with his wife Alice, and of a broad range of intellectual and policy issues. Everyday life offers him a major laboratory. When he thinks, he wrinkles his face, and a smile of delight slowly emerges. Those who know him smile in return, because they know they are likely in for a treat. Schelling can turn instantly incisive on a vast range of subjects in economics or politics or policy, or everyday phenomena that are puzzling to others. In the last category, he has explained that an errant mattress by the turnpike can cause a massive jam if each gawker—who has waited 30 minutes—is not unwilling to inconvenience others, and takes a mere 10 seconds.

Surely, the Nobel biography and this book got their dates wrong. Schelling, a trim crew-cut mountain climber, is certainly not in his 80s. Actually, Nature, pushing parity, simply got it right. She just decided to keep his body age in synch with his ever active mind. For incisive views on the importance and possible survival of taboos against nuclear weapons in a world where many nations, often at each others' throats, have them; or for an insightful discussion of the problem of global warming, one can do no better than to listen to Thomas Schelling's current thoughts. To learn how to think about a range of other policy issues, one should sneak into a seminar where Schelling is in the audience: At the end come the wrinkles and the smile. Next come perfect paragraphs of insight. Often Schelling relates the speakers' thoughts to other phenomena that we know well.

One Schelling motto—many are merited—might be: Strive hard to understand the everyday phenomena that you have encountered thousands of times. That will help you understand rarer or more distant phenomena that have the same structure at heart. If we understand what makes the parent's threat of no trip to Disneyland credible or not, we will have better understanding of why a tripwire in Europe might or might not work to stop a Soviet invasion. Four or five decades ago, when Schelling was focusing his laser intellect on mechanisms to avoid nuclear war with the Soviet Union, deterring the USSR was never far from the front of his mind. Yet he would often talk about how a parent threatens or makes promises to a child, or vice versa.

Schelling is the master of ricochet scholarship. He studies a real-world problem and develops a conceptual model. He then takes that conceptual model back to a dozen real-world problems to see how it applies, and then ricochets back to refine the model. He keeps the process going until he is happy with his model, and satisfied with his insights into the problems that most interest him.

Schelling is the Willie Mosconi of these intellectual caroms. None of us could approach his skill level, but all of us could learn from his example. If you are analyzing a policy, you should consider what your problem would look like in stripped down form. Look for an everyday analogue, and determine in what ways it is the same and how it is different. Go out in the real world to examine the information that participants have, the incentives that operate on them.

In the 1980s, Schelling, an ex-smoker, wanted to understand smoking behavior. For half a dozen years he ran a substantial research project that exposed him to the major empirical studies in the field, and he learned how others understood addiction processes, etc. He also worked backward from smoking behavior to study the problem of self command, and ultimately identified the problem of the "divided self": At this moment George wants to smoke, and may well do so, though last night George—in some sense a different fellow—promised to quit.

As usual, Schelling gave his essay describing such behavior a title both evocative and enticing: "The Intimate Contest for Self Command." The essay is literary. Though a strong conceptual model lay at its core, he did not bother with equations or formality, though others have added them in recent years. Indeed, more traditional economists came to Schelling's insights a couple decades later than he. In this case the subject is now labeled "hyperbolic discounting." The basic notion in both Schelling and this later work is that the immediate always is weighted heavily relative to tomorrow, even though today we do not think tomorrow should weigh so heavily against the day after. Since in one day tomorrow becomes immediate, we frequently find ourselves to be dynamically inconsistent, doing today what we promised ourselves not to yesterday. Our best laid plans are foiled, our New Year's resolutions abandoned. That is why people who prefer to quit still smoke, why so many Americans plan to save but never get around to it, and why this foreword was late to the publisher. Schelling provides the metaphor of the divided self, two people wrapped in the same body: the person who wants to eat his cake struggling with the person who promised to maintain his diet. Recent research reveals that contemplation of or receipt of immediate payoffs registers in different areas of the brain than news on payoffs to be reaped in the future, which helps to explain why we are so often dynamically inconsistent.

Scholars in social science also have much to learn from Schelling. Pardon me if I now state the implications of his approach for scholars in social science. In a 2006 essay on Schelling celebrating his Nobel Prize (*Scandinavian Journal of Economics*), distinguished economist Avinash Dixit advises budding economic theorists: [If incremental contributions are your goal, e.g.,] "generalizing an existence theorem by relaxing the condition of semi-strict quasi-concavity to one of mere hemi-demi-proper pseudo-concavity, then stick to the technical journals. If you want to change the field in more fundamental ways, then obtain your primary motivation from life, and use it to look for fundamental shortcomings of previous thinking in the field." Schelling is the high priest of economists who draw lessons from life. Just as Leonardo DaVinci drew remarkable figures of the human anatomy, Schelling sketches equally remarkable portraits that detail the anatomy of human interactions. For example, since the dawn of antiquity humans have engaged in threats and promises, in tacit communication. But only when Thomas Schelling took the time to puzzle out what we as sentient creatures were doing, did we come to understand the full function of these everyday practices. For example, he outlined the patterns of payoffs, and of actions to change payoffs that make cooperation more likely.

Experimental economics is now the rage in the profession. Decades before this efflorescence, Schelling conducted experiments in his classrooms and reported their results in his writings. Responding to questionnaires distributed to his classes starting in the late 1950s, Schelling's students tried to figure out where to meet each other in New York City without prior consultation. (Empirical results suggest under the clock at the Biltmore; alas this favored meeting spot is now torn down.) The students also tried to find tacit agreement on a number from 1 to 100, on one box in a matrix of boxes, etc. Thomas Schelling gave that questionnaire to my undergraduate class in 1959. Like hundreds of others in the years that followed, I became a disciple on the importance of tacit communication, which was the lesson of the exercise. In an example of contagion that must have pleased the originator, dozens of us have presented portions of the questionnaire to others, and the process continues. But Schelling was not interested in this tool merely for its brilliant pedagogy. He was conducting research that would enable him to ricochet back to the real world. He recognized that tacit communication would have to play a central role in reducing the potential for nuclear exchanges between the United States and the Soviet Union. Such communication was essential to prevent one side from launching a missile because it misperceived the other side's actions and intentions. Such communication was also required to make the deterrent threat credible.

Schelling seems to have x-ray vision when it comes to understanding the mechanics of human processes that are imperceptible to others. In his book *Micromotives and Macrobehavior,* he studied a variety of phenomena where uncoordinated individual actions—that is, people responding to micromotives—lead to outcomes that are far from what anyone desires. For example, in many a high school lunch room blacks and whites sit separately. Schelling points out that this is the inevitable outcome if members of each group find homogeneity distasteful, but prefer to sit at a table where its own members comprise a modest majority.

Over a number of years one could stop by Schelling's office at Harvard's Kennedy School and see him engrossed over a checker board covered with pennies, some heads up and some tails up. The pennies represented whites and blacks, and he moved them about to study what sort of segregation patterns develop given various types of preferences and alternative definitions of neighborhood. He was pursuing the second stage of an intellectual ricochet, from observed patterns of significant though unwanted segregation to an abstract representation of such a process on a checker board.

Schelling is quick to state that he is not a game theorist, just a thinker who uses game theory. But in fact his work anticipated many important game-theoretic concepts and models. His work on the credibility of threats and promises was the forerunner to the extraordinarily important concept of subgame perfect equilibria. Subgame perfection requires that each player follow a strategy that is optimal on a look-forward basis. He pushed us to recognize tipping phenomena. He identified the importance of focal points for facilitating cooperation and communication. Merely in doing his own work, he has provided many models that have become focal points for both scholarly analyses and policy discussions. You might say that he learned from the world, and the world learned from him, but that would be severe understatement.

I had the good fortune to have Thomas Schelling as my principal advisor for both my undergraduate and graduate dissertations, and then to have him as a close friend and colleague in the many years that followed. Like all of his students, including students who have never met him in person, I have been inspired by the clarity of his thinking, his courage in addressing difficult and controversial topics, and his unflagging belief that the best way to help the world is to identify the underpinnings of its problems. Those who know Thomas Schelling personally love him for his kind ways and his remarkable generosity in providing comments and sharing ideas. Those who know his ideas marvel at his remarkable creativity. And all, including those who have never heard of him, are indebted to him for his work in preventing nuclear war.

In the 1950s, there was much that the United States and the Soviet Union did not understand about each other or about their relationship, as they embarked on a multiple-decade adventure where either party could wreak intolerable losses on the other. This was precisely the type of relationship whose anatomy Thomas Schelling was prepared to explicate. His greatest insight was to recognize that the two great enemies were strongly interdependent, more interdependent than any two nations on earth ever had been, with a monumental joint interest in avoiding a nuclear exchange. As the pages of this book reveal, Schelling worked tirelessly for many years to prevent such a nuclear war, or indeed any other. He wrote books and articles, some at a scholarly level, others accessible to anyone with a policy interest. He worked with U.S. government agencies and non-profit groups, and he attended international conferences, both those designed to pursue particular objectives and those intended primarily to build international understanding.

When the history of the world from 1950 through 1990 is written, it will be recognized that the great historical event of the era was something that did not happen: Despite grave dangers, no nuclear weapon was launched against an enemy. The intellectual models of conflict and cooperation provided by Thomas Schelling, and his willingness to work tirelessly to get policymakers from all corners to understand their implications, deserve considerable credit for ensuring this nonevent. Today, he is seeking to extend the taboo on using nuclear weapons to a new era afflicted with dozens of potential nuclear nations, many hostile to one another.

Thomas Schelling has made remarkable contributions to scholarship by facilitating our understanding of how the world works at the levels of the individual, the dyad, and the larger group. He has provided us with deep insights into problems such as addiction, bargaining processes, and racial segregation. His greatest contribution to the world, however, is the work that he did over many years, and that continues: He helped make the world a safer place to live.

ACKNOWLEDGMENTS

I would first like to thank Tom Schelling for allowing me the chance to enter his world so personally, as I sought to bring his ideas and experiences to a larger audience. Those of us who teach history rarely get such opportunities to do more than talk second-hand about people who have played a role in shaping it. I would also like to thank his gracious wife, Alice, for her kindness and tolerance of my many interruptions in their family routine.

My gratitude I express to those listed in the sources for sharing information in interviews, letters, and emails. Special thanks for Richard Zeckhauser's contributions, both in writing the foreword and in the source materials he provided. Others who provided assistance that I would like to mention are Sarala Nair for her research aid; Siddharth Mohandas for his reading of early drafts and constructive comments; and Gretchen Needham and Robyn McCarthy for their editing of the final manuscript.

I would especially like to thank the Stockers, Tom and Pat, for their hospitality and encouragement throughout. While health hasn't always cooperated with me, I am indebted to my sister Pat for making the completion of the book possible.

Finally, thanks to my wife, Jane, for her tolerance and support.

CHAPTER 1

THE BEEP HEARD 'ROUND THE WORLD

The road to Thomas Schelling's Nobel Prize began in the fall of 1957 in the most unexpected of places. A man governed by pure reason, Schelling was unmoved by the emotions and fears gripping the times—fears of a secret *I Led Three Lives* world of "cells" and spies and a constant internal communist threat that compounded an overseas evil. Ensconced in Yale's ivory towers, Schelling was more concerned that autumn with the details of game theory

Sputnik: Traveling Companion

than with the state of world affairs. Yet halfway around the globe, monumental changes were under way that would eventually draw him onto the international stage.

"It's going to be the small one this time," Yuri thinks. Most of the men are choosing the larger one, but they're wrong. Raucous cheering erupts when the two combatants are thrown in. The fighters circle each other briefly, then attack furiously, going for the kill. Yuri was right: The big one is dead. Although the smaller one won't last long, he's clearly the winner. Sometimes the small ones kill the big ones . . . sometimes the big ones kill the small ones . . . One can never be sure with scorpions. The next two combatants are the same size, so which one would it be this time? There's one way to find out: Toss them into a glass jar together so everyone can watch.

It's not great entertainment, but few diversions are available to escape the pressures and monotony in this ultra-high security area known as the "Baikonur Cosmodrome" near the village of Tyuratam. Before long, a crowd would gather around to watch the spectacle again. Abundant in the sandy, dry flatlands of Kazakhstan, scorpions are easiest to trap on the paved road leading into the mining town of Baikonur some 200 miles away.

As he leaves the lab and retires to his boxcar for the night, Yuri doesn't feel the same sense of release from boredom he usually enjoys after the scorpion fights. He knows something is different, but Ostashev hasn't mentioned anything. Yuri's boss always lets them know when something special is going on, so they can look particularly busy in case an important official shows up. The tanks now sitting on the railroad cars look like the same ones there last May when Sergei Korolev himself was present, and those cars had held alcohol and liquid oxygen. Last May's effort was a success, so everyone on Ostashev's team knows they can repeat the process. But now Mikhail Yangel from Dnepropetrovsk is lurking around. What could that mean? Something big must be going on.

Yuri and his fellow workers will have to wait and see: Ever since construction first began at the Soviet's base at Tyuratam in 1955, secrecy has been a top priority. The base's "Site 2" houses assembly and processing materials surrounded by barracks and other living quarters, but the mystery project at "Site 1" is known to the workers only as "the stadium."

At Site 1, the pace picks up. More engineers and technicians arrive, and work crews begin assembling structures on the pad. The scorpion dueling continues, but such distractions become less and less frequent. A big day is approaching—a very big day, because Korolev himself has returned, followed by a railroad car bearing his R-7 rocket. Yuri recognizes the man from a distance, the autumn sun reflecting off the round, balding head atop that heavy frame. Years of imprisonment after Stalin's purge trials of the late 1930s had given Korolev a hardened look. And with Korolev's arrival, Ostashev is suddenly called away—to Moscow, he says.

On October 4, 1957, at precisely 10:28 P.M. the alcohol mixes with the liquid oxygen and ignites. The explosion lights up the night sky, throwing up a billowing cloud of vapor and dust. The noise is deafening, and the ground trembles violently as a quarter of a million pounds of engine thrust pummel the desert floor. A massive 31-meter rocket slowly rises, gradually gaining speed and shooting off into the darkness when its first stage drops away.

At Tyuratam, where secrecy and security were absolute and went hand in hand, the workers had just witnessed the second successful launch of an Intercontinental Ballistic Missile. The genie was released from the bottle—and the race for space had begun.

The second stage of this Soviet rocket has been modified, however, to carry a 184-pound, highly polished aluminum sphere the size of a beach ball. Filled with temperature-controlling nitrogen and attached to the rocket's nose cone with a special spring-separation system, the ball contains two radio transmitters. When it reaches 500 miles above Earth, the missile releases its little companion—its "fellow traveler," or *Sputnik* in Russian—and the small sphere becomes the first man-made object ever to orbit Earth. Traveling 18,000 miles per hour, it circles the planet every 96 minutes. In Moscow, Ostashev celebrates with ice cream and brandy, sending a message to Yuri and his fellow workers: "Congratulations. The road to the stars is now open."

Americans had gone to bed that Friday night knowing Marshal Dillon would get the bad guy next Monday on *Gunsmoke*, and that *I Love Lucy* would keep them laughing. When they woke up the next morning, everything was different. REDS ORBIT ARTIFICIAL MOON, headlines blared. The world had changed.

People didn't know what to think. Was *Sputnik* looking down on them during its seven daily passes over the United States? Were the Russians going to launch an attack? What was a satellite, anyway? And there was that grating *beep, beep, beep* broadcast every 90 minutes on two different public radio frequencies from its transmitters in space. What Americans did realize was that the Russians were beating them. Not since 1949, when President Harry Truman announced that the U.S. monopoly on atomic weapons was at an end, had Americans experienced a similar jolt to their sense of security and safety. In a Cold War-world divided into good and evil, with each side capable of completely destroying the other, the evil side had just taken an ominous stride forward.

President Dwight Eisenhower tried to calm the panic by saying that orbiting a satellite was really nothing special, and that the United States still held a commanding lead in science and technology. Americans were not convinced. Michigan Governor G. Mennen Williams captured the common sentiment in a poem:

> *Oh little Sputnik, flying high*
> *With made-in-Moscow beep,*
> *You tell the world it's a Commie sky*
> *And Uncle Sam's asleep.*

America's shock was compounded 29 days later when *Sputnik II* launched—this one a much more complex 1,120-pound satellite, carrying complex instruments and a living (though doomed) passenger, a black-and-white dog named Laika. It couldn't have been more painfully obvious that Russia's sophisticated technology and powerful missiles left the

United States trailing. How long before the Reds could launch missiles capable of reaching U.S. shores?

In a bid to recapture public confidence and international prestige, the United States rushed desperately to get its own satellite in orbit before year's end. The Defense Department announced the test launch of Project *Vanguard*, which would carry an American satellite into space, for December 4. Unlike the Soviet launch, this wouldn't be held in secret in some remote location. Press from around the world gathered at Cape Canaveral for hourly briefings, and television networks moved in their cameras to capture the event for an eager national audience. Mechanical problems delayed the scheduled launch countdown for 48 hours, however, and the foreign press mocked the U.S. effort with new names for the rocket: *Flopnik*, *Stay-putnik*, *Kaputnik*, *Sputternik*. Even at home, a joke circulating the nation's capital suggested we rename the rocket the *Civil Servant*— "because it wouldn't work, and you couldn't fire it."

Finally, on December 6, the *Vanguard* rocket rose three feet off the launchpad, shook briefly, then fell back to the ground. The nose cone separated, and the rocket burst into flames. The firemen rushing in to fight the blaze discovered a small ball spinning on the grass near the missile. It was the grapefruit-sized satellite, with one of its antennas released as though it had been placed in orbit and was transmitting to earth.[1]

International humiliation was intense, and the Russians enjoyed the moment. The Soviet delegate to the United Nations asked whether the United States would like foreign aid to help with its space program. The Cold War was a two-fold struggle: both a contest in which each side strove to demonstrate its system's superiority to the rest of the world, and a race to develop the military capability necessary for advancing each side's international interests against the other. The Soviet's success with their new technology represented unprecedented gains on both fronts.

The United States continued to rush to get something in space. Eisenhower dropped his ban on military space vehicles and turned to Wernher von Braun and his team of German scientists who had emigrated to the United States following World War II, asking them to have something ready within 90 days. Less than two months later, on January 31, 1958, *Explorer I* successfully launched from Cape Canaveral. The first U.S. satellite, a small instrument for measuring radiation, was in orbit. The launch offered some consolation, but there was no doubt which side had the lead. The "space race" was on and having the best rockets was critical, because missiles promised to be the weapons of the future.

Sputnik's impact was felt throughout American society, and public education came in for heavy criticism. Soon after *Sputnik I* went up, *Life* magazine ran a series of articles titled "Crisis in Education." The cover of the March 24, 1958, edition contrasted two high school students, one a stern-looking Moscow boy and the other a casual, smiling American student from Chicago. The story depicted the Russian youth conducting optics experiments in physics class and mastering a second language, while the American boy strolled around, holding hands with his girlfriend and rehearsing for a musical. Confounded by a simple math problem in school, the American was seen in one illustration stepping away from the blackboard laughing; the caption read, "Stephen amused the class with wisecracks about his ineptitude." The article concluded that American "standards of education are shockingly low."

At issue was whether U.S. schools had chosen to produce well-adjusted students, or well-educated ones. That administrators and teachers were losing their focus on academic achievement, especially in math and the sciences, and ignoring the most talented students was a major criticism. Schools were giving too much emphasis, it was said, to providing a "well-rounded" education, with electives such as general health and nutrition. As standards fell, America was losing the race to produce the scientists and engineers needed to compete successfully against the Reds. It wasn't only *Life*. Article after article in the media described a rigorous Soviet education system that emphasized math and science in a no-nonsense manner.

Revising school curricula to compete with an imagined superior Soviet education system was one way of handling the public's panic and uncertainty. But there wasn't time to wait for a new generation of technicians and scientists to gain an edge over the Soviets. Something must be done now. To deal with the immediate threat, brilliant and talented people were stepping forward to come to the aid of the country. Many in the academic community had much to offer—academics such as Yale economics professor Thomas Schelling.

As Paul Samuelson, America's first recipient of the Nobel Prize in Economics, said, "Once the vital game of survival in a nuclear age challenged Schelling's attention, mere economics could no longer contain him."[2] What Schelling brought to the contest was a completely rational approach and a new methodology for analyzing situations of conflict and cooperation—game theory.

∾

By the time Schelling got involved in 1957, tensions were reaching their highest and most dangerous point. Begun as World War II drew to an end, the struggles that would become known as the "Cold War" had hardened into a new kind of battle between the two surviving superpowers for political dominance over its dangerous and sinister recent wartime ally. One American response to threatened aggression would be the "Truman Doctrine," a call for America to take a stand against communism wherever it threatened further expansion. Americans didn't immediately accept Truman's plan for containing communism, however, and considerable public and congressional debate followed the president's speech.

Industrialist and financier Bernard Baruch was among those who supported the proposal. Realizing the president needed help "selling" his idea to the American people, Baruch called on an old friend, journalist Herbert Bayard Swope, for help writing a speech on the subject. Swope came up with the perfect phrase to describe the situation in which America now found itself. On August 16, 1947, Baruch delivered his speech to the state legislature in Columbia, South Carolina, and said, "Let us not be deceived—today we are in the midst of a cold war." *Cold War*. Picked up by widely syndicated columnist Walter Lippman, the phrase soon entered the popular lexicon.

Yet *Cold War* became much more than just a new expression. It became the label for a generation, perhaps the most dangerous generation in all of human history—a generation during which human existence itself seemed to hang in the balance, dependent upon individual personalities and wills, mistakes and misunderstandings, and trivial disputes. The Cold War featured gamesmanship and threats, and always danger, danger that continually increased as nuclear weapons grew more powerful and delivery systems more effective.

There were the events: the Cuban Missile Crisis, the Korean War, the summit conferences, the Berlin Crisis, the fall of Saigon, the Soviets in Czechoslovakia and Hungary. There were the places: the Berlin Wall, the Ho Chi Minh Trail, the Bay of Pigs, the 38th Parallel. There were things: *Sputnik*, the "hotline," fallout shelters, hydrogen bombs, Intercontinental Ballistic Missiles. There were organizations, plans, agreements: NATO, the Marshall Plan, the Strategic Arms Limitations Talks, the Warsaw Pact, the ABM Treaty. There were terms: brinkmanship, the space race, overkill, megatons, "mutually assured destruction," deterrence, peace rallies, "massive retaliation." There were quotes and phrases: "We will bury you," "the evil empire," "I am a Berliner," "Make love, not war."

And there were the characters, heroes and villains with their supporting casts: gallant John Kennedy, cool in crisis in Berlin and Cuba . . . sinister-looking Leonid Brezhnev, ordering Soviet tanks to crush resistance in the USSR's Eastern European satellites . . . energetic Henry Kissinger and his follow-up to "ping-pong diplomacy," opening relations with communist China . . . Nikita Khrushchev, pounding his shoe on a table at the United Nations . . . Richard Nixon, relentlessly pursuing alleged Communist spy, Alger Hiss, as a young congressman and taking on Khrushchev in the "kitchen debate" as vice president . . . Joseph Stalin, until 1953 the person with influence over more people than anyone else on earth, a ruler who possessed nuclear weapons and whose past demonstrated a willingness to sacrifice millions of his own people in the pursuit of his goals . . . Douglas MacArthur, whose forays near the Yalu River brought the Chinese into the Korean War against the United States . . . Robert McNamara, the "whiz kid" of the Defense Department, bringing a new look to America's defense planning . . . wily Ho Chi Minh and Fidel Castro, foes the United States couldn't vanquish . . . and many more, the statesmen, rulers, diplomats, and military leaders whose names dominated the headlines.

These events and people defined the times. Their stories are compelling and important, but an understanding of the Cold War is incomplete without some knowledge of the men behind the unfolding drama. Less is known about the strategic thinkers whose ideas quietly influenced the decision-makers. These individuals envisioned where situations and certain ways of thinking could lead, and they helped those in authority understand what was involved and then devise strategies to stave off disaster. In a world where nuclear holocaust was the price of failure, what could have been more critical than strategy? And among the nuclear strategists of the Cold War, none was more important than Thomas Schelling.

Yet when *Sputnik* went up and America needed heroes in the titanic struggle against communism, Tom Schelling had been an unlikely candidate. A wiry 37-year-old of average height, bespectacled and sporting a crewcut, he had a bookish, tweedy look about him, a pleasant manner, and a gentle smile that came easily. He was always scribbling on notepads, but when really concentrating, he would stare blankly and purse his lips. Schelling did not cut a figure that would inspire confidence in a struggle against the Russian Bear.

Schelling's relation to the Cold War spans its most dangerous period and guided his path in strategic studies. He was a young Harvard economist when he headed off to Europe in 1948 with the Marshall Plan, America's

successful program to help revive the war-torn economies of Western
Europe, bringing them politically closer and enabling the formation of
NATO. From there, he went to the Truman White House in a NATO-related
position, remaining for a time when Eisenhower came to office before the
academic world lured him away. Schelling moved to Yale and, while there,
first established connections with the RAND Corporation. A think tank
established by the military after World War II to get top civilian minds
thinking about military-related problems, RAND was described by the
Soviet mouthpiece newspaper *Pravda* as "America's institute of death and
destruction."

It was at RAND, the leading center of a form of strategic analysis called
game theory, that Schelling's reputation was firmly established. An
approach for studying how people interact to make decisions, game theory
is based on models and assumptions of rational choice. It proved to be a
highly useful methodology for Schelling: He saw its applications for both
advantages in conflict and for cooperation. He would attempt to enlarge
the practical scope of game theory in his 1960 book *The Strategy of Conflict*,[3] in which, according to the Nobel Prize committee, he "set forth his
vision of game theory as a unifying framework for the social sciences."[4]
The Strategy of Conflict set the standards for strategic studies. From Yale,
Schelling joined the faculty at Harvard, where he spent the bulk of his academic career, with occasional visits and one longer stint at RAND, and
then moved to the University of Maryland.

By the late 1950s, Schelling was focusing his work on nuclear strategy
and had become recognized as a leading figure in the field. He dedicated
much of his strategic work of the late 1950s and '60s to the prevention of
nuclear holocaust. He also participated in the high-stakes gambling that
came with nuclear arms, such as when he saw a "chicken dilemma" developing in Berlin in 1961. His ideas included a "hotline" for direct communication between U.S. and Soviet leaders and the concept of "save the
cities" during bombing campaigns. He developed games to train people to
make decisions in crisis situations that could lead to nuclear confrontation; the participants in his training games included not only generals, but
such civilians as Henry Kissinger and Robert Kennedy.

His influence on President John F. Kennedy during the Berlin Crisis
arguably led that administration to take a stand that threatened nuclear
war with the Soviet Union. The influence of his role in the Vietnam War is
subject to debate—from his advice to Robert McNamara on whether or
not to initiate a short bombing campaign against North Vietnam, to his
work on interactive decisions involved developing the strategy that led to

both the bombing of North Vietnam and the "madman theory" of that bombing as the war carried on. A crowning achievement would be his work to help overcome the "prisoner's dilemma" of the arms race (see Chapter 13, "The Prisoner's Dilemma of Nuclear Arms").

Drawing him into the use of game theory was Schelling's work aimed at establishing a theoretical framework for deterrence and preventing the thoughtless use of nuclear weapons. The idea of using a weapon powerful enough to end life on Earth is so horrible that most people consider the prospect unthinkable—so isn't the obvious solution just to get rid of such weapons? But throughout the Cold War the possibility remained that some crazy person would decide to use them, or that some situation would escalate beyond control, or that a mistake would be made, or that one side's technological advantage might make it seem "safe" to use such weapons. Each side's awareness of the other's fear of nuclear annihilation also offered strategic opportunities that could be exploited. Unthinkable as nuclear holocaust was, someone needed to think about it. Tom Schelling did.

When the Cold War wound down, Schelling found other uses for his analytical skills and game-theory tools and abilities. Applying his strategies across a broad range of problems, he provided insights both practical and-incisive into questions of segregation and integration, organized crime, self-control, and global warming, among other issues. The diverse application of game-theory principles developed by this Cold War strategist, who could see their relevance across social science boundaries, was recognized with the award of the 2005 Nobel Prize in Economics.

CHAPTER 2

EARLY YEARS

A cre after acre of the Irish coun-tryside was covered with black rot from 1845 to 1849. A fungus destroyed the potatoes that were the staple of the Irish diet. It was the Great Rot that was causing the Great Famine. The dead were sometimes found by the roadsides with grass in their mouths, after the lack of food reduced them to gnawing on weeds. Many were buried in the clothes they wore, as parish priests used money that would have gone for coffins to buy food for the poor. In villages where the poor grew weak from hunger, cholera and typhus spread, wiping out entire popula-tions. In a country of eight million,

Schelling at two, Mare Island
Naval Base, California

more than a million-and-half eventually died, and another million-and a half emigrated to English-speaking countries. The largest share of those who left went to America.

When they reached America, most of the Irish settled in the big cities on the East Coast. For the few with the means to head west to the expanding American frontier, there was the opportunity to carry on with the farm life they had known. One pioneer who managed to move on was James Henan. Henan and his wife, Mary, appear on the 1850 census roles for Mt. Morris, Illinois. They had four children, and only their youngest daughter, Susan, married and had children. In 1861, Susan married the son of German immigrants who had settled in Maryland then come to Illinois, Henry Schelling. Henry wasn't born "Schelling." It was a name he had adopted, but the family name would be Schelling from then on. His parents were Joaquim Shilling and Francesca Catherine Schafer. This union of Irish and

German immigrants would still be evident two generations later in the slightly ruddy complexion and square jaw of Thomas Crombie Schelling.

Susan and Henry had 11 children between 1862 and 1884, the last born named John. They raised their children in the small Illinois town of Leaf River. Most of their children ended up struggling at farming, but John had other aspirations. He took a competitive exam and won an appointment to the United States Naval Academy at Annapolis, Maryland. Commissioned as a naval officer, the young John Schelling married Zelda Maude Ayers, a strong woman who lived to be 107, in his hometown in 1912.

Their first son, Robert, was born in Norfolk, Virginia, in 1917. America was just entering World War I, and the junior naval officer was called for duty on a minesweeper. When the war ended, the Navy reassigned the young Schelling family to the West Coast, where most U.S. battleships and destroyers were stationed. After readjustments to peacetime living and battles over ratification of the Versailles Treaty, life was settling down in postwar America. The election of President Warren G. Harding in 1921 brought the "return to normalcy." Contestants showed their knees in Atlantic City, New Jersey, at the first Miss America pageant that year, and Charlie Chaplin released his first feature-length movie, *The Kid*.

For the Schellings, the return of "normalcy" meant other adjustments. Oakland, California, was their new home and it was there, on April 14, 1921, that Tom Schelling was born (followed, eighteen months later, by the birth of the last of the Schelling children, Nancy). Appropriately, the far-sighted inventor Thomas Edison had said the very year of Schelling's birth: "There will one day spring from the brain of science a machine or force so fearful in its potentialities, so absolutely terrifying, that even man, the fighter who will dare torture and death in order to inflict torture and death, will be so appalled, and so abandon war forever."[5] With what eerie accuracy these words of great insight would describe the momentous events of Schelling's life and his role in them.

The family spent the 1920s in California, as the Navy moved them up and down the coast from base to base. Their final move was to San Diego, where Schelling's father commanded a division of four destroyers. Summers included family visits back to Illinois, where Schelling sat by the radio with his grandpa, listening to the Chicago Cubs baseball games on station WGN. His attraction to those radio sessions didn't stem from any interest in how the Cubs were faring in the pennant race. If he sat quietly and wasn't a disturbance, he was allowed to share his grandfather's popcorn. Schelling's father only showed up once during the seven or eight summers they spent there.

With his father frequently away at sea for months at a time, it was, he recalls, "very much a mother-oriented family." His father came from a culture where the mother took care of the children, and in those early years raising the family was mainly Zelda's task. When he looks back on it, Schelling does not recall doing any of the things, like tossing a ball around, that boys often did with their fathers. Years later, when he had sons of his own, he would be actively involved in their lives, taking them skiing and camping and helping out in Little League baseball. Overall, his father's influence was minor, and he doesn't believe that there is any connection with so much of his later work being related to the military and having grown up in military surroundings.

A year in Newport, Rhode Island, where his father was at the Naval War College, followed life on the California naval bases. After that came two years in Washington, D.C., first at the Army War College, then at the Navy Department. Throughout all the moves, Schelling's parents held high academic expectations for all three children: Anything less than an A was a disappointment. In Washington, the young Schelling entertained himself with weekly visits to the Avalon Theater, where 10 cents bought you an afternoon of movies—often double-features or serials (a successful device for keeping audiences returning, serials told continuing stories that ran up to 12 weeks). Schelling's favorite feature films were the Wild West tales of Zane Grey. He was less fond of "spooky movies," another popular genre of the time, as he was a bit afraid of the dark.

After two years in Washington, it was time for Schelling's father to return to a command position and for an assignment overseas. In 1933, the family arrived in Panama for a two-year assignment in what was commonly known as the "Canal Zone." By that time, young Tom's penchant for intellectual pursuits and games was beginning to show. Interested in anything that offered a mental puzzle, he enjoyed chess and Monopoly, began playing poker, and had become an avid reader. As at the cinema, Grey's Wild West stories and other tales of "showdowns and shootouts between gunfighters" captured his imagination. (Cowboy analogies would turn up in his writings on the nuclear confrontation between the Soviet Union and the United States years later.) He enjoyed reading so much he would often continue after being told to turn out his light. After his mother began coming in to feel if the light bulb was warm and had been turned off recently, he would sometimes hide under the covers with a flashlight.

Zelda Schelling's attempts to make a musician out of her son met with little success. Foreshadowing his future in game theory and bargaining theory, eight-year-old Tom persuaded his mother to commit to a contract:

He would take piano lessons on the condition that when his 12th birthday arrived, the decision to continue or quit would be his. Schelling quit studying piano on his 12th birthday.

PERSONAL COLLECTION OF THOMAS C. SCHELLING

At 15 in Canal Zone on "Glasseye"

Tom's 15th birthday in the Canal Zone brought with it a special present: a horse named "Glasseye," blind in its bluish right eye. He rode Glasseye daily for the next 14 months, quartering him at the army base's facilities for its mules. He became an adept rider, and between that and his involvement in the Boy Scouts, grew comfortable with outdoor life. He began to develop his lifelong interest in outdoor hobbies that require physical activity.

In 1934, Schelling's brother Robert—always more "his father's son"—completed high school and was ready to leave home. Appointed to the U.S. Naval Academy, Robert headed off to Annapolis, as his father had done years earlier. John Schelling retired from the military the next year, and the family returned to an America in the depths of the Great Depression: Unemployment was at unprecedented levels, and men looking for work wandered the land; dust storms ravaged the plains, while bread lines and soup kitchens dotted the cities. The Schellings settled in San Diego, where they were largely insulated from the country's suffering. The Navy provided well for its officers, and the Mission Hills area of San Diego they called home was a pocket of affluence, isolated from the nation's plight.

The Schelling family was not a close one at that time. Robert was away, and though Schelling and sister Nancy always got along well, she was a year and a half younger. His father was around, now that he was out of the Navy, but they still had little to do with each other. Their family time together was limited to Sunday evenings in the living room. They would gather around the radio listening to Jack Benny and Mary Livingston on NBC's *JELL-O Program*, followed by another immensely popular variety show featuring ventriloquist Edgar Bergen and his dummy, Charlie McCarthy. The idea of listening to a ventriloquist on the radio, which today defies credibility, didn't affect the audience of the day. Radio in the 1930s was a social activity, like a group socializing without actually being together. Nearly everyone was doing the same thing. Schelling would listen in the evening in part so he could talk about what he heard the next morning on the streetcar or wherever he first encountered others.

Tom entered San Diego's Old Gray Castle, as the high school was called, and found the diversity a refreshing change from military bases. High school was a good experience for the naïve and pleasant young man. He found outlets for his quizzical and absorbent mind, and good teachers who motivated him to think more clearly, to reason, and to be articulate. Schelling's high grades pleased his parents. He thanks his English teacher from grades eleven and twelve, Miss Olson, for training him in the concise writing style that would characterize his work throughout his career. She taught him to write a five-paragraph essay, and when she returned his work, he recalls, "It would come back with all kinds of hieroglyphics, each one of which meant something—I loved it!"[6] He found outlets for his interest in writing by editing the sports section of the yearbook and writing for the school paper, *The Russ*. He joined the debate team and was elected president of the Boys' Federation, a large student organization. Among his courses was one called "Propaganda," a study of the rising fascist and communist powers in Europe. His growing awareness of the world around him led him to get his own subscription to the Sunday edition of the *New York Times*.

While the country around him escaped its Depression misery with fantasy and happy endings at the movie theaters, his favorite film introduced him to new themes—causes fought with terrorism. Schelling still recalls John Ford's 1935 drama of the Dublin slums, *The Informer*, as "the greatest film I ever saw." Set in 1922 Dublin with the IRA fighting a campaign against the hated British Black and Tans, the film tells the story of a desperate former IRA member who turned in his best friend for a reward the British were offering. His friend is executed, and the informer's reward money squandered. With other IRA members hunting him down, the informer seeks sanctuary in a church. There he encounters his dead friend's mother. He confesses his betrayal to the mourning woman, and she prays for his soul. It was a story with big themes: nationalism versus terrorism, compassion versus revenge, desperation versus loyalty—hardly a story that would interest most young boys who had just finished their sophomore year in high school. Then again, Tom Schelling wasn't a typical young boy.

The great forces of poverty and racial discontent weren't evident in San Diego's Mission Hills area. The Schellings carried on, aware of the country's problems, but living the comfortable and secure lives of the privileged. Schelling's only firsthand knowledge of the Depression came from a friend of his—a migrant from Arkansas, or an "Arkie"—who had come to his high school, and had become president of the student body. His awareness of racial issues was equally limited, as few nonwhites attended his school. Tom's only contact with them came in the Reserve Officers Training Corps, a military course in which young men put on uniforms, learned to march and salute, and practiced close-order drills. His father had encouraged him to take ROTC, and he ended up enjoying it. Schelling's mannerisms have always had a slightly martial air, with head held high and shoulders back. He became adept enough at performing the manual of arms, a series of sharply conducted movements with a rifle, to win a second-place medal in a citywide competition. A platoon commander, he was one of only three cadets who had risen to the rank of lieutenant. Three black students once came to him with complaints of ill treatment. He recalls that they displayed hurt feelings more than a desire for vengeance and thinks they probably approached him because he was a "nice guy." Tom saw himself as tolerant and open-minded, not just the "very intelligent young man" classmates recall.

Schelling's moderate political views and tolerant attitude sometimes strained his relationship with both his father and with his very conservative Republican grandfather, who had come to live with them and shared his son's prejudices and general cultural stereotypical views. As Schelling recalls, "My father shared what I would call the typical xenophobia of naval officers of that time: anti-Semitism, anti-Italian, anti-anything, except what you might call Nordic, German, English, Scandinavian, and so forth."[7] In an incident that reflects on both of them, Schelling wasn't even aware that his own very best friend was Jewish until his father's expression of "extreme displeasure" at the fact. It was his mother who eventually apologized for his father's outburst at him for having such a friend.

Another aspect of Schelling's life his parents disapproved of began during high school. He "went steady" with his first girlfriend during his junior and senior years, but his parents never met her. He borrowed the car nearly every Friday and Saturday evening those two years, but his parents never expressed curiosity about his romantic interests, except to help bring things to an end. He recalls being, "very much in love with her." We "spent lots of time sitting in the car kissing—we never did anything else," he says, adding with a laugh, "I've often wondered what I missed."

This happy relationship changed one warm spring day during their senior year, when they and several friends decided to skip school and head for the beach. Schelling was injured roughhousing and ended up in the naval hospital with a broken collarbone. With his parents away attending Robert's graduation from Annapolis, and his grandparents staying with him, Schelling's grandmother came in to have a "heart-to-heart" talk about "nice boys" like him being sued or exploited for money by pregnant young girls. When his mother returned home, she had no sympathy for his relationship with his girlfriend. Their romance fell apart soon thereafter, probably, Schelling suspects, because his grandmother "poisoned the well."[8] Finding the right relationship would be a long process.

No doubt having learned from his own treatment, Schelling would be an encouraging and involved parent many years later with his own children, who went in directions other than their father's rigid academic path.

After graduation, Schelling enrolled at San Diego State College and was elected freshman class president. College life offered greater independence, and academics were not a priority that first semester. When grades came out and his were all Bs and Cs, he recalls a scene that could have taken place in almost any home with school-age children over the years: "I remember very distinctly my mother standing in the doorway to the dining room one afternoon and asking me, 'Why did you get such low grades?' And I remember saying something like, 'Oh, Mom, I didn't think you'd mind. What do you want?'" He earned all As the next semester, and his mother was content.

It was the lesson parents long for: "I hadn't worked as hard as I could, and when my mother displayed sadness, I couldn't disappoint her again."[9]

After a year at San Diego, he was ready to move on to something more challenging. Just before the outbreak of World War II in 1939, he enrolled at the University of California at Berkeley. His father had an insurance policy for education, but it wasn't necessary. Tuition for a full school year was $62.50, and Schelling and a friend found a room on College Avenue near the university to share for $12 per month. He got a job washing dishes and waiting tables for meals, but more as a social activity than for the money.

High school graduation photo, age 17

Although he still had little first-hand experience with it, Schelling was quite aware of the Great Depression by the time he arrived at Berkeley in 1939. His response to this newfound awareness marks the beginning of his transition into a social scientist and offers insight into what sorts of problems he would choose to take on and how he would approach them. Well into World War II, Schelling believed that the great problem confronting America was the Great Depression, not the war. War was a problem people knew how to deal with: They fought it. The Great Depression was different: It required understanding, which made it a more challenging and interesting intellectual problem. Why did we get into it? How do we get out? So the difference between the two was the question of which presented the greater intellectual challenge.

Solve the toughest puzzle—that became a Schelling hallmark. The most difficult issues and thus, to Schelling, the most interesting ones were those he could frame as problems that required detached, clear, uncluttered thinking and logical analysis. Such problems were truly complex puzzles, situations in which people had let their emotions or interests dictate the solutions they found. The war was easy, but the Great Depression didn't have adequate answers. Seeking the greater puzzle to solve would lead him into the study of economics.

His view of society's ills as literal puzzles to be solved, combined with his ingrained love of puzzles themselves, would characterize Schelling's work from this early interest in the Depression, through his transition to becoming a nuclear strategist, to his studies of the problems of segregation and integration, self-control and beyond. Schelling developed a capacity to frame issues in terms of logic problems and took great pleasure in the mental gymnastics and lateral thinking required to find the solutions. The logical deductions must come first, rather than the views on policy. His enjoyment of puzzles would be especially evident later in the course on strategy he taught for years at Harvard. Along with problems that dealt directly with public policy, he occasionally assigned logic problems, puzzles related not to content but intended to promote the divergent thinking that would help find ways to approach situations.

At Berkeley, Schelling joined the debate team, a society of primarily left-wing students. Not organized for formal competitive debate, the "team" was more of an informal current events discussion society. It became apparent to him later that the group's faculty advisor and several participants were communist party members or sympathizers.

At the end of his first year, Schelling took off on a road trip with traveling companions who might not have pleased his father, had he known of them: Tom Ludwig, the "Arkie" Schelling had known in high school and who had become one of his close friends in college, and Morris Glickfeld, a Jewish friend from the debate team. The three diverse friends hopped in Schelling's Model A Ford and took off on a two-month trip to the East, camping all the way. It was an eye-opening journey for the naïve Schelling. In Memphis, Tennessee, the threesome stopped to visit some of Ludwig's distant relatives. After the introductions, one cousin announced, "Let's get one thing straight. We don't believe we're descended from monkeys, and we don't believe in equal rights for niggers."[10] From there they headed to Nashville, Tennessee, where, while walking around town, they heard music coming from a church. They had stopped outside to listen when a police car pulled up and the officer said, "Get in the back of the car. You don't belong here." Apparently, the church was in an area described to them as "Niggertown."

They proceeded to Philadelphia, where the Republican National Convention was taking place, and heard Wendell Wilkie's nominating speech. Glickfeld made some comment that received a great deal of anti-Semitic response. Schelling had heard such things happened, but he didn't think they could happen to him or his friends. At one point during their journeys, they were separated in a large city—and thought about a method for finding each other should it happen again. In that experience was the germ of an important idea that would emerge years later when Schelling discovered game theory (see "Chapter 6: Game Theory").

When they returned from their road trip, the war in Europe was a year old and Schelling's father had returned to active duty in the Canal Zone. His older brother Robert was keeping up the family military tradition as a naval officer. And back at Berkeley, Schelling thought he had fallen in love... but things weren't to be. The object of his affections said she liked him, but was already engaged. It wasn't America's war yet, and Schelling decided he wanted to study overseas. Europe wasn't possible, but South America was, so he headed to Chile, stopping in the Canal Zone along the way to visit his parents.

His host family in Santiago did not speak English, which was a good experience for Schelling, who hoped to become fluent in Spanish. The family's father was a retired army officer and, as was not uncommon in Chile, adamantly pro-German. That source of disagreement wasn't a lasting problem, since Schelling moved out after three months. School was no challenge and didn't require his full-time effort. A good friend in Chile worked as a correspondent for United Press International, so Schelling asked him to help find something to do when he wasn't in class.

Life in Chile made the drama gripping much of the world seem like a storybook tragedy. Schelling certainly heard about what was happening, but many people in his host country didn't pay attention, as if events on the global stage made no real difference. The general unawareness was evident one fall night in 1941 when he became lost on an overnight hike in the mountains near Santiago. Two Chileans happened on him and gave him food and water. After a few moments of conversation, they asked where he was from. When he replied, "North America," they asked, "What side is America on in that war in Europe?"[11] It was all so far away, it seemed. The events of December 7, 1941, demonstrated that the crisis that seemed distant couldn't be avoided.

Schelling had taken a part-time job as a watchman at the U.S. Embassy, located in the same building as the UPI offices. While working one quiet Sunday afternoon, he answered the phone. Somebody at UPI began explaining that the Japanese had bombed a place called Pearl Harbor. Schelling went down to the second floor and started reading the cablegrams pouring in. It was soon clear that Pearl Harbor was in Hawaii and it was the U.S. fleet that had been bombed. After about half an hour, he was persuaded that the United States was at war with Japan—or, at least, that Japan was at war with the United States—and that it was up to him to do something about it.

The first thing to do was to call the U.S. ambassador. The ambassador had one real claim to fame: He had been the U.S. ambassador in Spain when the Spanish Civil War broke out. At that time, he was vacationing incognito at a beach resort and couldn't be found for 48 hours. Now Pearl Harbor had been attacked, and the ambassador was vacationing incognito at a beach resort. No one could find him. Schelling tried calling the naval attaché, who was also away. He next called the deputy naval attaché, who was playing golf. The staff at the golf club refused to go and find him. The army attaché couldn't be located. He finally found the assistant naval attaché, an ensign, and said, "Believe me. The Japanese have just attacked Pearl Harbor. I'm going to write down that you're the most senior person I could find, and you ought to come to the embassy, because there may be things happening."[12] The ensign said he would come, but that he did not believe it.

Schelling felt uncomfortable being the only American in Chile to know and believe America was at war. On his way home from the embassy, he passed the assistant naval attaché, the one official he had managed to reach. The ensign told him, "Schelling, I will have your ass for this."[13] The next day, the embassy was deluged with messages. The codebooks for decoding the messages were all kept in a huge safe, and the safe jammed. They had to call someone who knew how to open a safe. The only person in Santiago who knew how to open a jammed safe was a German.

With the United States at war, the FBI arrived to establish a counterespionage office in Chile, offering Schelling a job that he held for the next 15 months. The office grew from just Schelling and one agent to a staff of eight agents and a dozen secret *sub rosa* agents busy infiltrating organizations around the country. The intelligence community he had joined was an active participant in the war effort, their most urgent task being the discovery of secret signaling stations for German submarines.

Chile's beautiful weather was conducive to the love of the outdoors born during Schelling's stay in the Canal Zone, and he and his friends spent their free time fishing and hunting, Schelling sporting his new shotgun. While other young men their age were being outfitted with M-1s and facing an enemy that shot back, he and his colleagues were exempt from the draft and the Army. When Schelling left the United States, the age for registration was 21, and he hadn't registered. While he was away, the age was changed to 18. It wouldn't have mattered because, under the new Selective Service Act, the president could designate certain categories of people exempt from conscription, and embassy personnel fell within one of the categories. The ambassador had confiscated his passport, so he couldn't decide to leave. Then, in 1943, he began suffering from severe stomach cramps, and the initial diagnosis was ulcers. The ambassador gave him permission to go home.

Back home, it would be his time to go in the Army, and he was old enough to register for the draft. So when he arrived in California, he went to his draft board to sign up and find out how soon he would be called. He handed his papers to the sergeant at the desk, who leafed through them, then looked up and told Schelling he was Section Eight, and the Army didn't draft Section Eight. Section Eight? Schelling knew Section Eight covered psychiatric disorders. He was perplexed, until the sergeant explained that, in the Army's experience, people with serious ulcers bleed when under stress, becoming more of a liability than an asset.

Returning to Berkeley looked like his best option, and he decided economics was the most important subject to study. The field seemed to offer the best possibilities for finding explanations to the social problems that had interested him since high school. "Economic reasoning will carry you a long way, so training as an economist is good training for working on a large variety of social issues," as he explains it, adding, "Economic reasoning is usually based on the idea that people are rational, that they know what opportunities they have and what their own values are, and that they will make reasonable choices among alternatives. I find that extraordinarily helpful."[14] It was an analytically challenging discipline, which suited him well. He also found that many of the published economics papers he read had some characteristic of looking at complex social issues as puzzles, adding that the approach to finding meaningful understanding or developing successful policy involved solving the puzzles. By solving the puzzles one could logically approach resolving the more complex issues. This puzzle-solving approach appealed to him. He completed his undergraduate degree at Berkeley and began doing graduate work. With so many men in the service and so few women studying economics, the classes were small, almost like tutorials, and the learning environment excellent.

Graduate school was a time of transition when Schelling came to think of himself as a serious student, a scholar even. He soon realized that a sound understanding of mathematics would only benefit any serious study of economics; unfortunately, he had never studied anything more advanced than plane geometry and algebra in high school. So he began teaching himself analytic geometry, trigonometry, higher algebra, and calculus. As he expanded his understanding of mathematics, he began reading the few economics books available that were highly mathematics-based.

One of Schelling's professors, a Hungarian refugee named William Fellner, served as a model of the ideal economist, and Schelling was determined to excel in the field. Fellner was one of the first economists to apply predictive models to cooperative economic behavior, especially oligopolies. His work would be seen as a stage in the development of ideas that led to the great game theory achievement by John Nash, the equilibrium that bears his name, and for which he would be awarded a Nobel Prize in 1994. Fellner's work in predictive modeling also influenced Schelling, who would make extensive use of such an approach when his work began to incorporate game theory. Modeling is an especially valuable tool for analyzing group behavior, as it can represent this behavior through formulas or analogies when the aggregate behavior of the individuals involved cannot be viewed as a "collective individual." Some of these models are described as "first approximation," when they can be made more complex to come closer to match an actual situation, while others are starting-set models that illustrate the kind of analysis necessary in approaching a problem. Schelling's work would come to deal with both in time, with a debt to Fellner.[15]

Some of his interests hadn't changed in some ways from high school, and like young students everywhere, politics and the opposite sex attracted him. College campuses were centers of political activism, and Berkeley was no exception. One day when Schelling was in a labor economics class, chatting with a friend, an attractive young woman approached him and introduced herself. Women were more forward with so few men around. When she invited him to lunch, he thought things were really looking up. He went, but was disappointed to see a second woman present. The disappointment was compounded when the second woman said, "First, we think you ought to join the Party." Not long after that experience, another friend invited him to a gathering at which it was announced, "We're here to hear from somebody from 'back East' about a change in the 'Party line.'" Schelling contested what was being said, and the host burst out, "I don't know if you're one of us, but if you are, you'd better not talk like that." When the woman who had invited him said he wasn't "one of them," he knew he was in the midst of communist party members.

With his first year of graduate school coming to an end, he was ready to move on and consulted Fellner about what he should do next. Harvard, the University of Michigan, the University of Chicago, and Berkeley had all offered him grants for further graduate work. Fellner said, "Go to Harvard. If you can't afford it, I'll help you."

Schelling was ready to do something more active, however, and since he had only just started graduate school and the military wasn't going to take him, he decided he'd be of most use to his country in Washington, D.C. An old friend introduced him to someone in the Bureau of the Budget, which led to a job in the bureau's Fiscal Division. President Roosevelt had died in April of 1945, shortly before the war against Hitler's Germany was won, and there was a new man in the White House, Harry Truman. Schelling worked with two government economists responsible for knowing what President Truman was on record of favoring or disfavoring, as well as for writing the annual budget message. He spent a lot of time on the Hill at Senate hearings, watching labor leader John L. Lewis and others testify, and met with senior government economists. It was a heady position for a young man with little formal training, and he learned a considerable amount of macroeconomics—likely more than he would had he gone straight to Harvard.

The war was nearly over, but men were still being drafted. The available pool was getting small and, as victory finally came, there would be a need for more non-combat forces where physical demands might be minor. Schelling was sitting in his Washington office when he got a call-up from Selective Service to report to the National Guard armory in Baltimore for induction into military service. He had failed before, but thought it might not be so bad to go off and improve his poker skills, if nothing else. After he and the others arrived at the armory, they all stripped down to their shorts and shoes and socks. The Army had paperwork on some of the men who had been called, including Schelling, who was seated in a group with three other special cases: one was a hunchback, one had web fingers, and one had undescended testicles. Schelling was especially fit, having been on vitamins and a special diet since his ulcers had first acted up. A voice over the loudspeaker told him to report to the chief medical officer. He walked to the chief medical officer's room and then listened as the colonel apologized profusely for having wasted Schelling's day by having him come to Baltimore, when clearly he couldn't be accepted for any kind of military duty. They gave him a bus ticket back to Washington, and he left the other three men he had been seated with originally, as they waited to be inducted into military service.

When Schelling later emerged as a leading strategist, he offered advice that would affect servicemen, the soldiers in the field: It is fair to question the attitudes and understanding of those who make the decisions and give the advice, the policy makers and the advisors who see no action but send others off to face possible death. What was it about him? Did he feel guilty for not doing his part, for not seeing active duty in World War II? His father and brother had both served in the war. Schelling may have felt some embarrassment for his inability to participate, but that wasn't what bothered him. He didn't feel guilty about not doing his part in the war; he just had feelings of opportunity lost. He thought he'd missed what might have been the greatest event of his life. He was denied his chance to go through the kind of experience he believed a healthy young man wanted to have: "I would never know what it was like to be involved in life-threatening situations in warfare, and I think I felt I had missed out."[16]

This "I felt I had missed out" observation is interesting, coming as it does from a member of that "best and brightest" generation that ended up advising the Kennedy and Johnson administrations and avoiding a great cataclysmic war but that also made such mistakes in Vietnam. Schelling's brilliant contributions to the deterrence of nuclear war, while conventional war continued around the world, may come in part from the awareness that war may be "an experience any healthy young man would desire." If Schelling is right about this desire for the thrilling experience, perhaps it is the embodiment of any young man's hope that he, or at least his cause, will survive. Self-interest could be eliminated by nuclear war. Understanding how to get people to cooperate by acting in their own self-interest in a way that was mutually beneficial would be Schelling's later achievement.

By the spring of 1946, the war was over and, having spent a year and a half at the Bureau of the Budget, Schelling was ready to return to graduate school. That fall he headed to Cambridge, Massachusetts, and joined the ranks of the largest enrollment American colleges had ever seen. Veterans were enthusiastically responding to the GI Bill of Rights, new legislation intended to help the country's servicemen adjust to civilian life. Covering tuition and a living allowance, the "GI Bill" enabled millions of eager young men, who might not have considered college or been able to afford it, to receive a higher education. Half of all American college students that fall were attending school on the "GI Bill."

Optimism permeated the country as America struggled to get back to normal. Joe DiMaggio, his black hair flecked with gray, was back in the Yankee lineup after a four-year hiatus, and teenage girls in bobby sox were swooning over Frank Sinatra. Penicillin had been synthesized and was widely available, making Americans healthier. As the theater crowd in New York headed for *Annie Get Your Gun*, soap operas made their television debut and found loyal fans. With 30 million "war babies" born between the entry of the United States into World War II and the end of the 1940s, families were springing up in record numbers. Dr. Spock's *Common Sense Book of Baby and Child Care* would become the common guide for raising an entire generation of children.

While many of his fellow Americans engaged in such distractions, Schelling was busy working on his first published paper, an article titled "Raising Profits through Raising Wages?", which appeared in the July 1946 issue of *Econometrica*.[17] The trademark concise and literate writing style that characterized his nearly 200 published works in the years to follow generally avoided mathematical proofs in favor of metaphor and explanation. That isn't how his publishing record began. Schelling was young and doing his best to make his mark; it would be some time before his reputation was such that his thoughts were enough to impress on their own. The first article was esoteric, involving a 14-step equation and increasingly complex development of his view.

Equation six on its way to his 14-step derivation was:

$$Y \frac{g + r + m_w m + n_w + a_w + m_p + n_p a_p = MK1}{1 - h - h_w b_w - h_p b_p}$$

The proof soon moved on to:

$$\frac{dP}{db_w} = b_p \left| \frac{M\, dk}{db_w} + \frac{dM}{db_w} + \frac{K\, dM}{db_w} \right| + Mk\, dbp$$

That was only step eight of a 14-step progression. Even after going through the entire derivation, he said it was the foundation only, the background understanding needed "before we complicate our system" to make his argument.

As a full-time teaching student, or teaching fellow, at Harvard, Schelling's duties included instruction in elementary micro- and macroeconomics along with his own coursework for his degree. He also served as the resident tutor at Kirkland House, one of the school's student residences. In exchange for free room and board, he provided economics tutoring and handled minor disciplinary responsibilities.

Although the highlight of Schelling's course work came from studying with Wassily Leontief—recipient of the 1973 Nobel Prize in Economics— his most outstanding academic experience during this period at Harvard occurred outside of regular classes. Of the approximately 200 graduate students in economics, an elite group of about 20 would gather with a number of younger faculty members for weekly seminars. It was in these sessions that most of Schelling's real learning at Harvard took place— learning that came from fellow students. One such student was James Tobin, who would go on to win the Nobel Prize in Economics in 1981.

Reflecting on those early years, Tobin recalled the seminar group and Tom Schelling himself: "Tom and I were fellow graduate students and good friends in those incomparable years just after the war, our 'the war.' Even then, Tom was always several steps wider and a few layers deeper than the rest of us and our professors. He always perceived a new angle, a surprising implication, or a puzzling problem in arguments and propositions that satisfied most of us. His pleasure in his intellectual discoveries, as he told them in seminars, Littauer corridors, and lunches, was wonderful to behold. He showed his wonder and excitement by the twinkles of his eyes and the lilt of his talk."[18] That thrill of solving puzzles, the intellectual triumph apparent to others since Schelling's youngest days, was evident at Harvard as well.

In the spring of 1947, with his first Harvard year drawing to a close, Schelling met Corinne, the daughter of labor economist David J. Saposs. After a brief courtship, they married that September. Schelling was 26.

The following year, Schelling received Harvard's prestigious Junior Fellowship award, which carried a three-year stipend plus a bonus for married people. He would never have the opportunity to use it. In mid-June 1948, he received a call from Sidney Alexander, a Massachusetts Institute of Technology economist. Now in Washington, D.C., working on the Marshall Plan, which had been signed into law in April 1948, Alexander had received a new assignment in Paris, where a central office for the Marshall Plan was being set up. Unable to accept the assignment without finding a replacement for himself in D.C., he asked Schelling. Finding the offer too tempting to decline, he and his wife were off to the nation's capital, leaving the Junior Fellowship behind. The decision would ease Schelling into his first involvement in the Cold War—an involvement that would begin on the fringe, then move him to center stage 10 years later.

CHAPTER 3

THE MARSHALL PLAN AND THE COLD WAR

The Marshall Plan began following a commencement speech at Harvard on June 5, 1947, during which Secretary of State George Marshall announced a new program that would be "directed not against any country or doctrine, but against hunger, poverty, desperation, and chaos," the conditions that existed in the war-battered nations following World War II. The idea was to give massive economic

Destruction of Germany, 1945

aid to Europe without ideological attachments. It was to be a humanitarian effort; but, as Marshall said, poverty was a big ally of communism.[19]

The Marshall Plan invited European nations to work out joint plans for their own recovery, offering economic aid to those countries that successfully developed such plans. While the Marshall Plan was clearly intended to revive suffering Europe, the Cold War was definitely a consideration. Marshall noted that this successful program "should permit the emergence of political and social conditions in which free institutions can exist." The Soviets responded on September 18, 1947, with a UN speech by their deputy commisar for foreign affairs, Andrei Vyshinsky: "It is becoming more and more evident to everyone that the implementation of the Marshall Plan will mean placing European countries under the economic and political control of the United States."[20]

While Schelling was working in Washington, Sidney Alexander received a transfer from Paris to Copenhagen to serve as program manager for the Marshall Plan's Denmark office. He asked Schelling to join him there. Once again, Schelling thought the offer too good an opportunity to turn down, so he and Corinne were off to Denmark. His work there consisted mainly of interpreting economic statistics for Marshall Plan administrators in Paris and Washington—a job that required learning enough Danish to read journal reports. He was also responsible for analyzing Denmark's trade with other European countries and its need for funds to rebuild the animal stock depleted during the war. While working for the

Marshall Plan, Schelling did a bit of economics tutoring and realized how helpful a textbook with a mathematical foundation would be. He began work on what would become his first textbook, *National Income Behavior: An Introduction to Algebraic Analysis*, published by McGraw-Hill in 1951.

Corinne, also a student of economics, was not allowed to work because of a rule that prevented husbands and wives from working in the same office. Her father worked as a labor attaché at the Marshall Plan's central office in Paris. While Schelling's work focused entirely on rebuilding the Danish economy, his father-in-law was fully engaged in the politics of the Cold War. Communist activity in labor unions was a major concern, and most Marshall Plan missions had a labor attaché responsible for keeping labor movements anti-Communist and pro-United States. Such representatives were expected to promote pro-productivity, pro-reconstruction attitudes that would keep organized labor from looking to the East. Perhaps a bit ideologically, Schelling thought of the Marshall Plan not primarily "as a way of defending Europe against the Soviet Union, which, in a way, it was. But I thought of it more as a way to rebuild Europe after the war. I didn't think of it primarily as an East-West Cold War thing."[21]

During their year-long stay in Copenhagen, the Schellings made several trips by car to Paris for conferences. On one such trip, they stopped in Hamburg for the night, arriving in the barely lit city well after dark. The Schellings expected to see destruction from the war, but had no idea of the degree of devastation that morning's light would bring.

In 1943, the British had launched Operation Gomorrah against the German city, attacking with firebombs that raised the temperature to 1,000 degrees and ignited everything flammable in spontaneous combustion that resulted in fires raging for nine days. The initial combustion literally sucked the oxygen out of the city, creating hurricane-force winds that ripped children from their mothers' arms, collapsed buildings like dominoes, and uprooted every tree in their path. The resulting vacuum left people gasping for air on the pavement. Three more raids followed in rapid succession, and the British left Hamburg a smoldering ruin: 20 square miles of city center rampaged, bodies crushed under wreckage or baked in the open, a million without homes . . . and 50,000–80,000 dead, 20 percent of them children. A moral threshold had been crossed with weapons of mass destruction.

The next morning when they got up, Schelling asked someone, "Where do we go to see the ruins?" Every building they had passed driving into the city had been destroyed in the firebombing. Nothing remained but hollow shells. More than half of the city was destroyed, in fact, and everything had been cleaned out. Only the building facades were left standing; the rubble was completely removed and piled high along the river. Schelling later visited Bremen, Aachen, and other war-devastated German and Dutch cities. After that, he had seen enough of what war leaves behind.

Witnessing such devastation was especially terrifying with the world confronting the dangers of even greater mass destruction and human suffering. The United States had relied on its monopoly of nuclear power to contain Soviet aggression during the post-World War II years. For those reluctant to consider Russia a threat, or who wanted to avoid world affairs beyond the shores of America, 1949 was a year of shocks, a year that set the world on a path of uncertainty and fear from which it would never return.

The year's greatest surprise came on a warm afternoon in late August, when a specially equipped RB-29 touched down after a flight to conduct tests that measured cosmic radiation in the upper atmosphere. It began as a routine mission: Photographic plates designed to record radioactive particles were carried by the plane to high altitudes and exposed. As usual, the plates would show a sprinkle of light tracks, indicating the existence of radiation. But this day was different—this day the plates were completely exposed, literally saturated. Only one explanation was possible: A nuclear explosion had taken place. Since the United States hadn't conducted such a test, it was clear the U.S. monopoly on atomic weapons had ended. The one great military advantage the United States had held over the Soviet Union since the end of World War II was lost. The eventual development of a Russian A-bomb was expected, but not nearly so soon. Most scientists had put the likely date at 1952 and some as far off as 1955.

It wasn't until September 23 that the White House made an official statement. Charles Ross, the presidential press secretary, called reporters to his office that morning and announced, "Nobody is leaving here until everybody has this statement." The presidential press release read simply, "We have evidence that within recent weeks an atomic explosion occurred in the USSR." The administration did its best to play down the severity of the news, saying the test had been expected, just not quite so soon. Leading newspapers were generally cooperative in supporting the administration's efforts to control the public's fears. They argued that having a bomb was not the same as producing a number of bombs and being capable of delivering them. Yet controlling the public's sense of imminent danger was becoming an increasingly steep uphill battle, for communism seemed to be making gains on many fronts.

Earlier that year in China, Chiang Kai-shek's nationalist government had fled the country to Taiwan. On August 5, 1949—more than a month before the administration's announcement about the Soviet's atom bomb—Dean Acheson had released a State Department white paper announcing that the world's most populous nation had fallen to the communist forces of Mao Tse-tung. The secretary of state's paper warned of the likelihood that Mao's regime would "lend itself to the aims of Soviet Russian imperialism."

The events of 1949 concerned those who best understood the state of scientific development as well, a concern made graphic in what was to become one of the most emotive symbols of the era. Gracing the cover of the June 1947 issue of the *Bulletin of the Atomic Scientists* had been a seven-by-seven-inch orange clock face. Its hour hand pointed to twelve, and the minute hand stood at seven minutes before the hour. "The Clock of Doom," or "The Doomsday Clock," as it became known, was a dramatic symbol of the state of peril the world was in and the possibilities for horrific disaster it faced. The Doomsday Clock remained at seven minutes to twelve on the cover of every monthly issue for more than two years, until the Soviets exploded their bomb. When the October 1949 issue of the *Bulletin* came out, the clock showed three minutes to midnight.[22]

Busy with his economic reports, Schelling was one of those who kept his head in the sand, avoiding what seemed obvious to others and dismissing the communist threat as a real danger. "Even in 1949 it didn't cross my mind seriously that war would break out," he recalls.[23]

During his trips to France, Schelling got to know former Harvard Business School faculty member, Lincoln Gordon, then working as the assistant to Averell Harriman, head of the Marshall Plan's Paris office. Gordon asked Schelling to come work for him in Paris for a year after his time in Copenhagen was up. So, he and Corinne moved there in 1949 and were soon enjoying a life of much greater financial ease, complete with a new red Ford to get them from place to place. Housed in the elegant Hotel de Talleyrand on Place de la Concorde, the Marshall Plan offices were a block from the U.S. Embassy, where Corinne worked for the Plan's mission to France. Schelling worked with Robert Triffin, collaborating on what became known as the European Payments Union. A form of a clearinghouse bank to create multilateral trade between Marshall Plan countries, the union would make it possible to cancel a debit with one country by using a credit with another country as a result of trade. Schelling and Triffin aimed to create opportunities for a considerable increase in multinational trade.

Although the threat of communist expansion was a real challenge for America, back home the Cold War escalation was bringing out irrational fears in people as well. Politicians were willing to exploit those fears, and none was more adept at doing so than the junior senator from Wisconsin, Joseph McCarthy. The Senate Republican Campaign Committee had assigned McCarthy the topic "Communism in the State Department" for his February 9, 1950, Lincoln's birthday speaking engagement at the Women's Republican Club in Wheeling, West Virginia. It was during this speech that he announced, "In my opinion the State Department . . . is thoroughly infested with communists." He continued, "I hold in my hand a list of 205 names . . . known to the secretary of state as members of the Communist Party." Other charges soon followed.

Washington Post cartoonist Herb Block drew a cartoon showing the chairman of the Republican National Committee, Guy Gabrielson, Senator Robert Taft, and several other leading Republican senators pushing a confused Republican elephant toward a stack of tar buckets. On the top barrel, the largest in the stack, was the word *McCarthyism*. Block's word immediately entered the language, but the message of his cartoon was lost. For much of the country, anti-communist accusations were reason enough to condemn a person. Sacrificing reputations and careers to the witch hunts was a price worth paying because, if the charges were true, the dangers were too great.

The Marshall Plan wouldn't escape the witch hunts, and McCarthy staff, among other communist-hunters, visited Schelling's Paris office during 1950 seeking out "subversive elements." Schelling saw the visits as a sign of the times: All around him, friends lost their jobs, and he knew people who had been sent to prison.

Schelling was never caught up in the anti-communist fears that gripped so many people. He opposed the irrational nature of such paranoia but never considered it a menace to the state of the American government. He viewed the erosion of personal liberties accompanying the witch hunts to be their worst effect. On the personal level, his greatest concern was that somebody might unearth the fact that he'd been a subscriber to a communist-front organization when he was at Berkeley.

Communism's threat became real to Schelling on Saturday, June 24, 1950, when the American ambassador to the Republic of Korea cabled the State Department to say, "North Korean forces invaded Republic of Korea territory at several places this morning." A Japanese colony before World War II, Korea was divided at the 38th Parallel by the occupying U.S. and Soviet forces after Japan's defeat. When no agreement could be reached on how to create a unified Korea, separate elections were held in 1948 that created the anti-communist Republic of Korea in the South under Syngman Rhee and a communist Democratic People's Republic of Korea in the North under Kim Il-Sung. When communist North Korean forces crossed the 38th Parallel using Russian-made tanks and attacked South Korea, any questions Schelling had about the communist threat being imaginary vanished.

At the end of that summer, President Truman asked the head of Schelling's Paris office to come to the White House and serve as his foreign policy advisor. When Harriman left, he took Schelling's boss with him. Gordon said he'd try to arrange for Schelling to join them. By the time his Paris year was over, the Marshall Plan was winding down. While playing his role in the Plan, the young economist had witnessed and experienced much that helped him clarify certain ideas: The threat of Russian communism was real, and real dangers could result in irrational fears.

The Marshall Plan was a great success on two fronts, the humanitarian and the ideological. Prosperity returned to Western Europe, as most nations exceeded their pre-war economic outputs. A new confidence replaced post-war fatigue and dejection, as poverty declined and cities rebuilt their infrastructure. The communist parties in France and Italy were in decline, and the threats of the westward expansion of communism no longer had significant internal support. A Cold War victory could be claimed in Western Europe, and hope was returning to people's lives.

The international cooperation Schelling witnessed while working on the Marshall Plan made a lasting impression. Years later, when he began to develop theories of cooperation in nuclear strategy, the Marshall Plan cooperation would serve as a model. It served as his model again when discussing how countries could share benefits in overcoming global warming. Competition needn't be the only available option when mutual cooperation served the parties' interests better.

Another model of international cooperation had emerged at the end of the 1940s: the North Atlantic Treaty Organization, a Cold War alliance designed to protect Western Europe from Soviet invasion. The U.S. communist party's newspaper, the *Daily Worker*, branded the organization "International Murder, Incorporated." Schelling was soon involved.

CHAPTER 4

WHITE HOUSE YEARS

It was a new decade and time for the Schellings to return to America. Schelling didn't have a job waiting for him, but within two days of arriving home in late 1950 he received two letters: one from his former boss at the Bureau of the Budget, asking Schelling to join him on the newly formed Council of Economic Advisors; the second an offer from the White House. Schelling thought they looked like the two best jobs he could have had at that time, and he chose the White House position.

LIBRARY OF CONGRESS

Schelling began his Washington years in the administration of Harry Truman, a man he held in high regard.

The 1950s were a time of contradictions for middle-class America. Two rival strains of emotions and thoughts existed side-by-side throughout the decade. The country was enjoying unprecedented economic expansion and the consumerism that accompanied it. Recovery from the Great Depression and the war was complete, and America had achieved the highest standard of living in world history. A novelty in the 1940s, by the end of the '50s nearly every home in America owned a television set. Popular shows modeled the "ideal" happy family: *Leave It to Beaver, Father Knows Best, The Adventures of Ozzie and Harriet*—households where the father went off to work at a successful job and his wife stayed home to care for the family.

The great "white flight" from the cities to the suburbs dramatically influenced individual lifestyles and the culture at large. Abandoned by the whites, cities became home to the country's minorities as blacks headed north. Many Americans chose to ignore the racial tension beneath the surface of white affluence. Suburbia became as much a way of life as a place to live: Residents conferred social status on themselves while enjoying backyard barbeques and cocktail parties. With commuter trains less readily accessible, the two-car garage became a necessity rather than a luxury. This conservative consumer society found a genial spokesman in President Dwight Eisenhower.

Yet the communist threat simmered just beneath those happy days, seemingly close to boiling over. Escalating from year to year, the Cold War just got more and more serious. While the Korean War dragged on in the early years of the decade, fears about the Russian Reds remained the main issue. The Soviets were the ones controlling worldwide communism and enough atomic power to devastate America. Schoolchildren became accustomed to air-raid and fire drills, while local civil defense agencies prepared to deal with perceived Russian dangers. Americans bought Geiger counters and built their own bomb shelters. The Cold War was becoming a way of life. Accepting the 1949 Nobel Prize in literature, William Faulkner commented on the pervasive nature of the fear. For many young writers, he lamented, there was only one question to write about: "When will I be blown up?" The optimistic good times of easy living existing in conjunction with fear and pessimism about the future was the great middle-class contradiction of the 1950s.

Although they were beginning to share their fellow Americans' concerns about the dangers of war in Europe, daily life offered many distractions. The Schellings had been away for two years and had much catching up to do. People were now buying things with "credit cards." New characters had arrived on the scene: a modest little boy named Charlie Brown in the new comic strip, *Peanuts,* and a lecturing bear named Smokey. Jukeboxes playing 45rpm records added to the noise at soda shops and other gathering places, while office workers had a new writing tool in their hands, the ballpoint pen. Schelling knew the threat of communist aggression was thousands of miles away and reminded himself how foolish it was to fear the Reds in America. The hysteria that gripped the nation did touch him occasionally though. Sirens were common sounds in Washington . . . . Was this one an air-raid warning from the Civil Defense system of a Russian attack? He knew it wasn't possible but, with so much talk about the Reds, such a reaction to the sound became almost involuntary.

Schelling's new job came with a special perk, a personal parking place between the White House and the old Executive Office Building. Schelling, who thought of himself as a Democrat, had been a great fan of Roosevelt, and on the few occasions he met Truman, he thought the president "terrific." One of his new duties was to brief Averell Harriman on European topics and to proofread his congressional committee presentations.

Schelling tried to be precise and thorough, but he recalls Harriman snapping his fingers one day and telling him, "Tom, I can think faster than you are talking."[24]

Schelling's most important work in the White House was serving as "administrator in charge of European program affairs" from 1951–1953. As administrator-in-charge, he helped oversee an economic aid program similar to that provided by the Marshall Plan and, for the first time, dealt directly with Cold War issues. The program aimed to cover the foreign trade deficits of NATO countries that needed to be paid in U.S. dollars. As with the Marshall Plan, countries had to present proposals for dealing with their specific economic challenges in order to receive aid; unlike the Marshall Plan, they had to be explicit about their planned military expenditures. This form of aid enabled the United States to offer Cold War assistance by supplying NATO countries with weapons; such aid could also be used as leverage to guarantee that NATO countries maintained favorable policies. With decision-making authority over aid to NATO countries, Schelling used the promise of U.S. aid—or the threat of withdrawing it—as a tool to see that NATO commitments were upheld.

Schelling and his group were especially concerned with the war between the French and the Vietnamese in Indochina, which had begun in 1945, when World War II ended, and would last until 1954. They worked to aid the French economy, being drained by the war in Vietnam, and to provide dollar balance-of-payment assistance to France in the guise of securing supplies and equipment for the war.

Schelling's group also reviewed military requests from U.S. Army generals for new equipment both in Europe and at home. Foreign-aid budgets in the form of military equipment amounted to hundreds of millions of dollars for trucks, ammunition, and aircraft. For a bespectacled 30-year-old who had failed his army physical and was overseeing an equally young staff, his role as the final decision-maker on such requests from U.S. generals might have been intimidating. It wasn't. Confident in his own clear-sightedness, Schelling trusted his ability to make rational decisions despite any seeming differences in status.

On one occasion, a group of generals approached him with a $1.6 billion program for Europe, $1.3 billion in equipment and $300 million in ammunition. Schelling refused the request. The Army revised the program specifics to $300 million in equipment and $1.3 billion in ammunition. The generals' NATO plan called for fighting a 90-day war with supplies already in Europe, and Schelling had calculated that the original request would provide only enough ammunition for about five days. He realized the Army was just trying to get rid of old equipment, so he forced the billion-dollar change.

Schelling's first textbook, *National Income Behavior: An Introduction to Algebraic Analysis,*[25] was released while he was working at the Truman White House. Using the book as his thesis, he completed his doctorate in economics at Harvard in 1952. Robert Solow, 1987 Nobel laureate in economics, had been in Schelling's section when Schelling was a teaching assistant to Professor Gottfried Haberler, recalls the work as "elaborately detailed" and done in what he described as typical Schelling fashion, showing "that sort of extraordinary patience in getting the ducks exactly in a row."[26] It was also a conventional book and, at the time, Schelling's contemporaries viewed him as a conventional economist.

While Schelling was reviewing foreign-aid proposals in the White House and completing his thesis, American scientists and engineers were at work on a secret project, one that would mark the next great step forward in destructive power. The decision to develop a weapon so powerful that, in the event of total war, all other weapons would be obsolete, had been a contentious one. While developing the atomic bomb during World War II, some of the scientists involved realized that another form of nuclear weapon was a theoretical possibility. The atom bomb the United States had developed, and which the Soviets had succeeded in building, was a fission bomb—a device that released an incredible amount of energy by splitting atoms. A fusion-based weapon—one in which energy would be released by forcing hydrogen atoms together—might also be possible. Nuclear fusion is the power by which the sun generates heat and light, which meant that an H-bomb was theoretically hundreds, even thousands, of times more powerful than the A-bomb. After the Soviets ended the U.S. monopoly on atomic weaponry in 1949, the question of whether it was time to take the next step and develop this "superbomb," or "super" as it was often called, soon surfaced.

The debate over building a "super" centered around two of America's leading nuclear physicists, J. Robert Oppenheimer and Edward Teller. Oppenheimer, the former director of the Manhattan Project responsible for developing the first atom bomb, was opposed to proceeding with the new fusion bomb. The dapper, Harvard-educated scholar cited practical as well as ethical reservations about its development: "I am not sure the miserable thing will work, nor that it can be gotten to target except by oxcart." He asserted that the atomic weapons of higher and lower yield already developed would be an adequate defense against the Soviet Union. Teller, with his rumpled suits, bushy eyebrows, and leather foot from an accident involving a trolley car, was Oppenheimer's opposite in many ways. Hungarian-born, he had fled to the United States to escape the Nazis in the 1930s. Another veteran of the Manhattan Project, Teller was convinced of the workability of a fusion bomb and believed that if the United States didn't develop one, the Soviets would.

The conviction of former Roosevelt advisor Alger Hiss for his involvement with the communist Whittaker Chambers on January 21, 1950, settled the Oppenheimer–Teller debate. The communist threat appeared too real to take a chance on Teller being wrong. On January 31, only 10 days after the Hiss conviction, the White House released a statement from the president. Truman's historic words on the mimeographed sheet read: "It is part of my responsibility as Commander in Chief of the armed forces to see that our country is able to defend itself against any aggressor. Accordingly I have directed the Atomic Energy Commission to continue its work on all forms of atomic weapons, including the so-called hydrogen, or super bomb."

The general public began to comprehend fully the degree of danger involved two weeks later on February 12, when the man widely regarded as the greatest genius of modern times appeared on television to offer his thoughts. Clad in a sweater and with unkempt hair, Albert Einstein stepped down from his cloistered world to the level of everyman, explaining in the simplest terms the significance of Truman's decision to build a hydrogen bomb: "[R]adioactive poisoning of the earth's atmosphere and hence annihilation of any life on earth has been brought within the range of technical possibilities . . . General annihilation beckons."[27]

On November 1, 1952, the world's first H-bomb, code-named "Mike," was exploded on the atoll of Eniwetok in Micronesia. The heat at its center was five times greater than the heat at the center of the sun, and the explosion was the equivalent of five million tons of TNT—or five "megatons," in the new terminology. The mushroom cloud, the signature of atomic explosion, extended 100 miles across the sky and rose 25 miles into the stratosphere. The atoll of Eniwetok was obliterated. The U.S. lead was short-lived, however. Nine months after the U.S. test, the Soviet Union exploded an H-bomb in Siberia.

The thermonuclear age had begun, and doom hung in the air. A new satirical magazine called *MAD* (for "mutually assured destruction") was launched to capture the spirit of the times. Einstein's words took on a more haunting air: ". . . . annihilation of any life on earth has been brought within the range of technical possibilities . . . General annihilation beckons." The Doomsday Clock was reset at two minutes to midnight.

Schelling realized the news wasn't good, but it wasn't really his personal concern; there were puzzles to be solved that affected his own work and personal life, not something "within the range of technical possibilities." He couldn't have known how much the explosion of "Mike" and the emergence of the thermonuclear age would become more than just a "concern"—how much it would dominate his thinking and work for years.

The 1952 presidential election pitted the amiable Republican general, Dwight Eisenhower, against the Democrat "egghead," Adlai Stevenson. Americans decided they agreed with Eisenhower's "I Like Ike" campaign slogan. Despite worries about the Korean War dragging on, Americans found life better overall—it was certainly a bit more convenient, thanks to innovations like TV dinners and motorized lawn mowers—and thought Eisenhower would keep the country on a positive track.

Schelling decided to remain in the White House under the Eisenhower administration. The new year brought more than a new president, however: Schelling had a new boss, Harold Stassen. While Harriman had surrounded himself with cronies, Stassen accepted the people already there. Schelling's job didn't change under Stassen, but he did learn a good deal about politics. Stassen was an effective speaker who had, Shelling estimates, about 100 minutes of prepared things to say. He could use 20-minute pieces of his memorized speech differently, tailored for commencement addresses, congressional testimony, or whatever the audience. One of Schelling's jobs was to proofread Stassen's congressional committee presentations; they sounded good when Stassen was giving them (even when he was intentionally evading answering), but they were much different when seen on paper. Sentences broke off in the middle, ideas skipped around. Despite the continual recycling of his material, Stassen enthralled his audiences.

Such skill at reading and communicating with an audience were put to good use when Congress required a 10-percent personnel budget cut throughout all foreign operation administration. Unfortunately, the unpleasant task had been put off for so long that the required reduction was now 20 percent. To get the chore of laying off one-fifth of his staff over with, Stassen gathered his employees in a large auditorium. Having always tried to maintain good racial relations, he told them that discrimination would have no place in the decisions. Every employee then took two civil service tests, a logic test and a test of the employee's knowledge of public affairs. Stassen took everyone's tests into a room by himself to review, then let one in five employees go. In a tense atmosphere, Stassen's good communication skills prevented any problems with race relations.

Nineteen fifty-three brought even more changes with the news that Corinne was pregnant. Thinking they would be in Washington for years and that it was time to make a home, the Schellings bought a house. Ever since returning from Europe, though, Schelling's work had required long hours and many Saturdays in the office. Perhaps the time had come to move on to a position where family life and his career could be more easily combined. Academic life seemed to promise the right balance, so Schelling began looking around.

After the birth of son Andrew, Schelling knew that government work and family life were too much. Friends at Yale arranged a teaching position offer for him. He met with Stassen to tell him he'd been offered an assistant professorship at Yale starting that fall. Stassen said, "Take it." Then he offered the new father a little advice: "Always make sure when you're in the government that you have a career outside, so you can quit."[28]

No sooner had Schelling accepted the position at Yale than Bob Bowie, director of the State Department's policy planning staff, called to offer him a job. It was an attractive offer, and Schelling considered it seriously, even calling on Paul Nitze, who'd held Bowie's position previously. Nitze said the job was a good one, but not so extraordinary that it was better than going to Yale.

The Schellings left Washington and the seat of power, where there was always something interesting happening and somewhere interesting to go, and headed to New Haven, where there was . . . New Haven. They hoped the commute to New York would be short enough that they could enjoy the city's dining and entertainment scene. That proved something of a disappointment. Schelling soon learned that when he and Corinne wanted to go in for dinner or the theater, it was a long trip home. The train was a real milk-run, and especially slow at night.

CHAPTER 5

YALE AND BARGAINING THEORY

The nation breathed a little more easily when the Korean War was finally concluded by an armistice in June 1953. But there was no escape from concerns with the Reds. Just eight days before the war ended, Julius and Ethel Rosenberg headed to the electric chair for selling atomic secrets to the Soviet Union. Their execution symbolized the commingling of two great fears: internal communists and nuclear parity or inferiority. The Cold War was ever-present throughout the 1953–54 academic year, Schelling's first year teaching at Yale, and behind the scenes it all came ominously close to exploding. On five occasions, President Eisenhower rejected advice to use nuclear weapons against Red China in defense of the small islands of Quemoy and Matsu. The threat of communist expansion in Indochina continued to grow; the president warned that the fall of one more Asian nation to communism would lead to the fall of others until they had all gone—what he called the "falling domino" principle.

Safety and patriotism remained national concerns. Armistice Day became Veterans' Day. First Lady Mamie Eisenhower launched the world's first atomic-powered submarine, the *USS Nautilus*. By congressional resolution, the Pledge of Allegiance was changed from "one nation indivisible" to "one nation under God indivisible." Joseph McCarthy, the demagogue of suspicion and distrust whose blacklists and charges had ruined careers and lives, was condemned by the Senate for abusing his colleagues.

Meanwhile at Yale, Schelling was teaching international economics to both undergraduate and graduate students and focusing his own academic interests on bargaining and bargaining theory (the bargaining theme would run through much of his work from then on, especially his great contributions to Cold War strategic thought). Although he liked his students, Schelling found the institution less academically inclined than he had hoped and considered the administration somewhat anti-intellectual. An undergraduate-oriented gentlemen's school, Yale demonstrated its diversity, in part, by the variety of prep schools represented in its student body. Schelling approached his new career with enthusiasm, however, and it was a fortunate group of students who found themselves in his classes.

An early colleague remembers the Schelling of those days and his "broad smile: his delight in ideas, often transforming his face and activating his whole body, and eagerness touched with impudence."[29]

With the new year came significant events at home, as well as Cold War escalations abroad. In a monumental decision, the Supreme Court ruled in *Brown v. Board of Education* that the segregation of schools by race was unconstitutional, ushering in a new era in American history. For the Schelling's, 1954 was marked by the birth of their second son, Tommy. Corinne, who had accepted a teaching post at a small New Haven college when they moved, gave up the position after learning that one-year-old Andrew would soon have a little brother. (She had already put her plans for completing her PhD in economics on hold after leaving Washington.) In less momentous news, Schelling had his hair cut short and tapered in front in the new "crewcut" look—one that suited him and that he never changed from that time on.

Nineteen fifty-five was another watershed year in many ways. Albert Einstein, the man who made the nuclear age—and the nuclear terror— possible, died; and Walt Disney, the man who kept fantasy alive, opened his park in California. Everyone "Loved Lucy," even children in their coon-skin "Davy Crockett" hats and teens mourning the loss of their hero, James Dean. At Yale, Schelling's thoughts on bargaining had been fully developed, while in Washington, Congress overwhelmingly authorized the president to take whatever steps were necessary to defend Formosa, or Taiwan, against a threatened attack by communist China. Eisenhower ordered aircraft carriers to the region and, in a largely ignored bit of news, U.S. advisors were quietly being sent to Vietnam.

So, what was the United States doing in Vietnam? Just what was going on over there? Was the United States making a threat, or a commitment— and what was the difference? Would it be better to establish communication with the Viet Minh, the communists in the South? What would have been the effect had officials made public statements at home that locked the United States into a position? Was sending the advisors an overt statement of intentions?

These were all questions that would be asked too late, questions Schelling was just learning to formulate. Schelling's thoughts on bargaining theory might have given the advisors and their superiors material to work with. Strategic studies was an evolving area lacking clear definitions and theories. Such questions might have been better approached with an understanding of what Schelling called the "distributional" aspect of bargaining: There are bargaining situations with a range of possible outcomes available, he said, where agreement at any point is better for both sides than no agreement at all. He was hard at work defining and describing that range and how agreement could be naturally found or the range manipulated, even as the first advisors arrived in Vietnam.

The first widely acclaimed expression of Schelling's views on how to successfully find agreement, or to narrow the range of agreements, came the following year in "An Essay on Bargaining," published in the June 1956 issue of *The American Economic Review*. One of its readers was Daniel Ellsberg, who was so impressed with the young economist that he came to Yale to meet him. Thus began a long friendship between Schelling and the man who would play a role in ending America's involvement in the Vietnam War and would be included in the charges that brought an end to the Nixon presidency.

Among the many topics Schelling dealt with in his essay was the question of why certain agreements seem to be settled on naturally. A fundamental idea of Schelling's bargaining theory was that bargaining situations may not always have logical outcomes, and that when they don't, the solution is found in the tactics. In such cases, the question becomes one of what constitutes successful tactics. Schelling described how the ability to remove all of one's options may give one the upper hand in certain situations. He wrote of the differences between the tactical uses of commitments, threats, and promises, giving a vocabulary to the evolving discipline of strategic studies. Some consider this the point at which Schelling began to enter the realm of game theory. "An Essay on Bargaining" eventually became the second chapter of his greatest and most frequently mentioned work incorporating game theory, *The Strategy of Conflict*.[30]

Discussing the value of making commitments, he wrote that "the power to constrain an adversary may depend on the power to bind oneself." In bargaining, one way to establish a strong position is to eliminate your options to make other choices: "[W]eakness is often strength . . . and to burn bridges behind one may suffice to undo an opponent."[31] Decisions that cannot be changed, commitments must be made carefully because, "[c]oncession not only may be construed as capitulation [but] may make the adversary skeptical of any new pretense at commitment." The difficulty is making believable commitments, a problem with which public opinion can help: "When national representatives go to international negotiations knowing that there is a wide range of potential agreement within which the outcome will depend on bargaining, they seem often to create a bargaining position by public statements, statements calculated to arouse a public opinion that permits no concession." Yet public statements made by

officials often carry little weight, as they may
not be believed. Hence the importance of
overt acts when making commitments, said
Schelling, offering an example: "State that
any attack on a NATO country will be seen as
an attack on the United States. Who's going
to believe that? The answer came in the Truman administration. Station seven divisions
of U.S. troops in Europe. Any Soviet invasion
would have to go through the U.S. forces.
They couldn't get out of the way. The United
States clearly couldn't see seven divisions of

Eisenhower and Secretary of
State John Foster Dulles,
August 14, 1956

troops destroyed or captured and let it go at that. Make it true in a way the
Soviets and Germans would recognize."[32]

Schelling spoke of another tactic in his seminal 1956 essay: the threat.
Different from a commitment, the threat would only be acted upon when
it failed as a tactic. The one making threats has no incentive to do what is
threatened. It is the threat itself, not its execution, that gains its goal.
Schelling pointed out that the threat's magnitude, if extremely large, may
affect its believability, as in the case of the doctrine of "massive retaliation."

First spoken of by Secretary of State John Foster Dulles (who took the
concept to frightening levels when he discussed "brinkmanship" in 1956),
"massive retaliation" was the idea that any act of Soviet aggression would
be met by an immediate escalation to nuclear war. (Meeting Soviet aggression with nuclear war would also be a question in 1961, when President
Kennedy looked to Schelling for advice on Berlin as tension mounted.)
Schelling explained the problem of threats as ineffective deterrents
because of failures in self-control by drawing an example from his own
children: Parents threaten their children with no TV, an early bedtime, and
other punishments but often fail to enforce such threats consistently.
Drawing parallels between nuclear war with the Soviets and disciplining
his own children was typical of what would become Schelling's analytical
style. He looked to the patterns and common themes around him that
would illuminate his topics and make explanations most understandable.

Schelling also discussed a third arrangement sometimes required
between parties: the promise. The promise is used in circumstances where
the final action to be taken is outside of one's control, making it a weaker
tactic in some cases but necessary in agreements where an incentive to
cheat exists. Kidnappings for ransom involve risky promises, and everyday
promises come with borrowing money and entering into contracts.

The roles of outside agents in bargaining situations and the notion that there are times when appearing irrational can be the rational thing to do were additional discussion points in "An Essay on Bargaining." He presented these ideas and arguments in his early works in bargaining theory, but he would find applications for them in his changing emphasis to game theory and nuclear strategy. Always related to his work, bargaining theory is difficult to separate from later game theory.

With his first essay published and receiving high praise, Schelling was off to a six-week seminar in Amherst, Massachusetts. While there, he met the deputy head of economics at the RAND Corporation. Although Schelling was hardly familiar with the Southern California think tank, that would soon change: The meeting led to an invitation for Schelling to visit RAND the following summer.

In November 1956, President Eisenhower won an easy reelection over Adlai Stevenson. That same fall, the adult world stood by in shock as America's youth went wild over Elvis Presley rocking his way to the top of the charts. Fifty-four million viewers tuned in for his television debut on *The Ed Sullivan Show*. In New Haven, Schelling was the proud father of a third son, Daniel. He had also begun his study of game theory, the method of analysis he would find use for and relate to nuclear strategy and much else in the years to come. A half century later Schelling would be awarded the Nobel Prize in Economics for his integration of game theory into practical social science. Years before that award, Steven Pearlstein of *The Washington Post* would write, "The task of integrating game theory into popular economics fell to Thomas Schelling. Schelling found applications for game theory not only in arms control, but in designing environmental regulations, setting criminal penalties and reforming insurance markets."[33]

Schelling had actually been interested in game theory in the 1940s before leaving Harvard, shortly after the theory originated in a 1944 work called *Theory of Games and Economic Behavior*[34] by John von Neumann and Oskar Morgenstern. At Harvard, Schelling had taken a point out of their book and written about it, arguing that it omitted many important considerations. He showed what he had written to his Harvard mentor, Wassily Leontief. Leontief asked whether Schelling had actually read the book. Schelling said he had not, but that he had read several reviews. Leontief offered the sage advice that perhaps he should wait until he had read the book.

Years later at Yale, Schelling had the opportunity to meet the founder of it all, the legendary John von Neumann. The encounter occurred at a party for William Fellner's 50th birthday. Fellner, Schelling's professor at

Berkeley, had moved on to Yale, where they were both on the economics faculty. Coincidentally, Neumann had gone to grammar school with Fellner in Hungary and was a guest at the party. A prodigy and mathematical wizard, Neumann could divide eight-digit numbers by eight-digit numbers in his head and carry on conversations with his father in Ancient Greek at age six. He could also look at pages of the phone book then recite them from memory. He had mastered calculus at eight, and it is said that when he got older, he took two books with him when he went to the toilet. By the mid-1950s, his exhibitions of virtuosity included races against the new computers in solving complex computation problems. Schelling said that when he was first at the RAND Corporation, everyone had Neumann stories to tell, but that the Hungarian-born polymath "didn't perform any mental feats"[35] at Fellner's party. Schelling adds, with a chuckle, that he didn't mention his earlier criticisms of Neumann's work that evening either.

During his early years at Yale, Schelling had spent, by his estimate, 100 hours reading and rereading Neumann and Morgenstern's *Theory of Games and Economic Behavior*. Yet he found Duncan Luce and Howard Raiffa's 1957 work, *Games and Decisions: Introduction and Critical Survey*, much more useful in helping him understand game theory. Schelling and Raiffa were destined to become friends and colleagues, and Raiffa would later say of Schelling, writing in the *Journal of Economic Perspectives*:

> Tom thinks orthogonally to the rest of us. By now, I just expect him to be brilliant, to relate a problem that parents have with kids, or that general XYZ had in battle Q. The analogies keep tumbling out of his mind, as if he has an almost endless tabulation of concrete examples in his personal micro-micro-computer and each new thought automatically triggers a search routine.

CHAPTER 6

GAME THEORY

During the Arab-Israeli Yom Kippur War of 1973, oil-producing Arab nations unleashed a powerful strategic weapon, an embargo of oil shipments to countries supporting Israel. By the time the embargo was lifted in 1974, the price of oil had quadrupled, and Americans were trying a variety of schemes to cope with the apparent oil shortage. Homeowners lowered their thermostats, drivers were restricted to buying gasoline on alternating days, depending on whether they had even- or odd-numbered license plates, and no one was allowed to purchase gas on Sundays. On December 19, 1973, Johnny Carson opened *The Tonight Show* by quipping: "You know what's disappearing from the supermarket shelves? *Toilet paper*. There is an acute shortage of toilet paper in the United States." This was a joke, but the idea of a toilet paper shortage was disturbing enough to cause an unusually large number of people to decide they should stock up "just in case."

The next morning, 20 million viewers headed to the supermarkets and emptied the shelves of the available supplies, resulting in a short-lived toilet paper shortage, perhaps the only shortage ever caused by a single person. People made their decision to buy toilet paper based on the decision they anticipated other people would make, which was also to buy more paper. People also anticipated that others were making a decision that was being made by many viewers of the show: The mentality that "I'm deciding to buy more, and I know he's deciding to buy more, and he knows I'm going to buy more, and I know he's going to buy more" sent people rushing to get to the market first. People were thinking vicariously about what other people were thinking and what those people were thinking the same people were thinking—nobody wanted to be caught unprepared. The shortage was short lived, and Carson apologized for having brought it on.

During the Cold War, the United States and the Soviet Union stockpiled nuclear weapons at an astonishing pace.[36] A Brookings Institution study reveals some eye-opening facts. In 1956 and 1957, the U.S. army requested 151,000 nuclear warheads, and the U.S. stockpile peaked in 1966 at 32,193. "More than 75" secret "presidential emergency facilities" have been built for use during and after a nuclear war. And 11 U.S. nuclear bombs have been lost in accidents and never recovered. That's just the United States, and there was an equally armed rival. To understand the scope of such figures, consider that nuclear weapon explosions are measured in kilotons and megatons of TNT—in other words, in one thousand or one million tons of TNT. A single pound of TNT could bring down an airplane. The bomb dropped on Hiroshima was a 15-kiloton bomb. The largest bomb the United States has since tested had a yield of 15 megatons, or was 2,000 times as powerful. The Soviet Union tested even more powerful bombs. Each side in the Cold War confrontation wasn't just going ahead with its own armament, but trying to determine what decisions its rival would make. Each knew the other was doing the same thing—trying to decide what the opposition would do next—and that knowledge played a part in the decision it made.

What toilet paper and nuclear holocaust threats have in common here is that they involve situations related to game theory. The accumulation of both could be analyzed by the same methods, as they each involved vicarious, interdependent decision processes. The game theory approach to analyzing decision-making arose from the observation that many indoor games like chess and checkers share a number of characteristics. First, and most important, players' decisions are interdependent. For example, the best move to make in chess depends on the moves one's opponent has made or is anticipated to make. Second, the games are usually well defined with an explicit set of rules; the amount of information available to players is specified at every point, and the scoring system is complete.

Such characteristics often appear in the "real world" the social scientist studies as well. Investment in the stock market is a good example. Decisions to invest or sell are certainly interdependent, the rules are specific, the available information is specified at every point, and profits or losses amount to a scoring system. Game theory is the formal study of rational, consistent expectations that these people can have about each other's choices.

Game theory is a misleading name, since it is neither a theory nor a study of what are commonly thought of as "games." It comes from the title of the original book in this field, Neumann and Morgenstern's *Theory of Games and Economic Behavior*. Although the theory was inspired by observations of the interactive nature of parlor games like checkers and chess, such social science "games" include forms of competition that have much more serious consequences. Patterns of segregation and integration, wars, elections, and personal attempts to quit smoking or to get homework done on time all fall within the realm of "games," as seen by game theorists. A theory is a set of theorems and solutions, which is not an accurate description of game theory. Moreover, a theory is usually a theory *of* something (economic theory or the theory of relativity, for example). Many leading scholars in game theory disagree about which theoretical frontier game theory is developing on. Mathematicians and social scientists are the principal groups involved in the subject, but there is often little common interest to keep them in touch. While this may make game theory sound like a questionable approach to analyzing social studies, it is, in fact, highly useful. Game theory provides a framework for analyzing many types of situations. It is equally applicable to the study of sociology, economics, conflict theory, political science, and the natural and physical sciences.

Two assumptions about people are inherent as starting points in the game theory approach. First is the "rational actor," the assumption that people behave according to reason and are equally capable of complex logical thought. The second is what is sometimes called "situational ethics," the assumption that people are only concerned with outcomes, or final results. Critics sometimes disregard game theory as a valid approach for making complex decisions because of these assumptions. Yet the assumptions are merely starting points: Adjustments in problem solving can be added to methods and models when one learns that either or both assumption is not valid in a particular case.

One of game theory's basic concepts is equilibrium, the state in which some condition or some thing remains in balance. One sees equilibrium in the atmosphere, as the production of oxygen and consumption of carbon dioxide by plants equals the consumption of oxygen and production of carbon dioxide by animals. One might see equilibrium between the amount employers are willing to pay employees, and the amount potential workers are willing to work for. If a problem requires an equilibrium answer, it requires a solution acceptable to both or all participants.

Equilibrium is either "stable" or "unstable," depending on how it responds to being upset or thrown off. A stable equilibrium tends to respond by returning to its original equilibrium condition. An unstable equilibrium is the opposite. If upset in some direction, it tends to continue in that direction rather than revert to its starting point.

Picture a marble resting inside a bowl. The marble is at an equilibrium point. Jiggle the bowl, and the marble moves. Stop the jiggling, and the marble returns to the bowl's center. This analogy illustrates "stable" equilibrium. If the bowl is turned over, and the marble is balanced at the center of the top of the inverted bowl, it is still at an equilibrium point. Yet the response to the jiggling would differ. The marble would move away from the equilibrium point and not return (it would fall off). This illustrates an unstable equilibrium. Stable equilibria produce stable game outcomes.

Efficiency is another frequent game-theory concept. When used in its economic context, efficiency refers to an outcome in which the value of output from the resources involved has been maximized. Game theorists often refer to it as "Pareto efficiency" or "Pareto optimization," after the Italian mathematician Vilfredo Pareto. This more specifically states that the parties in a game with a variety of choices have reached a point where they cannot make a different choice, or move to a different position, without lowering another player's outcome.

The choices and decisions that individuals, or "players," make in game theory are made in the real world, and those choices are interdependent. The players are aware that their actions affect each other, and awareness of this effect is a factor in their decisions. The games are usually classified as purely competitive, called "zero-sum" games, games of cooperation/coordination, wherein players share common interests, or games that are neither completely competitive nor cooperative, what Schelling called "mixed-motive" games. Most earlier work in game theory had focused on zero-sum games.

Soon after Schelling became interested in game theory, he developed the concept of "focal points" (now sometimes called "Schelling points"), which earned him a reputation as a game theorist. Focal points are solutions to situations where agreement is sought, but where no contact between the parties involved could take place. Schelling knew the parties would have to try to think vicariously, to think as the other person or people would think. It was game theory; the players' decisions were interdependent. As Schelling said, "Each player is the prisoner or the beneficiary of their mutual expectations; no one can disavow his own expectations of what the other will expect him to expect to be expected to do."[37]

The focal-point concept wasn't something Schelling originated while teaching at Yale, however. The idea that what he called a "prominent" solution exists when people are trying to achieve a common goal without communicating with each other had come to him much earlier: during that summer road trip with his college buddies, Tom Ludwig and Morris Glickfeld. The group had been separated in San Antonio, Texas, unable to communicate, and they wanted a solution for finding each other should the situation rise again. How would they all choose the same place to meet?

They had spent a whole afternoon thinking about the dilemma individually—each concluding that the meeting place must be something every city has one of, but not more than one, that could be found by asking a policeman or fireman, and that, preferably, was accessible via public transportation. They each came up with the general-delivery window of the main post office. It especially made sense because they'd all promised their mothers they'd check for mail in three cities at general delivery. What struck Schelling at the time was that there had been a certain signaling quality about the circumstances that led them to arrive at their goal of a common answer without speaking to each other. Their thoughts had both independently and collectively focused on the general-delivery window.

When the focal-point idea crystallized at Yale, Schelling sat at his typewriter and began typing examples to test it. He wanted to determine what sorts of clues tended to create effective communication, and he suspected they could be derived as much by imagination as by logic. He ended up creating a questionnaire, an exercise of short decision-making activities that could be done by two people to determine whether they could arrive at mutually beneficial solutions to problems or situations when they didn't have the opportunity to communicate.

Schelling's questionnaire began:

a) Write down heads or tails. You win if you choose the same as your partner.

b) Circle one of the Xs. If you circle the same X as your partner, you both win.

$$X \quad\quad X \quad\quad X \quad\quad X$$

$$X \quad\quad X \quad\quad X \quad\quad X$$

$$X \quad\quad X \quad\quad X \quad\quad X$$

$$X \quad\quad X \quad\quad X \quad\quad X$$

c) You are to meet someone in New York at a stated time. You have not been instructed where to meet; you have no prior understanding with the other person of where to meet; and you have no way of communicating with each other. You will have to guess where to meet and hope both of your guesses are the same. Where will you meet?

He mailed the puzzles to a variety of friends and colleagues and, when they were returned, he scored them and sent the results back. John and Sally McNaughton, old Marshall Plan friends, ended with the highest score, and MIT economics professor Francis Bator was happy to finish second. Future Nobel Prize winner Herb Simon was less enthusiastic. His reply, among other comments, was "Don't you know you're always supposed to include a stamped, self-addressed envelope?"[38]

When *The Journal of Conflict Resolution* released its first issue in 1957, it included Schelling's questionnaire. Along with the questionnaire, Schelling devised other situations involving cooperative tacit decision-making to explore his ideas and tried them out at Yale. James Tobin recalled, "We had great seminars where he would make us decide where . . . and at what time of day we would meet . . . how we would divide a joint surplus or a mapped plot of land . . . For weeks no one talked about anything else. Game theory has never been as much fun or as relevant."[39]

Years before developing his formal theory, Schelling had put it to a practical test that recalled the summer road trip incident. He had planned to get together in New York City with Tom Ludwig, but when Schelling arrived in New York, he realized he didn't have the address. There he was, no idea where to go. Thinking over the situation, he concluded that Ludwig might remember the road trip of their younger days and that, if they were smart about it, they would be able to find each other. Back then, they decided the general-delivery window was the best place to meet, but general delivery was now a thing of the past. The closest thing Schelling could think of was Western Union. He called and said, "Do you have a way that I can leave a message for a person who may call in for a message?" The operator said, "Yes, what is your name?" He said, "Schelling." The operator replied, "Oh, we have a message for you from Mr. Ludwig."[40]

As Schelling demonstrated, focal points have often been useful solutions in situations where communication is indirect. In World War II, without discussion or direct communication, neither side used poison gas, as had been done in World War I. Sometimes a focal point has provided the basis for settlement of hostilities, such as with the 38th Parallel in Korea. Focal points are valuable on a day-to-day basis, by bringing husbands and wives together when they get separated in a department store, for example. As Cold War dangers grew, focal points and other forms of tacit bargaining became increasingly important.

A clear understanding of where lines were being drawn, literally and figuratively, and how unstated agreements could be achieved were becoming Schelling specialties, and lent themselves well to game theory. Schelling likes to describe himself as a user of game theory rather than a theorist. It was observation and empirical research that first convinced him of focal points, and their value lay in how they facilitated problem-solving, but the interactive nature of the decision-making process involved is game theory.

CHAPTER 7

RAND

In the summer of 1957, Schelling headed to the West Coast for a two-month visit at RAND, having accepted the offer made to him by the organization's deputy head of economics the previous year. The think tank was an outgrowth of World War II, when it had been demonstrated that modern warfare was a contest of science and new tactics and that keeping a new sort of thinker involved in military planning and research was critical. To maintain the relationship between academia and the military following the war, H. H. "Hap" Arnold, the commanding general of the Army Air Force, and Donald Douglas, president of Douglas Aircraft Company, cooperated in setting up Project RAND (for "Research and Development") in December 1945.

RAND's first report demonstrated its value in the emerging conflict, especially in hindsight. Eleven years before the Soviets stunned America with the launch of *Sputnik*, RAND published its *Preliminary Design of an Experimental World-Circling Spaceship*. Nine months later, Jimmy Lipp, head of Project RAND's Missile Division, wrote in a follow-on paper:

> Since mastery of the elements is a reliable index of material progress, the nation which first makes significant achievements in space travel will be acknowledged as the world leader in both military and scientific techniques. To visualize the impact on the world, one can imagine the consternation and admiration that would be felt here if the United States were to discover suddenly that some other nation had already put up a successful satellite.

In 1947, RAND moved to downtown Santa Monica, California, and broke its ties to both the Air Force and Douglas Aircraft. Incorporated as an independent nonprofit corporation, the RAND Corporation's stated purpose was: "To further and promote scientific, educational, and charitable purposes, all for the public welfare and security of the United States."[41] RAND operated in an extremely high-security environment, working on projects related to national defense, which increasingly meant nuclear strategy and nuclear war. "Public welfare and general security" had become an ominous phrase, and the high security under which it operated and the nature of its work gave RAND a minatory aura.

When Schelling arrived in Southern California, he wasn't sure what to expect. He knew little about RAND and had no background in the formal study of military strategy. He had come as an economist to work with other economists. Although RAND's two-story, white, nearly unmarked building was sterile and unwelcoming, a survey of the office's surroundings presented quite a different view. RAND was just a five-minute walk from the beach—and not just any beach, but 150 yards of golden sand stretching to the Pacific and running off in both directions into hazy outlines of hills. Tall palms and dark green bushes dotted with red hibiscus flowers lined the streets and beach path. Seagulls flew overhead. It promised to be a pleasant place for an East Coast professor to spend time.

Under the supervision of Charles Hitch, director of RAND's economics division, Schelling settled into his first project of the summer, a month-long economic study. He soon discovered that, despite the high security and highly classified nature of RAND's activities, the atmosphere inside the RAND compound was extremely casual, very much Southern California. Everyone wore Hawaiian shirts, and they all went by first names. There wasn't a necktie in sight. Just how informal RAND could be was apparent the day a man came in to apply for a job wearing only a wet swimming suit. Rather than being told to leave, he was hired.

Yet beneath all the informality hovered the ever-present theme of good versus evil. It was identical to being back in World War II fighting the Nazis, except the Nazis never had nuclear weapons.[42] The Allies had appeased Hitler before making a stand in that war, leading him to believe they were weak and could be exploited. The researchers at RAND understood that lesson and were determined it wasn't going to be the same with the Soviets. As Churchill had said, "An appeaser is one who feeds a crocodile, hoping it will eat him last." There would be no backing away this time: Nuclear war against the evil ones was a very real possibility to be faced every day.

The environment at RAND emphasized communication and interaction. Whatever subjects or projects were being tackled, it was all done in a spirit of camaraderie. Schelling found the place fun and exhilarating. People willingly worked hard and stayed late. RAND's leaders believed that the yeasty combination of intelligent, imaginative people brought together in situations where they could freely interchange ideas would stimulate new approaches for analysis and strategizing, leading to creative solutions to varied and complex problems. The institution's physical plant was designed with that in mind. The two-story building was a series of rectangles and corridors, with windows for everyone. Its horizontal structure forced people to walk from one place to another to go to conferences, go to the bathrooms, go to lunch, go anywhere; and, as they did, they were likely to have chance encounters or catch each others' eyes and stop to talk. It was normal for people to leave their office doors open unless they didn't want to be disturbed. If someone looked in and saw something written on a blackboard, he was likely to stop with a question or comment. Spontaneous conversations occurred all the time.

With such an emphasis on originality and creativity, new ideas were commonplace and often widely circulated. People prepared mailing lists, often of 50 names or more, and sent out their new thoughts for others to consider. The degree to which creativity was encouraged is apparent in some of the suggestions made for dealing with current problems: Schelling recalls being at RAND at a time when kidnapping and hijacking of planes were occurring frequently, and one idea put forward was to make it a capital offense to be the person kidnapped or taken hostage.

Lunch was an informal gathering, with cafeteria food on trays taken to an open patio. It rarely rained in Santa Monica. Animated conversations dominated many of the tables; at others, people gathered around chessboards. To a visitor's casual glance, it might look as if regular chess was being played. But this was something different, a game called Kriegspiel. *Kriegspiel* is German for "war game" and, although the game originated in the nineteenth century as a Prussian military board game, at RAND it was blind chess.

The game required three people: two players and a referee. Two chessboards were set up with a barrier between them, so the players could only see their own boards. The players made moves, only learning whether their moves had succeeded or whether their pieces had been captured when the referee told them so. The challenge of deducing an opponent's changing positions and attacking strategically without the opponent in view was formidable. A military strategy game on an extremely intellectual level, Kriegspiel was in many ways an apt metaphor for RAND.

A number of the period's leading nuclear strategists were in residence at RAND during that summer of 1957. Schelling's interaction with this exclusive group and their acceptance of him inducted the young economist into an elite fraternity. Theirs was the world of civilian strategists who devoted much of their intellectual lives to nuclear policy—thinking in a detached, objective way about preventing nuclear holocaust, winning a nuclear war, surviving a nuclear war, and every other related issue. It was an important group, one that confronted the most dangerous of all problems, and people listened to them. Schelling was there in their secret enclave, where they were free to think and talk and write while the RAND walls kept outsiders away. He had joined a warm, exciting think-tank world of ideas and analysis, where the topics of discussion were of ultimate importance and well beyond the theoretical: The ideas that emerged could lead to formal, official policy. At times, the strategists directly affected policy by offering specific advice or plans; other times, their influence came through a presentation of basic ideas, understandings, and strategies, which were then developed into specific policies by government figures and decision-makers or which guided their thinking.

The strategists themselves were a varied and colorful group. Hitch, who had arranged Schelling's visit, later moved on to become comptroller of the Defense Department under Secretary of Defense Robert McNamara. Hitch had been a professor at Oxford, but left in 1948 to found the economics division at RAND. His greatest achievement was systems analysis, a method of cost-effective analysis that cut across all departments at RAND. Bernard Brodie, earliest among the group's members in nuclear strategy, introduced the term "massive retaliation" in his 1946 book *The Absolute Weapon*. Brodie argued that atomic weapons could be used as weapons of deterrence, rather than weapons of attack. His interests were more straight theory than application and, although a bit vain, he was a great conversationalist and especially good at keeping things lively at lunch. Food was important to Brodie, and he had trout flown in from Salt Lake City. (While he liked the trout from Salt Lake City, his past experiences with the city itself were less favorable: The Mormons had excommunicated his wife, a military historian.) Albert Wohlstetter, who had joined RAND in 1951, was America's leading strategist throughout much of the decade. His study about the location of Strategic Air Command bases contributed to the decision to locate them far from the Soviet Union and keep them highly protected, so the U.S. military could launch a second strike in the event of a Soviet attack against the United States. He later came to advocate a reduced reliance on nuclear weapons and increased development of non-nuclear systems. In his January 1959 *Foreign Affairs* article, "The Delicate Balance of Terror," he summarized a number of RAND concerns about how the United States had become vulnerable to nuclear attack and offered a variety of solutions. A gourmet and a somewhat aristocratic and arrogant man, Wohlstetter was at his best when involved in debate. When conducting meetings, he would have the seats arranged in a circle with his own chair right in the center.

While Hitch, Brodie, and Wohlstetter were certainly interesting, the most fascinating and controversial character Schelling met that summer was the rotund and effusive Herman Kahn. Sam Cohen, the longtime RAND scholar who had recruited Kahn, said of him: "He was a mutation. A cosmic ray must have struck his mother's egg."[43] The best-known strategist of the 1950s, Kahn believed that an effective deterrent required the capability of launching precise attacks on Soviet military targets. He frequently expressed his disdain for the air force's nuclear-targeting policy, comparing it to a "Doomsday Machine." Kahn delivered dozens of lectures on nuclear war that shocked his audiences, describing nuclear war and its aftermath, asking whether the living would envy the dead. He thought survival a possibility and compared conditions with various tens to hundreds of millions killed, while suggesting that the most radioactively contaminated food would be eaten by the oldest survivors. He spoke of birth defects and asked whether it might be possible to love two-headed children twice as much. Princeton University Press published Kahn's lectures in the 1960 book *On Thermonuclear War.*

A critique in *Scientific American* said what many people thought: Kahn was a "Genghis Kahn, a monster who had written an insane, pornographic book, an immoral tract on mass murder: how to plan it, how to commit it, how to get away with it, how to justify it." Kahn helped foster the growing impression of RAND as a sinister, Machiavellian place where the risk to human life was not considered seriously in calculations of nuclear strategy. While that might have been what people thought of Kahn, and Schelling could understand why they did, he had a different view. He enjoyed being around the gregarious and brilliant Kahn (who was said to have the highest IQ on record). It was hard not to like the man.

Schelling had a long conversation with Kahn early on, where it was apparent to Kahn that Schelling understood what he was talking about, and from then on Kahn treated him as an equal. Being a newcomer around the most famous strategists of the time didn't mean Schelling would not immediately be accepted as a part of their group. Earning their respect was required, but Schelling's "Essay on Bargaining," among other published works, suggested he was worth their attention, and he could hold his own in arguments. The informal nature of the place and the frequent interaction broke down barriers quickly. Kahn, Wohlstetter, Brodie, and Hitch all took Schelling seriously from the beginning. He passed the probation period and was one of them.

Decades later, in 1998, the *New York Times* looked back on those years and recalled the special fraternity: "Brodie wrote that the main function of nuclear weapons was deterring wars, not fighting them. Nonetheless, he, Albert J. Wohlstetter, Herman Kahn, Thomas C. Schelling and others soon began systematically contemplating their use. In the 1950s and early 60s, they coined the chilling phrases 'counterforce' and 'second strike' for the nuclear doctrines they devised."

Daniel Ellsberg visited Santa Monica that summer, and Schelling introduced him to his new colleagues. Ellsberg was soon invited to work at RAND, where he would become another member of the elite group. Ellsberg recalls those early years of working with Schelling: "Our minds were intellectually dancing together."[44]

The RAND group was a diverse mixture of backgrounds, characters, and interests, yet those in it had much in common. Although part of their strategizing and analysis concerned winning and surviving nuclear war, along with an endless array of related topics, prevention was the major theme. Schelling recalls that "I think we typically thought of ourselves as interested in anything that would make deterrence work and be safe. And by that I mean we were as interested in what we could do unilaterally as well as what we might do in partnership with the Soviet Union. I always had liked the Strategic Air Command slogan, 'Peace is Our Profession.' They might not have believed it, but I did."[45]

RAND's reputation as a home for seekers of peace was not one easily maintained, with Kahn there and with Neumann, who was quoted in *Life* magazine as saying, "If you say why not bomb them tomorrow, I say, why not today. If you say at five o'clock, I say why not one o'clock."[46]

In keeping with RAND's operational style, Schelling enjoyed considerable freedom during his visit. The economic-development study concluded, Schelling was free to work on anything he liked for the second month of his stay. Among other pursuits, he chose to spend time in RAND's war-games facility observing the enactment of hypothetical conflicts: a communist Chinese attack on Taiwan, for example, in which the gaming facility tried various possibilities of a mainland China attack with different combinations of American and Taiwanese forces to determine expected outcomes.

Other games involved cost-benefit analysis, such as the one Schelling observed as it was played on a board the size of a ping-pong table. An attempt to analyze the trade-off involved in spending money on weapons versus spending it on intelligence, the game simulated the Soviet Union and the United States dividing their resources between procuring weapons and ammunition and procuring facilities for gathering intelligence, depending on how much intelligence they already had. The game's goal was to determine the optimal allocation of resources. RAND's war games were simulations to see the outcomes of different possible alternatives, not games involving decision-making or choices. The war games interested Schelling, for he saw a different application for them: Rather than using simulations to test the outcomes of various alternatives, they could be used to train people to make decisions in crisis situations.

This time at RAND was important in drawing Schelling into the specific study of military problems and of demonstrating the relationship between military strategy and his focus on bargaining theory. He also began to relate his new understanding of game theory to strategic thought.

RAND was in the lead in the development of game theory, and the most famous of all game-theory games was first played there in 1950. That was the year John Nash had written a paper at Princeton for his thesis advisor, mathematician Albert Tucker, that presented a solution to non-zero-sum games. This useful solution would be the "Nash equilibrium" that later led to Nash's Nobel Prize. At RAND, Melvin Dresher and Merrill Flood designed a simple game that demonstrated the equilibrium wasn't a reliable predictor of behavior in social dilemmas.

Tucker was at RAND, preparing to give a talk at Stanford on recent developments in game theory when he walked past a blackboard with the payoff numbers on it for Dresher and Flood's game. The results startled him: Their game raised questions about whether the rational thing to do was always to "act rationally." Acting rationally meant, in game theory, acting in a manner that led to the best personal outcome, and the rational thing seemed to be for the two sides to cooperate. Yet even though cooperation might lead to the best results, the game seemed to show that with rational actors, cooperation would not take place, and the best results would not occur. Tucker decided to include the game in his talk, but thought it would be easier to explain if he gave it a name and, instead of concentrating on the math involved, turned it into a story:

Two men are arrested and put in solitary confinement for a crime they did, in fact, commit. The police know they don't have enough evidence to convict the two. They can, however, successfully prosecute both on some lesser charge, such as possession of firearms, which carries a prison sentence of one year. The only way the police can get convictions on the principal crime is if the men to testify against each other. So, the men are separated and each prisoner is offered a deal. If he testifies against the other, he will go free for his cooperation, but the other prisoner will get three years in prison if he does not cooperate. Each man is told that the same deal is being offered to the other and that if they testify against each other, both will be sentenced to two-year terms.

Concerned only with his own welfare—minimizing his time in jail—each prisoner might then be thinking, "Let's not testify, neither of us. That way, we both get off with the light, one-year sentence. We can't communicate, but the other person probably has figured out we shouldn't testify. It's obvious. But if the other has figured it out, and isn't going to testify, why not testify against him? That way I would be out free, while he goes to jail for three years. That's his problem. But wait . . ." he's probably thinking the same thing. There's no way to know. Now what? And if we both testify against each other . . ." Now what? It's a dilemma. Each man wants to do what is best for himself.

The prisoners' dilemma was especially important to strategic thought at RAND, because of its application to relations between Russia and America. When Schelling arrived at RAND, there was an arms race between the Soviet Union and America that was a prisoner's dilemma that threatened disaster. Schelling now understood game theory and, like his elite colleagues, could put the Cold War in a game-theory framework. The United States and the Soviets could each have chosen to maintain their nuclear arsenals at current levels or to increase them. While cooperation, by maintaining the current number of weapons, would have been an economically sound option, the temptation was not to cooperate in a bid to gain a strategic and potentially decisive advantage by increasing the sophistication of the weapons and their delivery systems. This mutual "defection," in game-theory terminology, to seeking an advantage resulted in the arms race. As in the prisoner's dilemma, the communication failure made arms control an even-more-distant possibility, and the understanding of communication through thinking vicariously, as in focal points, or as in understanding signals, was an area becoming associated with Schelling.

Although the story itself was famous, the tale of the prisoners' dilemma had practical applications at RAND because it could actually be played out repeatedly as a game, and that was what required study. Game-theory situations can often be seen as two-participant interactions, with each party having only one choice to make. A matrix, the most widely used tool in game theory, readily illustrates such games. The participants, or "players," are represented as "Row" and "Column," and each quadrant of the matrix represents one intersection of the players' possible choices, or one of the four possible outcomes.

In a sample matrix, Column and Row each have two choices, A and B:

Column

A   B

Row

A

B

Schelling placed a number in the lower-left corner of each quadrant to represent the value of that intersection of choices to Row, and a number in the upper-right corner of each quadrant to represent the value of that intersection of choices to Column. The letters A and B can stand for many different things and can be replaced by any decision that involves only a single choice between two options. The interaction between the players' choices can only produce one of four outcomes.

The matrix for the prisoner's dilemma story would be as follows:

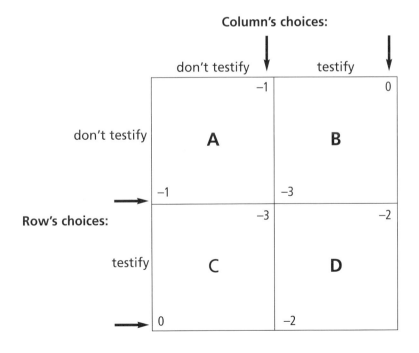

One prisoner is Row and the other Column. If they don't testify against each other, they'll end up in quadrant A, where each receives –1, or one year in prison. Row would be happier if the game ended in quadrant C, where he receives 0 years and Column receives three years in prison, or –3. If Column chooses "don't testify," and he chooses "testify," the game will end in quadrant C. Row doesn't really trust Column anyway, so he realizes that if he cooperates by selecting "don't testify," and Column doesn't cooperate, that would be the worst of all. So, "testify" is safest. He chooses the bottom row.

Meanwhile, Column looks at the game the same way. He'd really like to see the game end in quadrant B, where he gets 0. He could cooperate with Row, but he doesn't trust Row and really doesn't want to end up in quadrant C. Column chooses the right column. The intersection of Row's choice (the bottom row) and Column's choice (the right column) is the lower-right quadrant, quadrant D. Because of each prisoner's distrust of the other, and his hope for the one outcome best for himself, both players' outcome for the game is –2, two years in jail for each. It isn't a good outcome, but it is the natural, inescapable result of the game.

Schelling realized that the prisoner's-dilemma matrix could stand for Russia and America. "Don't testify" could be replaced with "maintain nuclear arsenals," and "testify" could be "increase nuclear arsenals." That would leave the superpowers in the lower-right corner where they both "increase nuclear arsenals." The outcome wasn't rational, but neither side trusted the other, and both hoped to gain the upper hand. The arms race was on. Schelling began to consider how the outcome could be shifted to the upper-left quadrant, "maintain nuclear arsenals." But even if they trusted each other once, how could they know it wasn't a trick by one side to get the other to expect it to be trusted a second time? The game was played over and over at RAND, using different conditions.

The relationship among RAND, game theory, and nuclear strategy is often made, and it is Schelling who would become known as the leading figure in the application of game theory to nuclear strategy. In *Neorealism and Its Critics*,[47] Robert Keohane said that "[g]ame theory has yielded some insights into issues of negotiations, crises, and limited war, most notably in the early works of Thomas Schelling," while game theorist Robert Axelrod's similar evaluation was that "I think you can say Schelling's work is well known and was probably helpful in establishing some of the ideas we have on arms control. But at the very top, you probably cannot find a secretary of state who can tell you what a Prisoner's Dilemma is."

Schelling's use of game-theory analysis, and the confidence placed in rational-choice theory and modeling by many RAND strategists, could raise questions about the strategic advice that sometimes emerged from the institution. Schelling would comment on the limits of that theoretical approach in his classic work, *The Strategy of Conflict*, half of which he wrote during a later stay at RAND: "The principles relevant to *successful* play (in mixed-motive games), the strategic principles, the propositions of a *normative* theory, cannot be derived by purely analytical means from a priori considerations . . . There is, therefore, no way that an analyst can reproduce whole decision process either introspectively or by an axiomatic method."[48]

The rational-choice/game-theory assumption was that players act in a rational manner to optimize results, leading to an outcome, or equilibrium, that could be anticipated with thoughtful analysis. Schelling wrote: "There is no way to build a model for the interaction of two or more decision units, with the behavior and expectations of those decisions units being derived by purely formal deduction." Games, including simulations of thermonuclear war, wouldn't follow that logical pattern when a player failed to optimize results, or when what were analytically irrelevant considerations proved to be more important than anticipated ones, causing a departure from the predicted results. Identifying each player's considerations correctly was critical to designing games, and this was not an easy task. Even when there was a single actor, such as the U.S. president or the Soviet premier, it was difficult to know what function he was hoping to maximize. Stakes as extremely high as nuclear war might incline the actors to theory-anticipating reasoning, creating the appearance of successful prediction by game theory models and raising the question of whether the models themselves were reliable tools.

Some critics of the rational-choice/game-theory approach to policy analysis commonly associated with Schelling say it fails "the grandmother test": It only arrives at what your grandmother already knew, or hasn't gone beyond what can be discovered without formal process. They question whether game theory and rational-choice theory have added anything new to the existing stock of knowledge. The causal institutions of rational choice are nothing that hasn't already existed in other areas of study. They say it has slowed down progress in advancing knowledge in the social sciences because it is method-driven, rather than process-driven, research.

By relying on the invention of methods to solve problems, researchers neglect pragmatic empirical research. Another challenge to the whole idea of rational-choice theory is the assumption of equilibria resulting from strategic interaction between players, and social laws deductible from a logic of individual behavior. The major challenge is the rational-choice assumption that the laws governing human behavior are in accord with deductive logic, and that such laws exist.[49]

An early rational-choice theorist, Schelling had perhaps expected too much of it as an answer to the questions of political science. He disagrees with critics who say it is not a useful guide for what happens in the real world. His view is that rational-choice theory provides a starting point, not that it gives assurances of how things will end. Departures from rational thought are also susceptible to systematic study, enriching rather than supplanting rational choice.

Whether Schelling was really using game theory for solutions or as illustration is a matter of how general a definition of the term is used. He made use of game theory, but often in support of his other forms of bargaining reasoning. The confusion comes in part from the fact that game theory had focused primarily on zero-sum, or pure, competition since it was first developed, and that Schelling's use of game theory involved varying degrees of cooperation. His oft-spoken rejection of the idea he was a game theorist fails to fit with widely held perceptions of him by experts in the field. He wouldn't be in the lead in the mathematical direction much of game theory was taking, always preferring words—examples or analogies that illustrated his points and were clear and memorable. As he put it, "I think most of the things I said, if they were influential, it was because they were pretty self-evident, once they were pointed out." Schelling was an observer and an imaginative interpreter, a man who saw lessons and metaphors all around him that he believed he could make as obvious to others as they were to him. Such an approach wasn't game theory as used by many, but it did involve thinking like game theorists do and using their symbols. It was vicarious and interdependent problem-solving.

In 1957, Schelling was more of an abstract thinker than most other strategists. His view opened the door to arms-control possibilities and was an expression of his non-zero-sum game theory approach, where players sought to find common interests rather than exist in direct confrontation. He was one of the earliest strategists to think that relations with the Soviets could involve common benefits. The general view at RAND was that the Soviets couldn't be trusted in any case. In some cases, America's reluctance to trust the Soviets may have been derived from the West's mistaken trust of Hitler prior to World War II.

During that second month of his RAND stay, Schelling developed an idea for modifying America's military strategy. The United States military policy in 1957 was "massive retaliation," which called for an all-out nuclear strike against the Soviet Union in the event of a Soviet attack anywhere against an American installation or America's allies. Secretary of State John Foster Dulles, who had proposed the "massive retaliation" doctrine, believed that such an overwhelming threat would deter the Soviets from aggressive action.

Schelling proposed a way to control and limit a nuclear war, if deterrence failed. He presented his idea, which became known as "save the cities," that August—and it eventually formed the basis for discussions leading to a dramatic change in U.S. military policy in the 1960s. Schelling pointed out that in a war with Russia, the expected outcome would be national homicide—something both sides wanted to avoid, thus making them partners in their attempts to avoid total destruction, as well as adversaries. Communicating to the other side that there was a common interest would require sending some sort of signal. Launching a bombing strike that avoided hitting cities would effectively signal the other side of an offer to establish an agreement that neither side would attack the other's cities. Such signaling could create a tacit understanding in which the two sides agreed to work together to avoid a war of total destruction. Communication through signaling and seeing adversaries as partners because they have some common interests would become common themes in Schelling's work.

CHAPTER 8

THE COLD WARRIOR EMERGES

Schelling returned to Yale in the fall of 1957, the fall of *Sputnik*. As the year drew to a close, the Cold War took on a new sense of foreboding. Khrushchev's rhetoric ("Who wants to overtake whom in science? The United States would like to overtake the Soviet Union."[50]) was more than mere gloating. Before leaving RAND at the end of the summer, Schelling had arranged to spend a year there beginning in the fall of 1958. He had finished five years at Yale, and Harvard had offered him a position as professor of economics and associate at the university's Center for International Affairs, which he would accept starting with the 1959–60 academic year. In early 1957, before he knew he wouldn't be continuing as a Yale professor, he had applied for a Ford Foundation Grant and received a faculty fellowship for a semester's leave to conduct research. Deciding to use the fellowship for the second semester of his final academic year at Yale, Schelling moved his family to London for a six-month stay in early 1958.

They rented a house near Charing Cross and converted an extra room into an office. Every morning, Schelling took the two older children to kindergarten and nursery school before turning his attention to game theory. He spent much of his time researching and writing, completing an article for *The Journal of Conflict Resolution* and essays that became chapters in *The Strategy of Conflict*. His typist also worked for Agatha Christie and, during the time she was typing Schelling's works on conflict resolution, she was also typing Christie's classic play *The Mousetrap.*

Schelling had spent the previous summer at RAND being exposed to the leading nuclear strategists of the time in the most intense and stimulating environment of the Cold-War era. The Russian's launch of *Sputnik* that fall moved them into the lead in a race that threatened annihilation. Those experiences and events had all interested him. They had not changed him.

It was during that period in London, working alone, that Schelling's intellectual transformation into a nuclear strategist occurred. Most leading strategists saw surprise attack as the greatest threat to peace and the most likely way a nuclear war would begin. Schelling recalls, "When I was in London thinking about surprise attack, I was doing it substantially as an intellectual puzzle. But as I worked through it, I realized it was a genuine, live problem. I became convinced that solving the intellectual puzzle was crucial to solving the practical policy issues."[51]

Schelling's decision to begin concentrating on nuclear strategy was motivated by the same factors that led him to become an economist. He realized as a young man that the problem of the Great Depression required a new approach, one undistorted by emotion. Lifting America out of economic depression was a puzzle to be solved—an intellectual puzzle, not a cause to believe in. Causes could clutter thoughts. Causes differ from purposes. Eliminate the emotional factors, and any puzzle can be better understood, the solution to the puzzle thus forming the basis for rational policy. That view would give Schelling the confidence to analyze and write about the most profound and ominous life-and-death issues as he emerged as a leading strategist. As Nobel laureate Paul Samuelson said, "Once the vital game of survival in a nuclear age challenged Schelling's attention, mere economics could no longer contain him."[52]

Returning to RAND for his longest stay in the fall of 1958, Schelling found the think tank imbued with a sense of mission and great urgency. The Reds were ahead, or so it seemed, and there was no time to lose in making sure the United States was back in a secure position. Georgia Senator Richard Russell later described the degree America's fears had reached: "If we have to start over again with another Adam and Eve, I want them to be Americans, not Russians." It was all scary, but it was also exciting, part of RAND's "golden age." The strategists and scientists were willing to work hard and to work together; 70-hour weeks were the norm. The feeling of good against evil couldn't be exaggerated and, as Schelling said, "Nobody doubted we were on the side of the angels."

RAND's reputation as a think tank had detractors. Some found the organization too cold and calculating, too private, and too detached in its dealings with subjects of such momentous importance. They had the impression that the strategists thought little of the human consequences of what they did, that they believed such considerations weren't their responsibility. Then whose was it? The view found expression in a song recorded by popular folk singer Pete Seeger:[53]

> *Oh, the RAND Corporation's the boon of the world,*
> *They think all day long for a fee.*
> *They sit and play games about going up in flames . . .*
> *For counters they use you and me . . .*

> *These brainy heroes transform us to zeros,*
> *So who gives a damn if we fall, after all,*
> *Who gives a damn if we fall.*
> *Their superior genes will be safe behind screens,*
> *With the rest of our line doomed to die.*

By the time Schelling returned to RAND in 1958, most leading strategists believed that only a balance of nuclear power between the United
States and the Soviet Union would create a stable peace. Schelling agreed.
The "delicate balance of terror," as Wohlstetter described it, and "mutually
assured destruction" could prevent nuclear holocaust. Schelling's role in it
all? According to a RAND Corporation document, Schelling "established
the basic conceptual structure of deterrence theory. In fact, one could go
farther. Schelling's ideas are at the heart of the complex, counterintuitive
logic of mutually assured destruction, which has underpinned American
nuclear and arms-control strategy for four decades."[54] That's an important
achievement for a figure who was beyond public scrutiny.

Economist and future Defense Department deputy assistant Alain
Enthoven was there, and remembers Schelling as calm and clearheaded,
clarifying differences between credible, effective threats and incredible,
ineffective ones, among other subjects.[55] Schelling spoke of how the
ancients used the practice of exchanging hostages as a method of guaran-
teeing each other's trust; he described the "balance of terror" between the
United States and the Soviet Union as "equivalent to a total exchange of all
conceivable hostages."

It was the maintenance of a "balance of terror" that made surprise
attack such a serious threat to peace. The advantage of surprise attack was
so great that it created a temptation to launch a surprise attack to avoid
being attacked by surprise, or to try to destroy the other before the other
could retaliate. Attacking weapons systems was thus a higher priority than
attacking people, as such targeted attacks could destroy the other side's
ability to retaliate. Schelling wrote: "If surprise attack carries an advantage,
it is worthwhile to avert it by striking first. Fear that the other may be
about to strike in the mistaken belief that we are about to strike gives us a
motive for striking, and so justifies the other's motive."[56]

Schelling thought it was important that people understood the dangers
of surprise attack and the difference between a stable " balance of terror" (in
which surprise attack could not destroy weapons systems) and an "unstable
balance of terror" (in which surprise attack could). As a strategic thinker, he
often saw his role as making situations and underlying logic understandable

so that rational choices could be made. Metaphors worked best, and he avoided complex mathematical explanations. In his discussion of surprise attack in *The Strategy of Conflict*, Schelling used a familiar scenario to illustrate his point. Westerns topped the ratings on television, and he'd liked Zane Grey stories since childhood. So, he wrote about the gunfighters of the Old West: "The 'equalizer' of the Old West (the 'six-shooter') made it possible for either man to kill the other; it did not assure that both would be killed . . . The advantage of shooting first aggravates any incentive to shoot. As a survivor might put it, 'He was about to kill me, so I had to kill him in self defense.' Or, 'He, thinking I was about to kill him in self defense, was about to kill me in self-defense, so I had to kill him in self defense.' But if both were assured of living long enough to shoot back with unimpaired aim, there would be no advantage in jumping the gun and little reason to fear that the other would try it."[57]

How to achieve stability drew a wide range of suggestions, many of which vividly illustrate the temper of the times. Among the more imaginative was Hungarian physicist Leo Szilard's idea that the Soviets place a hydrogen bomb under Chicago and the United States place one under Kiev. Then, if either side does anything too dangerous, "all you have to do is push a button, and there goes Chicago, there goes Kiev," Schelling said. A Quaker proposal suggested a yearly exchange of one million sixth-grade students, with the Russian students attending school in the United States and the U.S. students attending school in Russia. If one country fired a warhead at the other, it would be killing its own children. Schelling said, "I thought of the Quaker proposal as a nice way of illustrating the nature of mutual deterrence. They may have taken it literally, much more seriously. And considering back in those days people were pretty damn scared of nuclear war, this was not a preposterously unreasonably proposal."[58]

During his year at RAND, Schelling analyzed a wide variety of issues and wrote the first half of his seminal book, *The Strategy of Conflict*. He also returned to the "save the cities" idea he presented during his previous stay. He revised the idea from an offer that could lead to enemies avoiding the destruction of each other's cities to a focus on the strategic value of saving an enemy's cities during wartime. The cities could effectively become "hostages," the threat of their destruction affording considerable bargaining power. He wrote up the idea and circulated it around RAND in the usual manner, by memo. The response was good; he decided the idea was worth presenting somewhere, or bringing up in discussion at some point when individuals involved in policy decision-making were present.

As the greatest threat to a stable "balance of terror," surprise attack was the overriding strategic concern at the time. Yet Schelling was also concerned with another possibility during his year at RAND: that war could happen by accident. A mistake or a confused signal could lead to the launch of an unintended strike. Confusion over a possible, but non-existent, surprise attack could then lead to a strike supposedly made in reprisal. With both side's defenses in such a high state of readiness and at such hair-trigger alert, the possibilities for human or mechanical errors were numerous.

Both the United States and the Soviet Union had made careful plans for launching and defending against calculated attacks—but if an accident happened, and there had been no intent to start a war, it might still be impossible to keep the situation from spiraling out of control into complete disaster. With first strike being a real advantage, a truly tense situation could become a matter of "he thinks that I think that he thinks . . . ." until both sides were strongly tempted to launch strikes out of fear of being second.

A second risk was that each side's preparation against possible surprise attack might look like preparations for such an attack, prompting the other side to strike first. It was perilously possible that mistaken beliefs or suspicions could lead to a strike or a launch, which would lead to retaliation for something that hadn't happened, which would lead to retaliation for something that had.

Schelling attended the Surprise Attack Planning Conference in Washington in 1958, where he presented an idea he thought could lessen the danger of war occurring due to miscalculations during a crisis. Mistakes made about what one side thought the other was doing during a crisis could easily lead to disaster. Schelling suggested making arrangements for the use of direct communication in any crisis situation, with eyewitnesses in Moscow and Washington verifying what was and was not going on to make sure no misunderstandings occurred. His entire plan depended on the capability for direct communication between the two cities.

Yet, as he learned at the conference, no established direct communication between Moscow and Washington even existed. Schelling asked how it was possible that he could directly dial his mother 3,000 miles away to wish her happy birthday, but the president of the United States couldn't call the Soviet premier for urgent discussion.

Participating in events such as the Surprise Attack Planning Conference involved travel time, which Schelling used for reading. His tastes were mostly academic: Captain B.H. Liddell Hart's books on military strategy,

J.F.C. Fuller, Herodotus, Thucydides. On one plane flight in 1958, when he did not have a book along, someone handed him a copy of *Red Alert* by Peter George.[59] He found it fascinating.

> *"Give the orders to stop it, General," Howard said quietly. "There are men dying out there, men who trusted you and believed in you. Don't do this to them."*
>
> *Quenten shook his head. "They're unlucky, Paul, but they're honored too. They're dying to save our world. They're dying for peace on earth."*

It was a novel about a character named Quenten, a brigadier general in the Air Force who commanded a wing of Strategic Air Command bombers, the American planes that carried nuclear weapons. Quenten was dying and under the delusion that he could make the world a better place by ordering a nuclear strike against the Soviet Union. He sent the bombers. The U.S. president and his advisors decided the only way to avoid a nuclear holocaust was to shoot down all of the planes before they could drop their bombs. It was a difficult decision, but total nuclear war and human existence was at stake. The government's desperate plan almost worked. All of the SAC planes had been shot down but one, the *Alabama Angel*. The president managed to give it orders not to carry out its mission, but the *Alabama Angel* hadn't turned back.

Schelling thought that aspects of the novel were within the realm of possibility. He bought four-dozen copies of the 35-cent paperback to give to various people whom he thought would be interested.

In addition to his strategic work, Schelling had been doing other academic writing, and in 1958 his second textbook, *International Economics*, was published.[60] Robert Solow—who'd said Schelling's first text was conventional and that Schelling himself was seen as a conventional economist at the time of its publication—now said a "New Schelling" was emerging in this second work. Schelling discussed traditional topics in ways ordinary economists would never have considered. His writing style was unconventional as well. He wrote descriptively, filling his work with metaphors. The metaphors were often more easily recalled than the points they supported, but the messages were clear and the points they made were often obvious.

Although Schelling specifically studied military history for ideas and examples to use, it seemed that wherever he looked, he found something to support whatever topic he was analyzing. He could watch his own children play and find lessons that applied to nuclear strategy or to organized crime. Concepts that explained general social behavior turned up in the everyday behavior he saw around him, and it became a habit for him to use them in his thought, his speech, and his writings. James Tobin recalled such a Schelling's story concerning a traffic-slowing obstacle on the road back to Boston from Cape Cod. Any driver could have removed the obstacle in seconds, but once a driver reached it, he had no incentive to remove it, so it remained.

A. Michael Spence, the 2001 winner of the Nobel Prize in Economics, remembers a time when he was concerned about the non-market sorting methods people used to sort themselves. He brought the subject up over lunch with Schelling. Spence recalled, "After listening to me for a while, Tom started to talk about swimmers and surfers on a southern California beach. I can remember quite vividly thinking he was nuts. About fifteen minutes làter, it slowly dawned on me that this was a counter-principle of the principle I had enunciated."[61]

It wasn't just the metaphors that characterized Schelling's writing style. His work was concise and trim. He avoided anything that wasn't truly essential. Schelling said that Antoine de Saint-Exupéry, author of *The Little Prince*, best expressed his guiding idea for effective writing: "In anything at all, perfection is finally attained not when there is no longer anything to add, but when there is no longer anything else to take away, when a body has been stripped down to its nakedness."[62]

CHAPTER 9

HARVARD AND *THE STRATEGY OF CONFLICT*

The Schellings moved into their new house in Cambridge in the fall of 1959, and Tom began his career as a Harvard professor. He was well published by then, and many influential faculty members already knew him. He had been an outstanding graduate student and was still thought of highly. His experience in the government and at Yale were enough to earn him a joint appointment in the economics department and at the Center for International Affairs, where he was given time to pursue his work on nuclear strategy and deterrence and asked to develop a course based on his various experiences and interests

At the Harvard Center for International Affairs, in the early 1960s

in bargaining and strategy. He put together a course on strategy, conflict, and cooperation.

Soviet Premier Nikita Khrushchev, the leader of the communist world, made a visit to the United States that autumn. Khrushchev both terrified and delighted Americans, as he mixed his promise that "We will bury you" with his expressions of frustration at not being allowed to visit Disneyland and his pleasure at tasting his first hot dog. His final comment at the airport before his departure was, "Let us have more and more use of the short American word, OK." But it was "We will bury you" that most people felt summarized Soviet intentions.

Schelling spent most of his time at the Center for International Affairs. While most of his colleagues devoted themselves to one of several other areas of international study, Schelling—along with director Bob Bowie and assistant director Henry Kissinger—focused on national security issues.

While at Yale in June 1960 to give a speech, Schelling met an impressive graduate student, Morton Halperin. He invited Halperin to join the center as a fellow staff member. Government officials were brought in at times, and the center offered regular grants for year-long visiting staff as well.

The center was a comfortable place with a small regular staff and a good cook. Schelling's secretary was Alice Coleman, born Alice Modzelewska in Poland. She could remember sitting on her mother's lap when the bombs burst around her, signaling the outbreak of World War II. She had clear memories of time doing forced labor in Nazi Germany during the war and, since then, her family home had been in the hands of the communists. She and Schelling soon developed a working relationship based on mutual respect and friendship and destined to last for many years. Theirs was the sort of partnership often seen in offices where things run smoothly, when the competent secretary knows the work habits and needs of her employer well. Alice was bright and very protective of Schelling. In spite of their close relationship, she always called him "Mr. Schelling," never "Tom."

With strategists at both Harvard and MIT interacting regularly, Cambridge had emerged as one of the leading centers of strategic thinking in America. Schelling found Harvard's Center for International Affairs a lively and intellectually interesting place. Unlike at RAND, the center had no high security, only secured safes. Something of a creature of habit, Schelling treated his time there like a regular job, arriving at 9:00 in the morning and leaving at 6:00 in the evening. The center's enjoyable, even fun, atmosphere was dampened only by a running conflict between Bowie and Kissinger, who barely spoke to each other. Schelling got along with everyone, and the others found him interesting and pleasant. His colleagues respected him and he had good relations with all, but Schelling wasn't especially close with any one person. He did make a point of getting to know all of the visiting staff members and having them over to dinner at some point during their year in residence.[63]

Schelling's group was almost completely focused on arms control and nuclear weapons and, as always, Schelling was fascinated with ideas. At times, his lack of interest in the specifics of practical application was a source of frustration for his young colleague, Mort Halperin. Halperin found it somewhat challenging to get Schelling to be operational about the ideas they were developing and to concern himself with how those ideas could become public policy. Halperin also felt treated a bit junior at times, particularly with regard to writing. When he gave Schelling something to read, Schelling would do so carefully and thoughtfully, making valuable and insightful comments. When Halperin reviewed Schelling's writing, it was a frustrating experience. If he tried to tidy it up, Schelling resisted or wasn't very interested in his comments.

The year 1960 brought the birth of the Schellings' fourth son, Robert, and the publication of Schelling's most important book, *The Strategy of Conflict*. The Nobel Prize committee's 2005 press release summarizes its significance: "Against the backdrop of the nuclear arms race in the late 1950s, Thomas Schelling's book *The Strategy of Conflict* set forth his vision of game theory as a unifying framework for the social sciences. Schelling showed that a party can strengthen its position by overtly worsening its own options, that the capability to retaliate can be more useful than the ability to resist an attack, and that uncertain retaliation is more credible and more efficient than certain retaliation. These insights have proven to be of great relevance for conflict resolution and efforts to avoid war."

Schelling addressed a wide variety of topics in *The Strategy of Conflict*, many related to his ideas on the avoidance of nuclear war, or deterrence, which he defined as "influencing the choices that another party will make, and doing it by influencing his expectations of how we will behave." The importance of bargaining and tacit communication was a common theme throughout the book, and the idea of signaling as a method of communication showed up frequently.

He also expanded on the ideas of threats and warnings, commitments, and promises, first introduced as deterrent strategies in "An Essay on Bargaining." Bargaining and communication between enemies could take place through signals sent by actions taken. War was a bargaining situation where the opponents violently exchanged threats, promises, and commitments that could be exploited with considerable strategic value in gaining the superior bargaining position. Schelling discussed game theory extensively and devoted three chapters to "A Reorientation of Game Theory."

In this reorientation, he rejected the traditional reliance on zero-sum games as having failed to yield worthwhile results. Instead, he presented his focal-point or coordination game as a more promising option and proposed more consideration of what he called "mixed-motive games," games between the extremes. Bargaining was a fluid situation with the strategic game changing forms. While surprise attack was a serious threat to a stable peace, reasonable approaches could be taken to maintain a stable balance of power that would deter the temptation to launch such an attack. Randomization of threats, brinkmanship, limited wars, and limiting nuclear war were all discussed.

The Strategy of Conflict was almost immediately recognized as one of the foundation works in the academic arena of strategic studies, and Schelling was acknowledged as a leader in the field—a reputation that would only grow as the years went by. David Jardini later wrote in his work commemorating RAND's 50th anniversary that "Professor Thomas Schelling . . . established the basic conceptual structure of deterrence theory."[64] Schelling's RAND colleague Alain Enthoven said, "Tom Schelling was one of the most important contributors to our present understanding of strategies of deterrence. In fact, he was the leader in development of the theory of conflict and conflict resolution."

Years later in *Newsweek, The Washington Post,* and the *International Herald Tribune,* Fareed Zakaria wrote about nuclear deterrence and described Schelling as "its inventor." A list published in *The Times* of London in 1995 named *The Strategy of Conflict* as one of the one hundred most influential books in the West since 1945. Tyler Cowen of George Mason University summed it up with: "I once asked my class: 'If you had to hide a one hundred dollar bill in a book, so that your friend would find it, but you could not announce the book, which volume should you choose?' Many said the *Bible* but of course the game theorist picks Schelling's *The Strategy of Conflict.*"[65]

CHAPTER 10

DR. STRANGELOVE AND THE HOTLINE

During 1960, Americans had many distractions from the Cold War cloud hanging over them. One "King" returned and another left: Elvis was discharged from the army, but Clark Gable died. Barbie found a boyfriend in Ken. A new hero emerged from the Olympic Games, a loud-mouthed boxer from Louisville, Cassius Clay. AstroTurf first appeared on football fields, and beehive hairdos were all the rage. Life had a serious side, with sit-ins to protest racial inequality held in more than 100 cities and California passing a law to reduce harmful auto emissions. Whatever else was happening, though, the Soviet threat couldn't be ignored.

Over lunch with a magazine editor that fall, Schelling was discussing a favorite theme of his—the possibility of accidental war—and an article he planned to write about it. The editor suggested he begin the article with a review of the books people were reading about World War III. Schelling liked the idea. Americans were reading frightening novels with apocalyptic themes, tales about how the next great war would come about and what it would be like. He decided to read several of the most popular books to see whether they would work in his article. He had finished *Red Alert* and enjoyed it, so he started with *Alas, Babylon*.[66]

The 1959 novel by Pat Frank told the story of how a small group of survivors in a post-nuclear-war world dealt with having the advances of civilization vanish in a single day. Telephones and electricity were gone, money was worthless and soon replaced by barter, and medical supplies and food were running out. For all the survivors knew, they were the only people alive—anywhere. The book's title referred to a hellfire sermon two of the characters had heard as young boys about how the wicked cities of America resembled the biblical Babylon and would face the same destruction for their wickedness.

More popular, and more frightening, than *Alas, Babylon* was Nevil Schute's *On the Beach*,[67] and if Schelling was going to review popular fiction about World War III, Schute's novel couldn't be left out. Published in 1957, *On the Beach* was made into a movie in 1959 that was still attracting and terrifying large audiences in 1960. In the book, nuclear war had devastated the Northern Hemisphere, and the people of Australia were waiting several months for the radioactivity to drift south to kill them, too. Some people took cyanide to finish things quickly, while the remainder waited and died more slowly, suffering hideous deaths. A U.S. submarine surfaced and took an Australian naval officer and his wife and child and a friend of theirs on board to join them in an exploratory voyage for surviving life. Their journey resulted in failure and doom.

Schelling's article on accidental war—entitled "Meteors, Mischief and War," and published in the *Bulletin of the Atomic Scientists*—included reviews of *Red Alert, Alas, Babylon*, and *On the Beach*. A London newspaper, *The Observer*, reprinted the article, and it caught the eye of movie producer and director Stanley Kubrick. Kubrick had recently directed a major box office success, *Spartacus*. He was especially interested in Schelling's review of *Red Alert*, and he contacted the book's publisher in order to get in touch with the author, Peter George. He also wanted to reach Schelling to get the three of them together.

Peter George, a modest, likeable major in the Royal Air Force intelligence, was greatly appreciative of Schelling's commentary on his book. He told Schelling that the idea for *Red Alert* came one day when he was at a U.S. base for B-47 bombers having coffee in the officers' mess. A cup sitting near the table's edge when a B-47 roared overhead vibrated and moved until it fell to the floor and crashed. Someone said, "That's the way World War III will break out," and George had gone straight to the phone and called his publisher to ask for an advance so he could take a leave and write a book. He was interested in making people think about how to stop a war that appeared to have started.

Kubrick and George came to Schelling's office at Harvard to discuss how to make the movie. Schelling found Kubrick to be intelligent and thoughtful and, for a Hollywood figure coming off such a big-screen success, modest.

Written before either side in the Cold War had Intercontinental Ballistic Missiles or submarine-launched missiles, *Red Alert* featured weapons technology at the heart of its narrative that would soon be out of date: Missiles were quickly gaining prominence over bombers as the strike force for carrying nuclear weapons. Schelling and his guests spent several hours trying to figure out the tricky problem of starting the war and playing it out with missiles. They needed to allow time for dramatic War Room scenes, and the U.S. president would have to make the choice between trying to shoot down the planes to save the world from nuclear destruction or taking advantage of the surprise attack by sending a follow-up strike that could eliminate the evil Red menace forever. The book had dealt seriously with the choices that must be made quickly in such emergencies—there was no humor to the situation. Yet a missile attack would be over in minutes, and the plot would never be developed.

A secondary problem was that neither Schelling or George wanted to show the Air Force as demented or war-happy or out of control, and Kubrick at least appeared to agree. But there didn't seem to be any way to start a war without a psychopathic air force officer. "We had a hell of a time getting that damn war started," Schelling recalls. "We finally decided that it couldn't happen unless there was somebody crazy in the Air Force." That's when Kubrick and George decided they'd have to do the movie as what they called a "nightmare comedy."

When the afternoon session was over, Kubrick had what he needed from Schelling on nuclear war and accepted an invitation to the Schelling home for dinner. Schelling remained in contact with George afterwards, and the author and Kubrick soon headed to England to work on the screenplay. The result of their collaboration—*Dr. Strangelove or: How I Learned to Stop Worrying and Love the Bomb*—was released in 1964, and Schelling was anxious to see the movie. He wasn't disappointed and thought it a great film. The final scene was especially useful, with the American president and the communist premier trying to work together to prevent war. He thought that was a valuable message to leave with the audience. Cooperation was a real possibility in times of genuine crisis.

Ever since the release of Kubrick's film, people have wondered who the real Dr. Strangelove was. The most frequent suggestions (including speculation by strategists from the movie's time period) are Herman Kahn, Henry Kissinger, Wernher von Braun, and Edwin Teller. Each man possessed some quality, whether physical or in the ideas Strangelove proposed, that qualifies him as a candidate. Some combination of these people provides the best answer.

Dr. Strangelove was lauded as a great film on the big themes, but there were smaller points. Schelling had grimaced as he watched the scene with the U.S. president talking to the Soviet premier on the "hotline" he himself had proposed back in 1958. Nuclear disaster threatened, and the fate of the world hung in the balance. The American president picked up that "red telephone" on his desk and spoke immediately with the Soviet premier. Wait. He picked up that . . . Princess Telephone? The telephone sat on his desk in the Oval Office, and the American president spoke to the Soviet leader in . . . what language? While it made for good theater, Hollywood's version of the "hotline" bore little resemblance to the real thing.

The "hotline" was actually a leased transatlantic cable with Cyrillic-alphabet teletype machines at each end. In addition to the full-time wire telegraph circuit, a full-time radiotelegraph circuit served as a backup in the event the wire-circuit transmission was interrupted. The United States actually had two "hotlines," one in the Pentagon and one in the State Department. The Pentagon machine stood about five feet tall and resembled a wooden pedestal with a typewriter on top. The "hotline" rooms were manned at all times, and the machines themselves were activated several times a day with some regular phrase to ensure they were in constant working order. Schelling knew all about the "hotline," because it had been his idea. Times were tense, and the need for such direct communication seemed apparent.

The possibility of "urgent questions" needing discussion was increasing, as the United States faced problems around the globe in 1960. The Soviets were winning the space race, and, in a "missile gap," the United States lagged dangerously behind the Soviets in the production of Intercontinental Ballistic Missiles. Communism threatened Laos and Vietnam; President Eisenhower had called the countries "dominoes" whose fall would threaten the free world in the Pacific Asian region. Fidel Castro's communist Cuba was only 90 miles from U.S. shores, and a CIA-sponsored invasion was in the works. An American U-2 spy plane had been downed over Russia in May, resulting in Nikita Khrushchev's refusal to attend a scheduled summit meeting, while commenting, "If these provocations continue, we will have to aim our rockets at the bases."

Khrushchev had further dramatized the differences between the U.S. and Soviet systems in September, as he sat with his delegation in the General Assembly of the UN and angrily pounded his shoe on a table during a speech by British Prime Minister Harold Macmillan. New and often unstable countries, 19 that year alone, were being formed from the old European colonial empires, creating new battlegrounds for East-West competition. Soviet economic growth was booming along at a rate about triple that of the United States.

In the October 1960 issue of *World Politics*, Schelling published his "hotline" proposal for direct communication between Moscow and Washington, first put forward two years earlier at the Surprise Attack Planning Conference. He called for "two versatile, flexible, observation and communication forces, one for each side and located in each other's country, whose main function is to be available to meet whatever demands are placed on them in a crises." Two months later he presented a translation of the proposal to an East-West security conference in Moscow.[68]

November brought the election of a new president, the youngest elected president in U.S. history, John F. Kennedy. In Kennedy's words, "the torch has been passed to a new generation of Americans." Between his election and his inauguration, Kennedy read a report prepared by RAND, "Political Implications of Posture Choices," and underlined a single sentence: "Political history does not support that it is more dangerous to be strong than to be weak, more dangerous to threaten than to betray fear, more dangerous to be as 'provocative' as an Adenauer or a De Gaulle than to be as conciliatory as a Macmillan."[69]

On January 20, 1961, the RAND influence was evident in Kennedy's memorable inaugural address, when he said, "We dare not tempt them with weakness. For only when our arms are sufficient beyond doubt can we be certain beyond doubt that they will never be employed . . ."[70] The new president continued with a warning: "Let every nation know, whether it wishes us well or ill, that we shall pay any price, bear any burden, meet any hardship, support any friend, oppose any foe to assure the survival and success of liberty."

The Kennedy administration would come to regard Schelling highly as a strategist. *The Washington Post* wrote, "It was in John Kennedy's Camelot that Schelling really first burst upon the Washington scene."[71] Robert McNamara, in his book on Vietnam, said, "[Schelling's] view permeated civilian leadership under Kennedy . . . to a remarkable degree."[72]

Kennedy appointed John McCloy as disarmament advisor, and the former World Bank president was eager to make changes from the beginning. He asked Schelling to serve as chairman of one of six new committees, the White House Committee on War by Accident, Surprise, and Miscalculation. Schelling met with the seven committee members occasionally over several months and introduced them to his Washington-Moscow hotline idea. They included the "hotline" proposal as one of their recommendations in the committee's final report. As chairman, Schelling presented the report to McCloy and the rest of the State Department disarmament staff. When he got to the hotline recommendation, McCloy commented, "That's a good one. I'm on the board of AT&T."

Henry Owen of the State Department, one of Schelling's committee members, was especially interested in the proposal. Owen also represented the United States at the Geneva Conference of Experts on Surprise Attack. The Soviets, who expressed interest in the topic, had presented a proposal that contained something Owen found related to Schelling's idea. Russia's belligerent Foreign Minister Andrei Gromyko visited Geneva to offer his view on the dangerous possibilities of accidental war:

After all, meteors and electronic interference are reflected on Soviet screens, too. If in such cases Soviet aircraft, loaded with atomic and hydrogen bombs, were to proceed in the direction of the United States and its bases in other states, the air fleets of both sides, having noticed each other somewhere over the Arctic region, under such circumstances would draw the natural conclusion that a real attack by the enemy was taking place, and mankind would find itself involved in the whirlpool of atomic war.[73]

Owen got the direct-communications line on the agenda in Geneva, and it was initially approved five years after Schelling first presented the idea at the 1958 Surprise Attack Conference. Events in Cuba in October 1962, when the Cold War's most dangerous encounter took place, would make the urgent necessity of a "hotline" apparent. After Soviet soldiers and technicians were sent to Cuba to construct missile sites and President Kennedy blockaded the island, demanding the removal of the existing sites, the world held its breath for two weeks. American planes carrying nuclear bombs were airborne at the height of the tension, and Khrushchev gave in to American demands in an exchange of notes. Communication was clumsy and, on June 20, 1963, a "hotline" was formally approved and soon functioning between Moscow and Washington.

Schelling had advocated the direct-communication line for its practical benefits, but the "hotline" had symbolic significance of equal importance. It demonstrated a mutual awareness of dangers and a mutual willingness to confront them. He asked, "Who could devise a more vivid, simple ceremony to commemorate nuclear age relations than the delivery to the Pentagon of Cyrillic-alphabet teletype machinery, manufactured in the Soviet Union and lend-leased in return for American equipment to the Kremlin?"[74] It was an encouraging development at a time when there were few to be had.

CHAPTER 11

CHICKEN DILEMMA IN BERLIN

Throughout the real and looming confrontations of the times, one stood out above the others when John F. Kennedy was sworn in as president on January 20, 1961. The greatest danger of all was in Europe, and the flash point was Berlin. The divided city of Berlin, which Nikita Khrushchev called "a bone in the throat," had become the symbol of the Cold War.

John Kennedy meeting with Nikita Khrushchev in Vienna Embassy, June 3, 1961

When President Kennedy took office, Germany was a complex issue. After its defeat in World War II, the country had been divided into four zones of occupation: one each for the United States, France, and Britain, which combined to become West Germany; another for the Soviet Union, which became East Germany. Berlin was in the Soviet, East German zone, and the city itself had also been divided, with the Soviets controlling the eastern sector and the non-communist countries controlling the western sector. Travel between West Germany and West Berlin was unrestricted. If someone left East Berlin for West Berlin, he could then travel from West Berlin to West Germany, though it meant traveling through East Germany.

Hoping to reduce the tension over the divided city, Kennedy sent a con-ciliatory note to Khrushchev soon after taking office, in which he proposed a personal meeting between the two leaders for an "informal exchange of views." Kennedy offered assurances that "I intend to do everything I can toward developing a more harmonious relationship between our two coun-tries." The U.S. ambassador to Russia, Llewellyn E. Thompson Jr., delivered the note to the Kremlin on February 22, 1961. Thompson did not share Kennedy's optimism, and soon after delivering the president's message, the ambassador sent a top-secret cable to the White House. His warning to Kennedy was ominous: "All my diplomatic colleagues who have discussed the matter appear to consider that in the absence of negotiation, Khrushchev will sign a separate peace treaty with East Germany and precipitate a Berlin Crisis this year . . ."[75]

The boundary between communist East Berlin and non-communist West Berlin was the one place in Europe with relatively free movement from one system to the other. Yet the movement was all one-way: No one was fleeing West Berlin to escape to the repression and communism of the East. The West saw the continuous flight of refugees from the East as evidence of the communist system's failure; behind the Iron Curtain, the flood of refugees was considered an intolerable situation that must end. More than four million people had "voted with their feet" since the division of Germany into zones of occupation. East Germany had a population of only 17 million, while there were more than 55 million people in West Germany. The Western countries believed a Soviet military offensive to take control of all of Europe was a real possibility and that, if it came, such an offensive would begin with Berlin. The Soviets believed that the West planned to reunite divided Germany and rearm the country to serve as a barrier against the inevitable spread of communism.

When Kennedy's national security advisor, McGeorge Bundy, prepared a list of the 19 security risks facing the new administration, he ranked Berlin as the greatest risk of all. All the signs pointed to a crisis looming in Berlin, and Kennedy believed that if there were a nuclear war it would start in that city. On February 24, just two days after the U.S. ambassador delivered Kennedy's note to Khrushchev, the president approved Bundy's list.

Bundy soon sought out Schelling at Harvard to discuss how to deal with a possible Berlin crisis. Schelling told Bundy that the defense of Berlin didn't depend on 12,000 Allied troops accomplishing anything militarily, except that they could die. He said they shouldn't be talking about the defense of such a defenseless city, because the Soviets would be out of their minds to try to take Berlin by force unless they wanted a real war. And if they did want all-out war, it wouldn't stop with Berlin, something the communists surely knew. Schelling argued that if the Soviet Union appeared to be considering an attack on Berlin, the United States should carefully rehearse all available options to determine which were likely to be more dangerous than others. The most important thing to consider, Schelling maintained, was which actions might "give pause" to the East Germans and the Soviets. Did the West have options that would deter the Soviets and East Germans from initiating something too provocative or perilous in Berlin?[76]

By summer the Berlin situation was tense, and Kennedy met with Khrushchev in Vienna on June 3 and 4. The Soviet leader accused the Western countries of allowing West Germany to rearm in a way that posed a threat to the Eastern Block countries and with permitting a situation to develop in Germany that could once again lead the world into war. He charged the Western countries with using West Berlin as a base of operation against Eastern Block countries. He insisted that East Germany should have total control over travel between Berlin and West Germany, which would help stem the westward flight of East Germans. And he said that, if the Western countries refused to go along, Russia would sign a treaty with East Germany to ensure that East Germans controlled access from Berlin to West Germany. Khrushchev gave Kennedy time to consider his response.

Khrushchev doubted the new president's resolve and courage, and Kennedy was unsure of his position. On June 15, Khrushchev went on television and raised the stakes, warning that any country violating the treaty he expected to sign with East Germany would be held responsible for its aggression and face the consequences. Four days later, Kennedy said he didn't think it was worth going to war over whether East Germans would be able to examine the papers of U.S. citizens traveling to West Berlin.

Khrushchev upped the pressure by ordering new nuclear-weapon testing to be carried out on June 21. The Soviets sometimes used nuclear testing for psychological effect. It was their way of "signaling." Khrushchev soon made a personal visit to Sakharov, the Soviet's leading bomb designer, to tell him he wanted a 100-megaton bomb. Although the bomb wasn't ready before the crisis concluded, that October the Russians did test Tsar Bomba, the largest bomb ever exploded (and one of no real military use).

In such harrowing times, Kennedy's greatest fear was that he would be the one to initiate nuclear war. At the start of his term, there had been much talk and concern about the "missile gap"—but what was not well known was that the missile gap actually favored the United States. Not only did America possess missiles, but the total destructive power of its nuclear arsenal was moving toward an all-time peak, with a stockpile of weapons that possessed an explosive power of 20,491 megatons, the equivalent of nearly 41 billion pounds of TNT. With the country's massive destructive capability and ability to launch a first strike with a superior missile force, some in the U.S. military thought a first strike against Russia was the best option as the Berlin crisis continued.

Kennedy believed everyone would lose if war began, that Soviet missiles would be in the air before any U.S. missiles hit their targets. Early that summer, he walked out in the middle of the "net evaluation," a Defense Department briefing on the chances of nuclear war, and following that, after a discussion on the topic with close advisors, said, "And we call our-selves the human race."

Tensions continued to escalate that June and July. Rumors spread in East Germany of West German tourists resorting to biological warfare by bringing in polio. Every other passenger on trains headed for West Berlin was questioned, and the news was continually updated. At a Kremlin reception on July 2, the British ambassador to the Soviet Union told Khrushchev that the growing crisis could be resolved if all of the powers that had occupied Germany after the war cooperated. The communist leader replied with an ominous reminder that "only six . . . H-bombs . . . would be quite enough to annihilate the British Isles and nine would take care of France."

When Kennedy went to his Hyannisport retreat in late July to consider his options and prepare his speech on Berlin, his thinking took a twist, and Schelling's influence played an important role. According to Campbell Craig, chair in politics and international relations at the University of Can-terbury, writing in his 1998 book *Destroying the Village: Eisenhower and Thermonuclear War*: "Schelling was invited by the Kennedy administration to comment on the Berlin Crisis. His paper, 'Nuclear Strategy in the Berlin Crisis,' was included in Kennedy's reading packet for the trip to Hyannis Port in July." Historian James K. Galbraith describes what took place:

> Nuclear conflict was very much in the air that week. Another docu-ment of the time indicates the directions Kennedy's nuclear thinking was actually taking—quite the Cold Warrior, but at the same time far removed from pre-emptive strikes and the inflexible all-out attack envisioned by the Joint Chiefs. This is a paper entitled "Nuclear Strat-egy in the Berlin Crisis," by the economist Thomas C. Schelling, which was sent to Kennedy over the weekend of July 21, 1961 and which, as Bundy noted, made a "deep impression" on the President . . . [Schelling's paper said] "the role of nuclears in Europe should not be to win a grand nuclear campaign, but to pose a higher level of risk to the enemy. The important thing in limited nuclear war is to impress the Soviet leadership with the risk of general war—a war that may occur whether we or they intend it or not. . . . We should plan for a war of nerve, of demonstration, and of bargaining, not of tactical target destruction." The cumulative impact of this diverse advice can be seen in Kennedy's televised address to the nation on July 25, 1961.[77]

Schelling had argued in the paper that a function of nuclear weapons could be the threat of their use in order to prevent their use. That would be doing "what could be done to give pause to the East Germans and the Soviets, to make them reconsider any possible attack," as he had told Bundy earlier. He said the president could threaten the use of nuclear weapons to convince the Soviets that the risk of war was too great to make challenging the United States over Berlin worth the danger. It was a contest of high risks and a test of wills, a test where tactics equalled strength. Schelling was in California the week Kennedy was in Hyannisport—unaware the president was reading his words, and that they were influencing him to go to the brink, to risk a nuclear war where everyone's fate hung in the balance.

Making a commitment was a strategy Schelling had long advocated as a means of gaining the upper hand in bargaining situations. In a strategic commitment, one bound himself in the choice he could make in a situation where choices are interdependent. If the United States announced some policy or position before the Soviets made any decisions, the Soviets would know the results of any decisions they might make before actually making them. The United States, as Schelling had suggested, could threaten the use of nuclear weapons to convince the Soviets that the risk of war was too great. If the commitment was something that made the choices available to the Russians and East Germans dangerous, they might be forced to choose from options that were less dangerous, though the choices would not be preferable to them. Schelling was suggesting "brinkmanship," the deliberate creation of a recognizable risk of war, a risk that one did not completely control.

On July 25, President Kennedy announced in a televised appearance: "We have given our word that an attack upon that city will be regarded as an attack upon us all . . . For the choice of peace or war is largely theirs, not ours."[78] It was a commitment, and Kennedy had named it as such in his speech when he described "our commitment to sustain—and defend, if need be—the opportunity for more than two million people to determine their own future and choose their own way of life." He was specific: "an attack upon that city will be regarded as an attack upon us all." The United States had made a commitment to defend Berlin, and Kennedy was talking about nuclear weapons. America had bound itself to a choice and could not back away. The next choice was in the Soviets' hands. Kennedy included the consequences of the Soviets' choice, if they decided on war: "Now, in the thermonuclear age, any misjudgment on either side about the intentions of the other could rain more devastation in several hours than has been wrought in all the wars of human history."

The Soviets didn't challenge the United States in Berlin. Their response came on August 13 in the form of a barbed-wire barrier slicing the city in two. The East Germans soon replaced the temporary barrier with a concrete wall. With its watchtowers, guard dogs, and machine guns, the Berlin Wall became the grim physical symbol of the Cold War.

Schelling says the situation in Berlin had the characteristics of one of game theory's most studied games, the "chicken dilemma." The name "chicken dilemma" came from the teenage dueling practice depicted in movies about the 1950s, in which two teenagers drive their cars at each other, the one who turns away being the "chicken." If neither turns away, the result is disaster, as they would crash head-on. As with the prisoner's dilemma, each player has two options: He can cooperate (in this case, turn away), or he can defect (in this case, drive straight). The game is illustrated with a matrix:

	turn away **A**	drive straight
turn away **B**	2 / 2	3 / 1
drive straight	2 / 1	0 / 0

(Cell values as shown: top-left cell A=2, B=2; top-right cell A=3, B=1; bottom-left cell A=1 (lower), B=3; bottom-right cell A=0, B=0)

A player faces four possible outcomes in a game of "chicken." The best outcome is to drive straight while the other player turns away, or is "chicken." Next best is if both players turn away. If both are "chicken," neither is really humiliated. The next-to-worst outcome is being "chicken," turning away while the other player drives straight. Being "chicken" isn't good, but it's better than being dead. The worst outcome is when both players drive straight. In "chicken," rational players want to do the opposite of whatever the other player is doing. The dilemma is that in going for the best outcome, one risks the worst outcome—and if both players go for their own best outcome, the worst is assured.

The chicken dilemma is different from the prisoner's dilemma: It doesn't have a "natural outcome," a logical choice a rational player is forced to make. In such a case, game theory says you should avoid your minimum score, which for both players is the "zero" that puts them in the lower-right quadrant. By avoiding their minimum score, they end up in the upper-left quadrant where both turn away. That's the logical thing to do, resulting in the logical outcome. But, if you know the other player knows that turning away is the logical outcome, why not drive straight? That would give you your best outcome. But the other person is probably thinking the same thing. He might think he could drive straight without consequence. But since the other person is probably thinking the same thing, he would know you're thinking the same thing, too, so he wouldn't do it—so it would be safe for you to do it, after all. But then, he might have decided you wouldn't do it because he thought that you thought that he thought he wouldn't do it, so. . . .

One possible way of winning at "chicken" is to rip off your steering wheel and hold it out the window so the other driver can see you have no ability to alter your car's course. That's a commitment.

The chicken-dilemma game is a form of bargaining situation, where intentions take on great importance. In Schelling's paper, "Nuclear Strategy in the Berlin Crisis," he had written that "the role of nuclears in Europe should not be to win a grand nuclear campaign, but to pose a higher level of risk to the enemy."

President Kennedy announced, "We have given our word that an attack upon that city will be regarded as an attack upon us all," noting that "the choice of peace or war is largely theirs, not ours." His commitment was clear and in "chicken," rational players want to do the opposite of whatever the other player is doing. Kennedy announced that the United States was going to "drive straight," in chicken-game terms, and go to war over Berlin if the Soviets entered the city. Assuming mutual defection to be the most feared outcome and that both players want to do the opposite of whatever the other is doing, his public statement of the U.S. intention to defend Berlin was effective. It served, as Schelling had said, "to convince the Soviets that the risk of general war is great enough to outweigh their original tactical objectives."

When playing "chicken" at Berlin, Kennedy's "driving straight" did lead to the Soviets "turning away." The United States had proven willing to go to the brink, and the Soviets backed down. Yet the confrontation wasn't over.

In October 1962, it would rise to new heights in the Cuban Missile Crisis, in which the United States faced a repetition of the chicken dilemma.

Schelling believes that Kennedy and his advisors learned in Berlin that, if they did things right, there were limits as to how far the Soviets would push, because they didn't want a nuclear war—a valuable lesson for the Cuban crisis. Robert McNamara puts less credit in that assessment.[79] It may have been the Kremlin that learned from the crisis: Historian and former Kennedy advisor Arthur Schlesinger Jr., said that one of the reasons Khrushchev chose to place missiles in Cuba was "to acquire a potent bargaining counter when he chose to replay Berlin."[80]

Years after the Berlin crisis, a book was published in which the author claimed that Schelling had made a specific recommendation on Berlin: in fact, that Schelling had "called for replying to a Soviet move against Berlin with a demonstration nuclear drop on a Hiroshima-sized Soviet city."[81] Schelling was indignant when he heard the claim, coming as it did from a former colleague, but it wasn't the first time he'd heard such ideas of nuclear strikes attributed to himself. He didn't know where the stories originated or who first attributed the suggestions to him.

He does recall participating in a conference on limited strategic war and how it might be possible to keep a nuclear war limited, during which he may have made a comment as part of a broader discussion that sounded similar to this proposal, but he wasn't offering it as a proposal per se, and it wasn't related to Berlin. The only other statement in any way similar to the one described in the book that Schelling recalls having made involved talking about the possibility of exploding a bomb 100,000 feet in the air, possibly over Moscow, breaking a lot of windows, scaring a lot of people. Again, that comment wasn't in connection with Berlin.

One frightening possibility is that Schelling's supposed recommendation for a nuclear strike may have rested on the reading, or misreading, of his own work. Schelling's clear, insightful, and thorough explanations of the nature of tactics and strategy aimed to promote greater understanding of the issues and to contribute to more rational behavior. He frequently included examples of certain past actions and real-world strategic decisions, explaining how they had either succeeded or failed and discussing every conceivable result of the tactics used in such situations. Taken out of their detailed contexts, his analyses and hypothetical extrapolations of such historical examples could sound like strategic plans to adopt—and whether that happened at times was beyond his control. When it did, credit for the strategy would sometimes get back to him as though he had actually proposed it.

The Strategy of Conflict was widely read and in it Schelling had written: "Between the threats of massive retaliation and limited war there is the possibility of less-than-massive retaliation, of gradual reprisal . . . The idea that one might 'take out' a Russian city if Soviet troops invade a country." The notion that "one might 'take out' a Russian city if Soviet troops invade a country" was part of a much broader discussion. Had someone picked out this brief passage, considering it a concrete proposal? The dangers of an important strategist or advisor being misread or misinterpreted are ominously apparent. As evinced by Kennedy's reading of "Nuclear Strategy in the Berlin Crisis," the ideas discussed by a strategist of Schelling's stature and style were often just one step away from real-world application. Unfortunately, the questionable understanding and application of Schelling's ideas—finding things in his analysis of deterrence and warfare and considering them tactics he actually advocated—were problems that would recur on occasion throughout his career.

Looking back, Schelling recalls the danger of it all: "I don't remember being terribly afraid I was wrong. I did have a lot of occasions when I was afraid people would take me seriously and do it mistakenly."[82]

President Kennedy had not been mistaken in his interpretation of Schelling. With Kennedy's reading of "Nuclear Strategy in the Berlin Crisis," Schelling had provided the service he intended: He helped clarify a tense situation and promote understanding at a time when much was at stake and understanding was vital. Kennedy used those insights to make a choice that was all his own.

CHAPTER 12

WAR GAMES

As the Berlin Crisis unfolded, Schelling was studying signaled communication and how it could be more effectively and precisely conveyed. The interest he had developed in war games at RAND in 1957 had been revived when he moved to Cambridge, and it was the Harvard-MIT connection that encouraged his further involvement. A friend at the MIT Center for International Studies, Lincoln Bloomfield, had worked on some political games, and the center's director, Max Milikan, had suggested he and Schelling get together and organize a game. The Schelling-Bloomfield game was a political-military exercise involving a Soviet invasion of Iran. The Berlin Crisis now presented the opportunity to combine Schelling's interest in understanding signaling with the crisis training of war games.[83]

At the Harvard Center for International Affairs in the 1960s

In the summer of 1961, not long after McGeorge Bundy had called on him for advice, Schelling was on his way to RAND. Corinne's parents lived in Washington, so the family stopped there for a week on the way to California to let the children visit their grandparents. During that week, his old friend from RAND, Charles Hitch, invited the Schellings to dinner, along with another couple, the Rostows. An old friend of Schelling's, Walt Rostow was on the MIT faculty at the time Schelling and Bloomfield were conducting their first game and had worked with Schelling on the game's control team. Now the assistant secretary for policy planning in the State Department, Rostow would soon move on to the national security staff at the Kennedy White House, where he would be one of Kennedy's close advisors during the Cuban Missile Crisis. Berlin was on everyone's mind at the time, and the topic naturally dominated their dinner conversation.

Seeing Schelling again and discussing Berlin gave Rostow an idea: "You know that game we did in Cambridge? Why don't we do a game like that about the crisis in Berlin?" Those involved had all found the Cambridge game a valuable experience, useful as an exploratory device for simulating crisis decision-making, and Rostow thought the format might have applications for Berlin. Schelling and Rostow described the game to Hitch and, before the evening was over, both Rostow and Hitch suggested that Schelling stay in Washington and develop a game involving Berlin rather than go to RAND.

The prospect was an appealing one, but Schelling said he'd already rented a house in Santa Monica and made a commitment to RAND. He didn't have any specific role or project already scheduled at RAND, however, and suggested that perhaps he could devote himself to developing the game while there, trying it out on the RAND staff. The group agreed that was a good idea.

Before Schelling left Washington, Hitch wanted one more thing: to introduce Schelling to his new boss, Secretary of Defense Robert McNamara. Kennedy had brought in McNamara to reorganize the Defense Department, to increase its efficiency and give a new look to America's defense policy. The currently available approaches had weaknesses: The Eisenhower–Dulles policy of "massive retaliation" and the generally accepted concept of "mutually assured destruction" both relied on nuclear strikes to control Soviet expansion and to maintain a balance that would preserve peace between the two superpowers. The United States was ahead in the arms race, yet the military continued to press for a rapid build-up of strategic missiles.

The United States was unwilling to use nuclear weapons in small or regional conflicts, which meant that current policies were not guaranteed deterrents in such situations. Yet national security depended on controlling regional conflicts. If they got out of control and escalated, they could lead to nuclear confrontations. McNamara's solution was "flexible response": making available a range of conventional weapons for use against the Soviet Union or its allies. That would avoid reliance on nuclear weapons as deterrents in all situations. "Flexible response" was intended to offer a credible deterrent on a scale that didn't threaten a large war, thus preventing a nuclear confrontation.

Kennedy wanted to change another aspect of current policy brought to his attention by Schelling. Schelling's RAND paper, "Nuclear Strategy in the Berlin Crisis," included an observation that the current nuclear com-mand-and-control structure didn't ensure that the U.S. president had full and final authority over the bomb. Although it was assumed to be the case, control of the weapons was, in fact, far from being securely concentrated in the hands of the commander in chief. Schelling advocated centralizing control of the weapons under the president, which would improve his bar-gaining authority. Gaining operational control of the country's nuclear force became a priority for Kennedy.

Schelling had heard stories about the brilliant, efficient McNamara and was excited at the prospect of meeting him. The secretary of defense was famous for his quick grasp of issues and ability to analyze situations and make rational decisions. Hitch and Schelling went to McNamara's office for an informal visit. It wasn't much of a conversation. Schelling thought McNamara was either a good listener, or that he had nothing to say. The qualities he'd heard so much about weren't in evidence at that first encounter, but Schelling did think McNamara must have been a strong believer in analytic thinking, or he wouldn't have acquired so many people from RAND. Later encounters would reveal more about McNamara.

It was time to get to RAND and start on his Berlin game, so the Schellings headed to Santa Monica. As the Berlin game would involve the possible outcome of nuclear war with the Soviet Union, Schelling and his assistant, Allan Ferguson, needed to know the specifics of America's defense system in order to develop the game. The United States must not be caught by surprise if a major crisis developed into a war. It would be important to alert America's first line of nuclear attack, the long-range nuclear bombers of the Strategic Air Command. At that time, America relied on the "distant early warning," or DEW, line to detect an incoming Soviet attack and launch an SAC strike.

To better understand the workings of SAC, they called in two brigadier generals, operations officers who could explain SAC's attack plans. SAC was prepared with an Alert Force for immediate attack and a Ready Force for follow-up. Among the things Schelling and Ferguson learned from the generals was that if the Alert Force were launched when there was a warn-ing of a Soviet attack and then recalled, the force was dead for 24 hours. Its planes couldn't land because they were too heavy and had no capability for dropping fuel; once they burned enough fuel to land, the crews would be fatigued and the planes would require an emergency overhaul. The Alert Force had no spare crews. If Russia could trick SAC into launching an attack and then pulling back, the Soviets could launch a first strike.

Schelling thought there appeared to be a solution to this potential disaster: If the Alert Force had been mistakenly pulled back and an immediate U.S. strike was required, why couldn't the Ready Force take over for the Alert Force? The generals replied, "That's not their job." So . . . it wasn't the Ready Force's job. Schelling and Ferguson persisted, offering a hypothetical scenario: If SAC is warned of a possible, very dangerous attack, but knows that it would also be very dangerous to have the planes take off in case the warning was a false alarm, how would SAC's command decide what to do? The generals paused, conferring quietly. Schelling and Ferguson then suggested that perhaps the SAC could launch half the Alert Force? If the enemy knew this was SAC procedure, they'd realize there would be no unanswered first strike; and if half the SAC force struck, the enemy would know more were coming. When the first SAC group returned, the second could attack. The generals looked at each other for a minute, then one said, "Well, how could we do it? We could launch all the odd-numbered aircraft." The other added, "Maybe we could launch the odd-numbered wings." They discussed that for some time and then said they'd go home and think about it.[84]

Not only had SAC command never figured out how to launch half the force before, it hadn't occurred to them that they might even want to do such a thing. The United States depended on this force for survival in the event of a nuclear attack—and such was the state of its readiness.

Schelling finished developing his game and tried it out on the RAND staff. The consensus was that the game was good, and he was ready to take it back to the East Coast. Early that fall, shortly after the Berlin Wall went up, Schelling conducted the first of his war games. A government-sponsored political-military game, the Berlin game was held over the weekend of September 8–11, 1961 at Camp David, Maryland and included two teams of seven participants each and a control team of six.

The game's purpose was to provide people in leadership roles with practice handling tense, evolving, and confrontational situations. Decision-making during critical East-West confrontations, such as the highly volatile Berlin Crisis, was often done under very intense pressure, when situations were fluid, the stakes were extremely high, and choices must be made quickly. The dangers in acting irrationally, in overreacting, in making hasty decisions, and in misinterpreting the other side's actions or signals were extremely serious and very real. A common Schelling theme throughout the Cold War was that people in power must think about and prepare in advance to deal with the most dangerous of situations, those that could involve nuclear weapons. There wouldn't be time for research when a crisis suddenly arose. Schelling's war games were to be life-like and serious, with role-playing that involved very high stakes. He intended them to simulate highly believable Cold War scenarios.

The crisis simulated in the first Berlin game began as a showdown, with the Soviets closing off the *Autobahn* to the West and the United States reinstating an air blockade of Berlin. The participants were divided into two teams, the Red Team representing the Soviet Union and the Blue Team representing the United States. The control team members, headed up by Schelling, would run the game and act as referees. Each team received specific data—geography, military capability, recent history, political goals—so that its members knew something about the background for the game's situation. Then each received a "scenario," 15–20 typed pages describing a tense situation set in the immediate future which involved some plausible Soviet or American activity that necessitated a very important decision.

The teams were given two to three hours to think about what they wanted to do under the circumstances and write a detailed statement of their planned actions for the next 48 hours. Their decision could involve anything from sending troops into combat and calling for reinforcements to pushing forward a diplomatic initiative of some kind. If a team chose to respond militarily, they had to stipulate the details: the kinds of weapons, the number of troops, how each would be used, how long it would take to get them into action, whether they would have forces go on alert back home . . . everything. The control team reviewed each side's detailed statement to see what would have happened if each side had done what they said they would do. The resulting situation became the new scenario. The Red and Blue Teams took the new scenario and spent another three or four hours preparing statements for the control team, which then spent three or four hours projecting a new plausible situation.

By repeatedly creating new scenarios from the teams' statements, the control team could keep the crisis from petering out. If there was no interaction to make things worse, the control team could introduce an "act of God" or, at times, Schelling would feed them misinformation. With a little creative ingenuity, Schelling's team would carry the scenario ahead another 12 hours, 24 hours, 36 hours, saying, "Here is the new situation. Here is what happened." Schelling found he could usually get through three rounds in the course of a weekend.

The final stage of the games was the "post mortem," a group review and evaluation of the entire experience. It was during this stage that reflection and learning really took place. Everyone gathered in a large room, and each team reviewed all of the other team's documentation. Both sides learned where their own actions or intentions had been misunderstood, where they had misunderstood the other side, and where each had jumped to erroneous conclusions. They spent time considering what the other side had done right and what they'd done wrong. Schelling directed the conversation as they relived what had taken place, and the participants often found the results fascinating and surprising.

The Berlin game proved a success, and Henry Rowen (one of its sponsors, along with Rostow) wanted another. Schelling held the second game two weeks later, September 29–October 1, just outside of Washington in Rosslyn, Virginia. Occurring such a short time after the Berlin Crisis cooled down, all of the participants were extremely familiar with the situation.

In the second Berlin game, the Red Team's Soviet-controlled East German troops had cut off night access to a small satellite town in the no-man's land on the edge of Berlin and activated several Soviet divisions to move to Berlin. In response, the U.S. Blue Team was sending a company of soldiers straight down the *Autobahn*. The company, which had been told to defend itself at all costs and to fire if fired upon, had the option of calling for air support. The event touching off the tension was a minor skirmish that broke out between the U.S. troops and the East Germans. Although the event itself didn't seem significant, the underlying issues were: If Blue backed down, it would look as if the United States was surrendering Berlin; if Red backed down, it was a bluff that failed and demonstrated Soviet weakness. It was the sort of situation that required decision-making in a dangerous, uncertain environment.

Berlin game participants included officials from the White House, the State Department, the CIA, and the military, among them: Carl Kaysen, the deputy special assistant for national security affairs at the White House; John McNaughton, an assistant to McNamara at the Defense Department; Alain Enthoven from the State Department; intelligence officer DeWitt Armstrong; McGeorge Bundy, Seymour Weiss from National Security, and Henry Kissinger. Their immersion into Schelling's simulations was so intense that the teams would stay up nearly all night, getting by on only several hours of sleep.

Schelling's games didn't end with the Berlin scenarios. Within a year, he conducted a game with French, British, and German players, and ran another the following year in which the scenario featured four insurgencies running simultaneously in Latin America and Africa. By 1963, Schelling had run seven games, and he continued to do so from time to time on differing topics.

As the games and post-mortem discussions continued, certain patterns of understandings and misunderstandings became apparent. The post mortems revealed that, although both sides proceeded with caution, they regularly appeared more cautious than they actually were (or more cautious than they themselves thought they were). Schelling's explanation for this was that differences of opinion existed within each team; some members were more hawkish, some more dovish. This combination resulted in decisions that were a compromise between "bold, harsh, scary actions" and extreme caution. The teams began with relatively mild steps, escalating only if the enemy escalated. That led to mutual waiting. Each side only saw what the other side actually did, not what the other side had resolved to do if necessary. Since neither side began aggressively, each thought the other was winding down. Schelling thought about how tense the world seemed at the time, but he said, "After we'd done three of these games, all involving Berlin, the staff of the war games agency that sort of worked for me during these games had come to the conclusion that, 'It's awfully goddamn hard to get a war started.'"[85]

That the appearance each team gave the other and the beliefs they held about their own attitudes differed was a consistent trait of the game scenarios—and an extremely significant lesson. If the messages the teams thought they were communicating were not the messages being received, the consequences could be disastrous. The war games offered empirical support for one of the prominent themes in Schelling's work on deterrence: Clear signaling is critical to clear communication.

The dangers of failing to communicate through successful signaling were readily apparent in the Iran game he ran involving higher-level government officials. The game began with this scenario:

The Shah of Iran was reinstated in power. The CIA had successfully directed the coup to overthrow the government of Mohammed Mossadegh, whom it regarded as a threat to Western interests. The Shah was pro-West and eager to cooperate with the United States. Keeping Iran, Turkey, and Pakistan under the U.S. sphere of influence as a buffer against Soviet expansion into the Middle East was critical to America. Having another country on its border as a U.S. puppet and a base for U.S. military operations was an equally critical setback to the Soviets. With the Shah in power, the United States had the advantage. Soviet troops poured over the passes of the Caucasus Mountains and through Azerbaijan into Iran. The Turks were quick to respond, sending troops to help defend the northern Iranian city of Tabriz. The Soviet advance was stalled, not only by the Turks, but also by the guerrilla tactics of the local Iranians they encountered. Winning a war against guerrilla fighters in a large country would take considerable time and manpower and fail to exploit the Soviet's vast advantage in technology. The Soviets began to consider other options; as Iran was on their border, and they weren't going to allow another base for U.S. bombers and missiles so close to home. A U.S. carrier armed with nuclear weapons was patrolling the Persian Gulf.

The two teams responded to this scenario and, after reviewing their statements, the control team came back with a new scenario: The Soviet team had decided to bomb Iran. Brief use of conventional bombing against population centers would bring an immediate end to resistance, because the Iranians had no capability for retaliation and would realize that to hold out was futile.

The U.S. team was aware the Soviets were considering using bombers, because their troops were making so little progress. The commander of the carrier, who had been in contact with the Soviet troops since the invasion began, was given authorization to issue an ultimatum, stating: "The bombing of Iran from bases in Russia would lead to the following response: the United States will launch a strike against Russia with tactical nuclear weapons against the Soviet airfields used in the bombing raids." The Soviet Union didn't attack.

The head of the U.S. Blue Team was Richard Bissell, the CIA's chief of staff. In the post mortem, he said that even though the Soviet Red Team had almost decided to make the forbidden attack in Iran, the United States was already committed to use nuclear weapons in return. When Schelling asked about the momentous nature of that decision, Bissell said he wasn't completely sure his Blue Team really meant what they said in their threat to use nuclear weapons if the Soviets did follow their plan. On behalf of the American team, Bissell said that maybe they had faked it.

He wasn't completely sure what they really meant? Maybe they were faking? This was a scenario involving the use of nuclear weapons and confrontation between the world's two superpowers. A better time for near misses was during Schelling's simulations than during the actual events. The importance of sending and interpreting clear signals so that messages were communicated without misinterpretation was evident.

Schelling didn't maintain written records of the war games. His team wanted to be free to use classified information in their scenarios. Also, they didn't want any of the participants to be associated with anything that could be identified as contrary to established national-security policies. Role-playing demanded freedom to act contrary to established policy, and even role-playing a communist could possibly get someone into trouble.

Schelling's games continued intermittently after the Iran game, always with the same purpose: to provide decision-making experience for those involved in tense and dynamic situations. When the War Games Agency in Washington took over some of the games' functions, Schelling thought he had passed along the responsibility for running them and could concentrate on other interests. Yet the brigadier general heading the agency began having trouble getting participants. He didn't have the drawing power of an academic. Schelling had also been successful because he could call on friends of his, including Kissinger, Rostow, and McNaughton, to recruit participants. Having proven himself able to get assistant secretaries and high-ranking military officers to take part in his games, Schelling was asked to serve as the agency's director.

Agency officials wanted to try a new approach to the games, hoping to attract high-ranking participants at the deputy-assistant-secretary, brigadier-general level. Rather than expecting such senior people to take part in the entire exercise, however, the games were conducted as usual with the special participants brought in for the last few hours. Having been briefed about the course of the game up to that point, the new participants then took part in the final sessions and wrap-up. The War Game Agency's approach made it easier to attract high-ranking officials, but the games themselves lost some of their value. The late participants only looked over the final options rather than really making decisions. Among the military leaders Schelling got to participate in the agency games was Maxwell Taylor, the chairman of the Joint Chiefs of Staff, along with the chief of staff of the Army and the commandant of the Marine Corps.

Schelling ran an insurgency game for the agency on Halloween 1963, a time when civil rights had joined the Cold War in dominating American's thoughts and beliefs. The country was just going through the integration of universities in the South. The game's participants included the head of the U.S. Information Agency; David Bell, director of the Bureau of the Budget; and Attorney General Robert Kennedy. The game was a fourfold one involving two insurgencies in Africa and two in South America.

Afterwards, Kennedy called Schelling aside and said, "You know, this would be very helpful in preparing for problems in desegregating Southern universities." He talked about bringing "his brother," the president, into some games also. Schelling never heard from Bobby Kennedy again. Three weeks later, on November 22, the president was assassinated in Dallas, and Lyndon B. Johnson took office.

Earlier, in June, President Kennedy had returned to Berlin, where the Cold War had come so close to disaster two years earlier. His words captured the essence of the struggle and touched not only the crowd he spoke to, but the worldwide audience he addressed, when he said, "All free men, wherever they may live, are citizens of Berlin . . . I take pride in the words, 'Ich bin ein Berliner.'" (There were a few who got a chuckle out of Kennedy's words, for *Ich bin ein Berliner* can also mean "I am a jelly doughnut," *ein Berliner* being a popular local pastry, as well as "I am a citizen of Berlin.")

CHAPTER 13

THE PRISONER'S DILEMMA OF
NUCLEAR ARMS

In 1961, Schelling and Morton Halperin had published a book titled *Strategy and Arms Control*.[86] The two of them were working together more, and Schelling later introduced Halperin to RAND. They had taken part in the Summer Study on Arms Control at MIT, at which many of the participants came to believe that the prevailing views on arms control were incorrect. It was commonly thought that arms-control agreements with the Soviet Union couldn't be achieved: Proposals from either side were just political posturing and included what Halperin called a "diplomatic joker," something in the wording that would ensure its rejection. The seminar participants believed that, if properly designed, negotiated agreements on arms control could contribute to peace. Halperin suggested that Schelling write a short book outlining that position, and Schelling agreed to do so if Halperin would help.[87] *Strategy and Arms Control* would be the only time Schelling ever collaborated in writing a book.

Strategy and Arms Control began by making it clear that it wasn't a book about disarmament. "Arms control," Schelling and Halperin argued, meant something broader: the adjustment of military postures and doctrines to induce similar adjustments in a potential enemy for the benefit of both countries. Whether the process involved reductions or increases of certain kinds of military forces, both sides sought stabilized deterrence. Shared interest was what made arms control work. Schelling and Halperin discussed strategic aspects of war and how arms control could apply, looked at arms-control proposals and what they attempt to achieve, and discussed the difficulties of making agreements work effectively. When the book was released, the co-authors distributed copies around Washington. Among those in the government who received copies were Paul Nitze, John McNaughton, and McGeorge Bundy. McNamara's views on the subject came to resemble closely those discussed in the book.

Schelling's insistence on arms control, rather than disarmament, as a path to real progress was evident in his related thinking about deterrence. Throughout everything happening in those Cold War days, as crisis followed crisis and escalations carried on, one constant was that Schelling was developing and refining his ideas about deterrence and nuclear strategy. He was thinking about how to make war less likely, or less destructive if it happened. He wasn't alone in that, though his methods relied more on bargaining and game theory than others did. Where he was more nearly the unique strategist was in thinking about what happens when nuclear weapons are actually used.

The general public assumption was that "mutually assured destruction" meant what it sounded like, that once nuclear weapons were introduced into combat, all was over. Schelling said that mutual annihilation was only one possible outcome—because nuclear war could be limited, not total—and he paid much more attention to how the use of nuclear weapons might affect Soviet decision-makers. His thoughts on limited nuclear war were purely rational. He was solving the puzzle, the first step to policy. It was an intellectual challenge. Schelling didn't think he was wrong, but thought that if he was wrong about the possibility of limiting a total nuclear war, it didn't really matter. Being wrong couldn't make things worse. He explained how the use of nuclear weapons didn't have to mean Armageddon:

> The main thing about limited nuclear strikes is if you're ever tempted to use nuclear weapons in a place like Europe, don't judge them according to what they do on the battlefield . . . if you ever use nuclear weapons, the main thing to think about is, what are the Soviets going to think you are doing? What are they going to think is coming next? Because, once nuclear weapons go off, the main consequence is going to be in the minds of the Soviet leaders, and not on the battlefield.
>
> If you use them, you should primarily use them so that the Soviets get the message that you want them to get. That could mean using them earlier than you normally would, because if you foresaw that you might need nuclear weapons on a drastic scale in 24 hours, maybe finding a way to introduce them on a smaller scale now would be more effective, only because, if you do it now, you have control. If you wait 24 hours, you may not have control.[88]

Such rational, unemotional talk about the possible use of limited nuclear strikes suggests how those who don't pay close attention to his work might find it frightening. He was talking about introducing nuclear weapons against the Soviets "earlier than you normally would," and the question of when you should introduce your nuclear weapons (earlier than normal) wasn't an idea often discussed. Schelling believed that in the tense Cold War world, someone had to consider all the possibilities. He wasn't

presenting a specific policy for the use of nuclear weapons; he was express-
ing ideas that might have policy implications. What Schelling meant to convey, he makes clear:

> Now, that was not proposing to use nuclear weapons to scare the wits
> out of the Soviets. I was simply saying, if you're ever tempted to use
> nuclear weapons, don't ignore the main consequence. I think that is
> the correct advice. I am not ultimately opposed to the use of nuclear
> weapons. I am mainly concerned, if you're ever tempted to use them,
> do it right, and make sure the President knows what he's doing. Until
> you have thought through what the affect will be of using nuclear
> weapons, what the primary objective's going to be on what the Soviets
> believe their response should be, you shouldn't use the damn things.[89]

In 1962, Schelling was jointly appointed by Walt Rostow and Paul
Nitze to chair a committee on strategic problems of the 1970s. Seeing what
the future had in store—to prevent being left behind by some new form of
"*Sputnik*"—was part of what the strategists did. The United States would
only remain a leader in the space race by looking ahead to see what was on
the horizon in both technology and in the changing strategic landscape.
The committee spent part of the summer touring, interviewing officials at
the headquarters of SAC, Air Defense, and NATO. In Schelling's report, he
focused on the proposal for development of an anti-ballistic missile system, or ABM. He concluded that while the ABM might be a technical possibility, there was no certainty it would provide protection. His major
contention was that it was an offensive, rather than a defensive weapon
system, because it encouraged surprise attack. It would offer advantages to
the side that struck first, by allowing that side to alert and ready its air
defenses and missile defenses, its ABMs; the side that struck first would
only have to ward off enemy forces devastated by its attack, enemy forces
that were unlikely to be ready to go.

It was the same surprise-attack problem that had haunted nuclear
strategists for years. Schelling's goal was to deter war, and ABMs on both
sides would make each of the sides aware that whoever went first had the
greatest advantage. The best way to maintain deterrence was to assure that
each side had enough survivable weapons to guarantee the destruction of
the other.

His committee agreed that an ABM system would be destabilizing, and
Schelling said it probably wouldn't be necessary to negotiate a treaty with
the Soviets; the Americans should just make it clear to them that they had
no interest in proceeding with development of the ABM unless the Soviets

went ahead with one. It was his recommendation that both sides avoid the dangerous and expensive escalation. It should be made clear to the Soviets that, although the ABM sounds like a defensive weapon system, it really isn't, and it would be in their best interest not to develop one, or they would force the Americans to do the same. It was a prisoner's dilemma, and Schelling was suggesting a way to get out of the least efficient, most expensive, and dangerous outcome. It would take some convincing to get the American public to believe the ABM wasn't a defensive weapon, too.

In 1966, the Cold War took on a new dimension with Red China's detonation of a hydrogen bomb. With the Vietnam War on its border and the internal chaos of the Cultural Revolution, China's situation was becoming less stable. Schelling came out with another book on nuclear strategy, *Arms and Influence*, that more fully developed his ideas on the use of military power as a bargaining force. Through his writings and his increasing presence in Washington, Schelling had a voice in the affairs of the government throughout the Johnson presidency, although he wasn't always aware of the extent of his influence as a strategist. Washington insider Francis Bator had a better perspective on his influence. A senior member of the National Security Council from 1964–1967, Bator moved on to serve as President Johnson's deputy national security advisor with responsibility for European relations and foreign economic policy. His summary was that Schelling's mode of thought had a pervasive influence on the ideas and actions of the time.[90]

In 1967, Schelling was a member of the Defense Science Board's arms control committee, and one of the committee's most important topics for discussion was whether to go ahead with the development of an ABM system. Schelling had presented his reasons for opposing the system five years earlier when he chaired the White House's committee on strategic problems of the 1970s. Now, working on the arms control committee with McNamara's assistant, John McNaughton, Schelling argued against going ahead with the ABM by promoting a tacit moratorium—the position eventually adopted by the Johnson administration.

When Soviet Premier Aleksey Kosygin came to the United States in 1967 to meet President Johnson at Glassboro, New Jersey, McNamara met with Kosygin and his entourage. McNamara explained how the United States construed ABM to be an offensive, not defensive, weapon system and he recalls that he succeeded in convincing them. Until then, they'd held the standard view that there was nothing wrong with defensive weapons; only offensive weapons were bad. McNamara persuaded them that it was a slogan without content, that defensive weapons could indeed be offensive.

With his committee meetings, conferences, and advisory roles, Schelling was in Washington at least two days a week in the spring of 1967—a great deal of time to be away from his family and his work at Harvard. Nicholas Katzenbach, the under-secretary of state, asked him to come to Washington as his deputy, and Schelling agreed, making arrangements for a two-year leave of absence from Harvard. He wasn't sure exactly when he would start, but to be sure he got who he wanted, Schelling hired a staff of three. In discussions with Katzenbach about his role as deputy, Schelling offered what he thought were a variety of ideas that would provide valuable service and advice. Katzenbach always listened politely and nodded, but delayed announcing Schelling's appointment. Schelling called Francis Bator for advice. Bator, who knew the Washington power structure well, told Schelling that the position would be a "non-job," and he would soon find himself frustrated. Katzenbach wasn't really in the loop and didn't have good relations with Secretary of State Dean Rusk. It's hard to be taken seriously in Washington, and Schelling's role as deputy was ill-defined. Bator felt uneasy about the advice after giving it, but not because he thought he was wrong.

Schelling had already begun to wonder whether he was perhaps more ambitious than Katzenbach wanted him to be, offering more advice than he cared to hear. He reconsidered what had become a seemingly questionable appointment and decided to withdraw his name. After a long, pleasant chat during one of the meetings Katzenbach had summoned him to, Schelling told him he wouldn't be taking the job.

Throughout the later 1960s and into the '70s, the arms race continued and "overkill" capability grew. Multiple Independently Targeted Re-entry Vehicles (MIRVs), which could load as many as 60 nuclear bombs in a single missile, multiplied destructive power. Russia would eventually have a nuclear force capable of destroying all humanity 29 times over, while the United States could do the same 18 times. Since the 1949 explosion of the Soviet atomic bomb, the arms race had been a prisoner's dilemma. Neither side could trust the other not to go ahead with any development that might give it some strategic advantage. Anything that might offer a first-strike capability was especially threatening.

The question of whether ABM was defensive and could prevent first strike, or offensive and make first strike a safer option, remained a debatable issue. Though Schelling's committee on strategic problems of the 1970s had recommended against its development, and McNamara had argued effectively against it as well, in January 1970, President Nixon announced the United States was going ahead with the development of the

ABM system and the Senate approved it. During April, the Strategic Arms Limitations Talks (SALT) between the United States and the Soviet Union began in Vienna. The ABM was also a topic.

Over the years, Schelling had written on and discussed arms control and the arms-race problem often, and his views were widely known. Here was another example of a prisoner's dilemma:

	Russia	
	don't build	build
don't build	3 3	4 1
United States **build**	1 4	2 2

In this dilemma, each side was unilaterally motivated to choose positively to proceed with a new weapon, regardless of what the other side was expected to choose or had chosen. If Russia committed itself to the weapon, the United States would elect to have the weapon; if Russia unilaterally promised not to have the weapon, the United States would welcome their promise but would still go ahead and get the weapon. If each made an independent choice, both ended up with a score of 2 instead of 3. Neither regretted its choice. Had it been otherwise, the country would have had the worst possible outcome: the other side having the weapon system while it did not. If both sides should happen not to invest in the weapon system, each would have done the "wrong" thing (given what their preferences are), yet both sides would be better off in terms of those preferences than if they each change their minds. Each side gains more from the other's foregoing the system than from the other side having it.

Schelling's basic assumption in the nuclear-bargaining process was that long-term stability could be maintained one of two ways. The first option was mutual acceptance of some resting point. The political model for this was the settlement in Korea, where the North and the South tolerated the peninsula's division for nearly half a century. The second was the ability to maintain some strategic bargain over an extended period, as in the "balance of terror." Represented on the prisoner's-dilemma matrix as the lower-right quadrant, the "balance of terror" was called a "stable, inefficient" outcome: a point where neither side would change, but where the outcome's values were not as high as they could be elsewhere. His first view of stability, the natural resting point, was the upper-left quadrant. Though not stable in game-theory terms, it was the most efficient outcome, or the one with the greatest overall value. It was the instability of the upper left that caused Russia and America always to end in the lower right, to continue the arms race.

Some contract seemed necessary to ensure stability, to ensure that neither side went ahead with developing new weapons systems while the other didn't. The difficulty came with ensuring an enforceable contract. Schelling's view was that enforcement would require only the ability to detect whether or not the other side was proceeding with development. Improved technology, including satellite reconnaissance, could make detection non-intrusive. Abstaining as long as the other side did was the bargaining chip. Saying your side would not proceed with the system, "if and only if" the other side didn't, should be sufficient to make it clear that going ahead would only be an expense unaccompanied by any gain.

The Soviet Union and the United States signed the Strategic Arms Limitation Treaty (SALT I) and the ABM Treaty in 1972. Schelling's colleague, Albert Carnesale, was on the U.S. negotiating team for both and discussed Schelling's impact on U.S. arms policy. Like Schelling, Carnesale used a prisoner's-dilemma matrix to represent the problems the two superpowers faced. After drawing the matrix, Carnesale pointed to the "build-build" quadrant where the arms race had been deadlocked; he then shifted to the upper-left quadrant, where Russia and America cooperated and didn't go ahead with new weapons systems, and said, "It was Tom Schelling of this school [Harvard] that made this change possible."[91] Such was the sort of influence that led to words like those uttered by David T. Ellwood, dean of Harvard's Kennedy School, on the occasion of Schelling's Nobel Prize announcement: "Tom Schelling is a titan, and it is not the slightest exaggeration to say that his remarkable scholarship has made the world a safer and better place."

After the treaties were signed, the Doomsday Clock was set back. It read 12 minutes to midnight.

CHAPTER 14

VIETNAM ESCALATION

Flying under radar control with a B-66 Destroyer, Air Force F-105 Thunderchief pilots bomb a military target through low clouds over the southern panhandle of North Vietnam. June 14, 1966. Photo by: Lt. Col. Cecil J. Poss, USAF.

The greatest controversy surrounding Tom Schelling's career is the role he played in the Vietnam War. There are some who claim he was responsible for much of the worst that was done by America, that people have ignored what writer Fred Kaplan calls "the crucial role he played in formulating the strategies of 'controlled escalation' and 'punitive bombing' that plunged our country into the war in Vietnam."[92]

Kaplan's view of Schelling's importance is at odds with the vast majority of informed opinion, when he writes, "it's a legacy that can be detected all too clearly in our current imbroglio in Iraq . . . Tom Schelling didn't write much about war after that (Vietnam bombing campaign). He'd learned the limitations of his craft. If Donald Rumsfeld and Paul Wolfowitz had studied history better, they, too, might have appreciated those limits before chasing their delusional dreams into the wilds of Mesopotamia." A strong heritage to attach to a man of peace.

Schelling can only be held responsible for doing what he has always done: making strategy clear and understandable, so that those chosen to make policy decisions know what they are dealing with.

The war in Vietnam increasingly dominated the news in 1964, the same year that Schelling's alleged influence on major policy decisions made by the United States in its conduct of the war began. To claim he personally advocated specific policy decisions that were made would be false. To claim that strategies presented in his works influenced some of the important decisions made in the course of the war, is another matter. There is evidence that they did, but only that tactics were found in explanations or examples he used.

America's involvement in Vietnam had a long history, dating back to the 1940s when, as part of his containment policy aimed at halting the spread of communism, President Truman rejected Ho Chi Minh's requests for recognition of his declaration of independence from France. In 1950, when Vietnam was part of the French colony of Indochina, Truman sent 35 military advisors to help the French in their war efforts against the Vietnamese as they struggled to gain their independence. In his position as administrator in charge of European program affairs at the White House, Schelling was responsible for overseeing U.S. financial aid to France that was nominally directed to its war efforts in Indochina. That form of aid, totalling $1 billion, was what Congress was most willing to provide. After the French suffered a disastrous defeat at Dien Bien Phu, Indochina was divided into Laos, Cambodia, and Vietnam.

By mid-1954, it was clear that the French had lost. At a conference in Geneva, Switzerland, to determine Vietnam's future, it was decided that Vietnam would become an independent country. Elections were scheduled for July 1956, at which time the Vietnamese would choose their own government. Prior to the elections, the country would be divided along the seventeenth parallel, with separate governments administering each half. All Viet Minh soldiers, those who had fought against the French, were to go to the North, and all soldiers who fought for the French were to go to the South. The United States and the South Vietnamese refused to guarantee they would abide by the Geneva Accords, as the accords recognized the communist North government.

The dual governments became a permanent situation. The Southern leader, Ngo Dinh Diem, was supported by U.S. money and advice, while in Hanoi in the North, or the Democratic Republic of Vietnam, the communists were led by Ho Chi Minh. The year 1957 brought the first communist uprisings in South Vietnam, and Americans were wounded in an explosion. Two years later, the first Americans were killed there, and the unpopular Diem government was being supported more and more by American aid. In 1960, the National Liberation Front, known also as the Vietcong, was formed and began a guerrilla war in the South with weapons increasingly supplied by the North. The following year Vice President Johnson visited Vietnam to assure Diem of U.S. support. Diem requested more direct U.S. involvement. President Kennedy's advisors recommended an increase in the number of U.S. troops involved, and in 1962 that figure surpassed 10,000. American casualties began to mount.

Political and social instability was contributing to the South's inability to resist the communist forces without increased American aid. The

United States would have to take steps to save the situation. Kennedy had thought so, and now President Johnson was in the Oval Office. He was going to see that something was done. Kaplan described what came next and Schelling's involvement in *The Wizards of Armageddon*.[93] He repeated his claims in an article called "All Pain, No Gain," in *Slate* after Schelling was awarded the Nobel Prize.

Kaplan states that on May 22, 1964, McGeorge Bundy sent a memo to Johnson to inform him that a group under John McNaughton was working on a plan to broaden the war in Vietnam: "An integrated political-military plan for graduated action against North Vietnam is being prepared under John McNaughton at Defense. The theory of this plan is that we should strike to hurt but not to destroy, and strike for the purpose of changing the North Vietnamese decision on intervention in the south." McNaughton, a friend of Schelling's since their Marshall Plan days in Paris, was described by Kaplan as "one of Tom Schelling's most dedicated devotees."

An idea discussed by Schelling that McNaughton is said to have adopted was "the power to hurt" as an important aspect of limited war. In *The Strategy of Conflict*, Schelling wrote: "The threat that compels rather than deters, therefore, often takes the form of administering the punishment until the other side acts, rather than if he acts . . . Inflicting steady pain, even if the threatener shares the pain, may make sense as a threat, especially if the threatener can initiate it irreversibly so that only the other's compliance can relieve the pain they share." He would later write: "The pain and suffering have to appear contingent on his behavior; it is not alone the threat that is effective—the threat of pain or loss if he fails to comply—but the corresponding assurance, possibly an implicit one, that he can only avoid pain and loss if he does comply." Schelling was observing that, historically speaking, a strategy of attacking an enemy's will to resist rather than its military strength—of attacking to cause pain that the enemy could only escape by a change in behavior—was a powerful psychological tool in warfare.

This Schelling view of targeting the will of the North Vietnamese also showed up in the Pentagon Papers, where Schelling's idea on the bombing was reported as: "The U.S. must be willing to pause to explore negotiated solutions, would North Vietnam show any signs of yielding, while maintaining a creditable threat of still further pressures. In the view of the working group the greater pressure to come was at least as important as any damage actually inflicted, since the real target was the will of the North Vietnamese government to continue aggression in the South."

Kaplan says, "[Schelling's] theory had been translated into official U.S. war strategy." The United States was going to inflict pain on the communist North to break its will and convince it to change its ways.

McNaughton sent McNamara a memo on September 3, saying they should look for incidents that would justify U.S. retaliation to begin the new strategy. One had already been reported that would be adequate.

In early August, two American destroyers, the USS Maddox and the USS Turner Joy, reported they had sunk North Vietnamese boats after being confronted aggressively. Although more-recent information has made it clear there were no North Vietnamese attacks at the time, they filed erroneous reports of unprovoked confrontation and attack in international waters by communists. President Johnson ordered a reprisal attack of air strikes against oil tanks and naval facilities in North Vietnam.

Unprovoked communist attacks in international waters . . . America was outraged. In August, Congress passed the Gulf of Tonkin Resolution with a unanimous vote in the House of Representatives and an 88–2 vote in the Senate. The resolution authorized the president to "take all measures necessary" to repel attacks against U.S. forces and to "prevent further aggression." Johnson said the unprecedented resolution gave him so much control it was "like grandma's nightshirt—it covered everything." In effect, Congress abdicated its constitutionally mandated responsibility to declare war, giving the president total control.

On November 1, the Vietcong launched an attack on the U.S. air base at Bien Hoa, and Bundy convened a meeting to plan the U.S. response. The group, which included McNaughton and McNamara, decided to launch a bombing campaign to break the North's will and get them to stop their flow of aid to the South. The plan, presented by Bundy, called for a gradually intensifying bombing campaign as a signal to Ho that, if he didn't call off the supplies, things would get worse. The question was how to be sure the North understood the signals being sent by the bombing.

In December, McNaughton visited Schelling, considered to be the authority on limited war and signaling, to discuss what kind of bombing campaign would send understandable signals and how long such a campaign should last. What happened at that meeting and its results are recalled by Schelling one way and reported by Kaplan slightly differently.[94]

Schelling remembers it as one of the few times he was called on for very specific military advice, rather than strategic policy views. McNaughton told him the administration was thinking seriously about engaging in a bombing campaign in North Vietnam and that Secretary McNamara wanted Schelling's advice on how to do it. Schelling asked what they wanted the North Vietnamese to stop doing that a bombing campaign would accomplish. McNaughton told him what he already knew: They wanted the North to stop supporting the Vietcong. McNaughton added that they wanted a campaign that would last no longer than several months.

Schelling asked how they would know the North Vietnamese had stopped supporting the Vietcong. McNaughton said that the Vietcong should gradually become less effective. Schelling persisted, asking how long it would take to know, by observing the Vietcong, that the North must have withdrawn support. McNaughton said he didn't know, but it could be six months or a year. Schelling's final question was how they were going to have a bombing campaign that stops at the end of three months as if it had succeeded, when they wouldn't know whether it had actually succeeded for six months or a year? McNaughton said he had to report something to McNamara. Finally, Schelling gave his advice: "You should report that he couldn't accomplish what he wanted to accomplish in three months. That's what I would report."[95] McNaughton returned to Washington to make his report.

Kaplan's recounting of the Schelling–McNaughton meeting is that McNaughton came to Schelling to ask what kind of bombing campaign would be most successful in sending the correct signals to North Vietnam and how long such a campaign should be. They spent much of their hour-long meeting discussing what the United States could try to stop the North from doing, how they would know the North had stopped, and what there was the North couldn't just stop doing, then start again when the bombing ended. Schelling said a short campaign of several weeks would be long enough, as it would either succeed within that time or it wouldn't. Three weeks was the maximum. Kaplan alleged that any other questions were too much for Schelling to handle, stating: "So assured when writing about sending signals with force and inflicting pain to make an opponent behave, Tom Schelling, when faced with a real-life war, was stumped."

Kaplan says that after the three weeks of bombing they had adopted, McNaughton wrote to McNamara to say, "The situation in Vietnam is bad and deteriorating ... We must have kept promises, been tough, taken risks, have gotten bloodied, and hurt the enemy very badly." The next month McNaughton, McNamara, William Bundy, Maxwell Taylor, and the Joint Chiefs of Staff concluded that the bombing campaign would carry on much longer, perhaps as long as two more years.

Schelling's actual advice probably had little influence in this case. Schelling says, "Well, I think a lot of people think I had direct influence on Robert McNamara, Secretary of Defense, either because I had access to him, or because he was reading what I was writing. I didn't have access to him, and I doubt whether he read anything that I wrote." In 1990, *The Washington Post* wrote, "It was said that Robert McNamara was influenced by [Schelling's] thinking more than by any other."[96] McNamara doesn't go as far, but says, "People were paying attention to him."[97]

After Schelling said "no," the idea that a short campaign could be successful was scratched and a long, sustained one began: Operation Rolling Thunder. Schelling says, "Yeah, but that's not my influence, that just means they had decided independently of me they were going to bomb. And if they merely had a mild curiosity whether they could stop in two months, all I did is tell them no." But couldn't people have misinterpreted what he said? Schelling comments, "But what 'people' are you talking about? The only 'people' I know would be John McNaughton, and I don't think he would have let himself be misunderstood by McNamara any more than I would have been misunderstood by McNaughton." McNamara does not recall any advice from Schelling, which supports Schelling's recollection.

Schelling's discussion with McNaughton had been for specific advice about the actual bombing campaign in the North, and his comments had little impact. The idea of attacking an adversary's will through the infliction of pain is another matter. "Inflicting pain" was not a policy Schelling recommended in Vietnam. It was something he wrote about as he discussed policies generically. If decision-makers tried to put something they thought they had learned from him into effect, and they did so poorly and things went wrong, that was beyond his control. Schelling happily takes responsibility for anything he wrote that influenced the conduct of the war, but not for the way the war was conducted. He never felt he'd written anything he shouldn't have. So to say that "inflicting pain" and the tactics it led to came from Schelling, as Kaplan does, has a certain element of truth, but few elements of responsibility. When the strategist passes along his thoughts and advice, they become the property of others. Along with the loss of ownership in the ideas is a loss of responsibility for their influence. In Vietnam, the strategy it led to was massive bombing.

Schelling is a blend of confidence and modesty. He has considerable confidence in his powers of analysis and ability to find solutions where few have been seen previously. The confidence is well placed, and his ability to see new solutions is a quality uniformly recognized by those who know him and have worked with him. The modesty can be seen in his self-deprecating descriptions of his own importance. In a comment that captures a recurring theme in his views, that he has not been misunderstood nor has he been responsible for creating situations of great danger, both sides of his personality can be seen: "I never saw how anybody who listened to me would misunderstand. And it never occurred to me that people would quote me as if I were an authority for something. I have no way of knowing whether or not people were directly influenced by me in making decisions, and whether, if they were, they got me wrong. I think it's unlikely."[98]

Schelling was in London for a conference when the real "pain" started that spring and was a visiting professor in Israel as it increased during the summer. The first bombing raids of Operation Rolling Thunder were launched on March 2, 1965, and the sustained heavy bombing of the North would last until the end of October 1968. Operation Rolling Thunder would be the longest prolonged bombing campaign ever conducted by the U.S. Air Force. During that period, nearly one million bombing sorties were flown and three-quarters of a million tons of bombs dropped, destroying more than half of the bridges in North Vietnam, nearly all of its large petroleum storage facilities, two-thirds of its power-generating plants, and killing an estimated 52,000 people. The campaign inflicted a great deal of pain on the North Vietnamese, but the pain failed to alter their will to resist.

Things could have gone worse in Vietnam. While the United States was bombing, the presence of Soviet soldiers and equipment in the North threatened a showdown of greater proportions. Yet some successful tacit communication did occur. Schelling describes the tacit cooperation between the United States and the Soviet Union during the Vietnam War as one piece of evidence that both sides had moved away from confrontation toward a stable relationship. The Soviets tried to present no embarrassing targets to American aircraft or naval vessels when they supplied North Vietnam, and both sides pretended there were no Soviet personnel at North Vietnamese anti-aircraft sites.

The bombing campaign failed dramatically. Schelling had written that inflicting steady pain could be an effective tactic even if it caused suffering to both sides, especially if one side had control over it and the enemy could end the pain by agreeing to specific terms or demands. It wasn't a success in Vietnam. As he later said, "We wanted to convince them that we could tolerate more pain than they could, but the Vietcong weren't rational." As the U.S. bombing increased, the amount of supplies moving from North Vietnam to the South did not slow.

McNamara later wrote in jest: "A story being circulated at Harvard during the 1960s was that a missed opportunity had occurred when Harvard failed to offer a scholarship to Ho Chi Minh, in order that he might have the opportunity to study with Professor Schelling. If he had, according to the Cambridge pundits, he would have known that Washington was trying to send him a *signal* via the bombing. As it was, Ho and his colleagues, in their ignorance, thought the United States was trying to destroy their country."[99]

CHAPTER 15

LIVING IN THE '60S

With Schelling's involvement in the Cold War consuming so much of his thought and energy, his presence began to give off conflicting impressions, a perception that would persist from then on. His longtime colleague at Harvard, Joseph Nye, would later say, "Tom is a unique combination: a man with a steel-trap mind and a twinkle in his eye. His brilliance is matched by gentle humor."[100] Such was the immediate impression given by his soft-spoken manner and quick smile, his questioning and frequent chuckling, and the interest he showed in people he met. But Schelling could be perceived otherwise. It was his analysis without judgment, his view of the problems of nuclear strategy and survival as puzzles, the detached logic of his approach that left people feeling differently. His friends said that to those who didn't know him, he could at times appear "cold and unfeeling" or give off an aura described by some as "chilling."

Life wasn't all drama and Cold War in the early 1960s. The gentle side his friends saw was always there. Along with Corinne and the four boys, Andrew, Tommy, Daniel, and Robert, there was also the dog, Champ. The kids had named him Champ, because they thought he looked like a boxer. Schelling got the family to do some hiking, and Daniel convinced him to start jogging. Theirs was not a family like the one he'd grown up in, where parents had little time for or interest in their children's lives. Skiing became a big activity for them all in the early '60s, and the Schellings rented houses in the mountains for ski season. These were good years for the family.

There were small moments of stress, of course, such as one memorable day at a Little League baseball game. Schelling's son Robert played, so he did some volunteer umpiring in the league. One evening on his way to a dinner party, Schelling stopped to see the beginning of Robert's game. The regular ump hadn't shown up, so he agreed to do the first three innings only. He was due at the dinner party, so they'd have to find someone to replace him after that. What made it especially stressful and embarrassing was that his son was pitching. Schelling put on the face mask and kneepads and crouched down behind the catcher to call balls and strikes. The regular ump never arrived, and in the last inning, with two outs, Robert's team was behind by one run. With one man on base, his son came up to bat. Schelling knew that if he had to call his son out, his team would lose, and Robert would take the blame. He shut his eyes when the ball came in and . . . *crack!* Robert hit a home run! Schelling took off his pads, ran to his car, and raced to the dinner party, exalted, elated, saved. He might not have handled it well, but he had survived.

In 1962, the year America was enjoying the new *Tonight Show Starring Johnny Carson* and talking about the 100 points Wilt Chamberlain scored in a single basketball game, Schelling and Corinne took a brief trip to Greece. It was a luxury vacation, hosted and escorted by the former head of the Greek air force, who managed the queen's special funds. The couple received special treatment at the queen's expense, all made possible by Schelling's colleague and friend from the Center for International Affairs, Henry Kissinger. Schelling and Kissinger were close both personally and professionally. The two nuclear strategists conducted seminars and worked well together and occasionally socialized. Kissinger was extremely bright and could absorb other people's ideas like a sponge. He would soak them up, pull them together, and feed them back, usually without giving credit as though they were his. He picked up a lot from Schelling, but didn't mention it when he used Schelling's thoughts.

It was also in 1962 that Cold War tensions reached new heights not far from America's shores. Soviet missiles were spotted in Cuba, and President Kennedy went on television on October 22 to announce that a missile launch from Cuba against any country in the Western Hemisphere would be regarded as a Soviet attack on the United States—and that the U.S. response would be an all-out attack on Russia. With Soviet ships approaching Cuba, Kennedy ordered a blockade to stop them, a step that could easily lead to real conflict. The missiles had to be removed, but it was the pending confrontation at sea that looked as if it might spark a war that would end in nuclear holocaust. Kennedy's blockade took effect on October 24. The world held its breath as the Soviet vessels came closer and closer to Kennedy's limit, and exhaled a collective sigh of relief when the Soviet ships turned back.

Secretary of State Rusk, who was advising Kennedy during the crisis, reportedly said, "We've been eyeball to eyeball, and I think the other fellow just blinked." It had been brinkmanship—or blinkmanship—played out at a new level, a reprise of the chicken-dilemma game. Schelling was with McNamara in Florida at a 25th anniversary meeting to discuss the Cuban Crisis; he says McNamara's face still flushed at that time when he talked about the crisis. Schelling recalls, "Kennedy was said to have said he thought the chance of nuclear war was one in three, and my response to that is Kennedy just doesn't understand fractions."[101]

It was also in 1962 that "save the cities," from Schelling's 1957 proposal, became U.S. policy. Schelling had wanted to present the proposal since refining it at RAND during his 1958–59 stay there, and had the opportunity to discuss the idea that cities were strategic assets that might be used in war at a conference attended by Paul Nitze, assistant secretary of defense. He had discussed this at greater length with Nitze's assistant, his old friend and McNamara's disarmament advisor for international security affairs, John McNaughton.

McNamara formally announced "save the cities" in a speech to NATO defense ministers. He told them that in nuclear war, city avoidance would drastically reduce casualties on both sides. Whether the Soviets would cooperate was uncertain, but they had a strong incentive to do so, as neither side would want to sustain a large number of civilian casualties. Schelling thought McNamara's speech missed the important point. The "save the cities" idea wasn't about avoiding civilian casualties as war carried on; it was about the cities' strategic value as hostages or bargaining chips. War was a violent form of bargaining, or game theory, and city avoidance wasn't intended to create something like a set of rules for war. War had never been a matter of saving civilian populations; it had been a matter of defeating armies in the field before civilian populations were at risk. That was the great change brought about by modern technology: Civilian populations were at risk within minutes of the outbreak of war. If the chips were used correctly, options existed, not just for the possible reduction of casualties but also for forcing desired outcomes. One of those outcomes could be bringing war to an end.

In spite of the differences in emphasis, McNamara agrees that there was a connection between Schelling's proposal and the policy he announced in his 1962 speech.

In August 1963, Martin Luther King Jr. stood on the steps of the Lincoln Memorial and told a crowd of more than 200,000 that "I have a dream," motivating the civil rights movement and capturing its ideals for posterity. In 1964, Bob Dylan captured popular sentiment with his song, *The Times They Are A-Changin'*—a fitting anthem for a year in which the surgeon general announced that cigarettes cause cancer, the Catholic mass was celebrated in English for the first time, and the Beatles came to America.

On college campuses across America, the anti-war crowd began protesting U.S. involvement in Vietnam. In 1965, the movement was just gaining momentum, with teach-ins and small demonstrations. At Harvard, whenever there were anti-war demonstrations, the presence of National Guardsmen or other military on campus, the Center for International Affairs was a key target for protestors. It sounded to students like it was involved in something because it was "international." Around the country, student resistance grew as draft boards increased their calls. Chants of "Hell no, we won't go" and draft card burnings became popular forms of protest. While motivation for the war protests in the mid-1960s ranged from political awareness and morale objection to avoidance, protests took place on the civil rights front too, as the morale conscience had been aroused. And for the otherwise interested, there were the trips. Ralph Nader was stopping the bad ones, attacking General Motors and its unsafe Corvair, while Timothy Leary promoted "good" ones, encouraging people to "tune in, turn on, drop out" with LSD.

Times were changing for Schelling, too, as his work began to branch out in new directions. President Johnson set up a crime commission headed by James Vorenberg of Harvard Law School to study ways of reducing crime. One proposed study involved deterrence theory and how it might apply to the Internal Revenue Service. Deterrence theory meant Schelling, so he was invited to Washington to consider its relationship to crime. By the time he arrived, that study had fallen through, but Schelling was invited to stay and ended up in a working group on technology and crime. He quickly got sidetracked to organized crime. To prepare for his participation in the working group, he had begun to study organized crime and read Senate hearings, and he soon decided the public had the wrong idea about what constituted organized crime.

He observed that it was a generally accepted view that organized crime was in the business of providing illicit services to willing customers who passed the costs along to their customers . . . and that if these criminals disappeared, there would be a lot of unhappy customers. Their activities, such as illegal gambling and prostitution, supposedly constituted "victimless crimes." Schelling said that was not the case. Organized crime was not in the business of actually providing illicit services; it was in the business of preying on those who did provide those services. The providers engaged in activities that lent themselves to organized crime, because they couldn't go to the law to complain, and they couldn't hide or they'd have no customers. The real money behind organized crime came from preying on those who operated in a black market, offering a legally prohibited service. It was more profitable to prey on the providers than on their customers.

Schelling raised the question of whether attempting to reduce the consumption of the illegal product or service outweighed the cost to society of creating conditions different from those that fostered organized crime. Until then, the standard assumption was that eliminating consumption of the illegal service was the only route to solving the problem. Schelling would later present his ideas on the subject to a more general audience in his 1984 book *Choice and Consequence: Perspectives of an Errant Economist.*

At the time, his views were published in the commission report and then the now-defunct *The Journal of Public Law.*[102] "That made me an authority on organized crime," he recalls. Elliot Richardson, attorney general of Massachusetts, asked Schelling to send him a copy of what he'd written and invited him to dinner. They later appeared together on television in Boston to discuss organized crime. By the time Schelling wrote another paper on organized crime, he was one of only a few in the country who had studied the topic. He spoke on the subject before a variety of audiences, including the National Police Chiefs' Convention.

Schelling was beginning to venture, from time to time, into areas outside of nuclear strategy.

CHAPTER 16

CRITICAL MASS AND RACIAL TIPPING

At RAND in the summer of 1967, Schelling began to look at another problem that drew him away from Cold War strategy. Again, his approach was not to view the issue in question as a campaign, but as a puzzle. Vietnam wasn't the only issue tearing the United States apart. Closer to America's collective soul was civil rights. Two years earlier, in March 1965, Martin Luther King Jr. led a courageous march from Selma to Montgomery, Alabama, and in August of the same year it was "Burn, Baby! Burn!" in Watts. Stokely Carmichael called for "Black Power" in 1966, and in '67, San Francisco enjoyed the "Summer of Love," while Detroit endured the worst race riots in the nation's history. Segregation was still the nation's curse. Despite Supreme Court rulings, laws, marches, and songs, neighborhoods were still segregated and riots still broke out.

Schelling considered discrimination and segregation from a different perspective, as was so often the case. The focus was commonly on "Why?" What were the factors behind the attitudes that led to racism and the segregation it bred, and what could be done to address those attitudes? Schelling asked, "How?" In American cities, where blacks and whites commonly lived in separate areas, a seemingly reasonable conclusion about the existing attitudes was that housing patterns reflected people's attitudes and preferences. He wondered whether that was a safe assumption.

Segregated housing exemplified a situation of dichotomous grouping, where individual preferences led to collective results. Such groupings and preferences show up in society in many areas on many levels. How do these arrangements work out? Schoolchildren offer one example. Consider a school that has two large, adjacent cafeterias. There are 120 girls and 100 boys. All the students prefer to eat lunch in an environment with a 1:1 girl–boy ratio and will choose to eat in whichever room has the more nearly equal numbers.

The girls go to lunch first. To avoid overcrowding when the boys arrive, they distribute themselves evenly between the two rooms, with 60 in each room. The boys begin to arrive. By the time three-quarters of the boys have arrived, there are 40 in one room and 35 in the other. Later arrivals notice a slight discrepancy and choose the room with the more nearly equal numbers. Since 60–40 is more nearly equal than 60–35, that's where they go. Soon there are 50 boys in one cafeteria and 35 in the other. The difference is obvious to the next 10 boys who arrive and, preferring the 1:1 ratio, they join the 50 boys already gathered in one cafeteria. That makes it 60 boys and 60 girls in one room, with 35 boys and 60 girls in the other. The final five boys arrive and, of course, choose the room with the equal ratio—thus upsetting the equality by making it 65 boys and 60 girls in one cafeteria.

With 65 boys and 60 girls in one cafeteria, and 35 boys and 60 girls in the other, 10 of the boys in the second room feel too uncomfortable being outnumbered almost 2:1 by the girls. They decide to move to the other room. This upsets the near equality in that cafeteria, by changing the numbers to 75 boys and 60 girls, and leaves behind a room with 60 girls and only 25 boys. Some of the boys can't cope with such a situation; they'd feel more secure being part of a 5:4 majority than a 1:2.5 minority. So, 15 more boys change rooms, leaving 10 behind. One room now has 90 boys and 60 girls, and the other has 10 boys and 60 girls. A ratio of 3:2 is closer to even than a ratio of 6:1, so the last 10 boys move into the crowded cafeteria.

Half the girls are now outnumbered 1.6:1, while it's a "girls only" lunch for the other half. The boys outnumber the girls 100 to 60 in one room. Overall, this isn't very close to the 1:1 ratio everyone had hoped for. Perhaps the situation would go one step farther, with the girls left dining alone deciding to move in order to get nearer to the 1:1 ratio. This would leave one cafeteria empty, and one crowded with 220 students.

The artificial nature of this situation comes from it being based on the unlikely overwhelming nature of a single factor of motivation (the desire for a 1:1 ratio) operating under a number of constraints. Yet its importance is that it illustrates key points Schelling was developing about "how" group behavior occurs, rather than "why" that behavior occurs. The conclusions he drew from such thought problems had significance for problems of segregation and integration as well: Individuals make decisions based on their own desires for outcomes (what he would term "micromotives"); sometimes, when taken together ("macrobehavior), these decisions lead to outcomes completely different from the desires that motivated them.

The relationship, then, between individual decisions and a collective result is not always as transparent as it was assumed to be. Looking at a city in which all the blacks of all income levels lived in one area, a seemingly reasonable conclusion about the existing attitudes in that city might have been that people preferred to live in segregated neighborhoods. If that city were to adopt policies related to integration/segregation, it might base its decisions on that assumption. Is this assumption correct? It could be. But it is also possible that every person in the city would individually prefer to live in an integrated neighborhood. Suppose each resident had the following attitude: "I would prefer to live in an integrated neighborhood, so long as 51 percent or more of the people in it are of my race." It is, of course, impossible to create neighborhoods that are both 51 percent white and 51 percent black. The ultimate result of such an attitude would be that, while everyone in the city would prefer to live in an integrated neighborhood, there would be complete segregation.

This had considerable practical public-policy significance. Looking at how segregation could occur might offer some guidance for policy decisions and assist in understanding the nature of the problem. What are the mechanisms by which patterns of segregation and integration develop? When individuals make choices on a discriminatory basis, what are the collective results? How successful are individuals in achieving their desired outcomes? Are individual motivations and aggregate outcomes necessarily consistent? To what degree can we draw conclusions about individual preferences, or expressions of "popular will," from existing segregation?

It could be a game-theory problem, and Schelling developed a game to demonstrate it. Back home from RAND, he borrowed his son's coin collection, which included both gray World War II zinc pennies and regular pennies, and got out a checkerboard. He and his son put the board on a coffee table and moved the coins around. The pennies represented two racial groups, with each penny surrounded by eight other neighbor pennies that constituted its neighborhood. Schelling set up a varying scale of racial tolerance—how many neighbors of "different" pennies would be acceptable before one would leave its neighborhood and move to a neighborhood that suited its level of tolerance. Although he set the preferences so that everyone was happy to live in an integrated neighborhood, the final result of the experiment was segregation. His simple experiment demonstrated how the desire to avoid being in even a slightly minority status could quickly unravel into segregated neighborhoods. The final results were a poor indication of the community members' individual preferences. He assumed that if an individual was unsatisfied with the racial mixture of his neighborhood, he would move to the nearest available location that met his requirements.

Schelling's game is easy to reproduce and dramatically convincing. It begins with the assumption that all the blacks and whites have a moderate attitude toward integration. Each individual would be satisfied by having more than one-third of his neighbors be of his own race. This assumption creates the following guidelines:

No. of neighbors an individual has:	No. who must be his race:
1–2	1
3–5	2
6–8	3

Given these constraints, all 60 individuals could be satisfied by leaving the four corners blank and simply alternating the houses in an "every-other" fashion, as follows:

```
      1   2   1   2   1   2
  1   2   1   2   1   2   1   2
  2   1   2   1   2   1   2   1
  1   2   1   2   1   2   1   2
  2   1   2   1   2   1   2   1
  1   2   1   2   1   2   1   2
  2   1   2   1   2   1   2   1
      2   1   2   1   2   1
```

Procedure:

A. Set up your checkerboard in the same manner as the above illustration.

B. Assume 20 individuals move away from the checkerboard neighborhood. To do this, remove 20 coins by use of some method of random selection.

C. Assume five newcomers with the same racial tolerance as all the others move in. Randomly select five empty squares for them to occupy.

D. Fill the five selected squares by flipping a coin in each case to determine whether the newcomer is white or black.

E. At this point, you should have 45 occupied squares and 19 blank squares on your board; 40 individuals are where they were at the beginning, and there are five new arrivals.

F. One by one, in order from one corner, move coins to the nearest location that satisfies the requirements, observing how that changes the neighborhood in which it arrives, and what further movement that requires.

It is necessary to keep certain factors in mind when looking at dichotomous mixing. Given a fixed set of boundaries, it is not possible for both groups to enjoy numerical superiority. If that is a condition each group sets, the only logical outcome is complete segregation. Taken a step closer to modeling reality, if one wants to be at least a one-third minority, and the other wants to be a three-quarters majority, the only compatible outcome is also complete segregation. These outcomes are not expressions of individual tolerance. They merely represent the obvious fact that sectors of the population involved cannot add up to more than 100 percent. Another factor is that people who must choose between polarized options (such as all-black or all-white neighborhoods) often do so in a way that reinforces the polarization. This is not evidence that these people prefer segregation. It only tells us that if segregation exists and people have to choose an exclusive association, they tend to choose "like" rather than "unlike" environments. A third factor is that patterns of segregation may be established through relatively minor preferences. A fourth consideration to keep in mind is the definition of "neighborhood." People analyzing the same social conditions may arrive at different conclusions, based on their different perceptions of what constitutes a neighborhood.

With help from a colleague at RAND, Schelling computerized his game so he could repeat the experiment with different variables. He learned that when looking at segregated neighborhoods, it wasn't safe to assume one knew the attitudes of the people who made up those neighborhoods. When individual choices were combined, the resulting behavior may or may not reflect their individual motives. (An incidental benefit of this experiment was that Schelling learned to use a computer.)

Schelling saw that the model he'd created demonstrated how segregation could develop within the boundaries of one specific area, as people moved within it from place to place just like the pennies on a checkerboard. He also realized there were elements the model didn't demonstrate that should be considered. He wondered how neighborhoods changed when, instead of just moving within an area, people moved in and out of the area based on varying ratios of acceptable racial mix, the least tolerant individuals leaving first. Some move "off of the checkerboard or onto the checkerboard," changing the racial composition. When they did, how did their presence or absence change the ratio of the area's racial composition, inducing further movement in and out of the entire area?

To answer that, he developed a second model, more mathematical than the first. The model allowed for changes and possible equilibrium points, but generally found that neighborhoods unraveled into segregation, with initial presence and relative speed of entry as important determining factors in determining the racial outcome. Compatible mixes could exist but would tend to attract outsiders that would dominate.

Schelling's models lead to a disheartening and somewhat counterintuitive conclusion. They indicate that the chances of avoiding segregated outcomes are not necessarily increased by heightened racial tolerance.

Understanding the mechanisms of a population's movement in racial settings demonstrated that segregation wasn't always simple to explain by looking at outcomes and that integration wasn't as easy to achieve as it seemed it should be. He presented the two models in an article in the May 1969 issue of *The American Economic Review*.[103]

Anthony H. Pascal came to RAND to work on a project about segregation called "Science and Society," and he published a paper on Schelling's interaction models. Schelling was soon invited to the University of Pennsylvania as a speaker in the Fels Lectures on Public Policy Series. His lectures about factors affecting segregation and integration, titled "Micromotives and Macrobehavior," led him to write a book of the same name published in 1978.

Schelling also looked at how a neighborhood's racial composition could change so suddenly, how it could "tip" from one situation to another. "Tipping point" has entered the language as a cliché for any sudden turning point as a result of Malcolm Gladwell's popular 2000 book, *The Tipping Point: How Little Things Can Make a Big Difference*.[104] Since then, Secretary of Defense Donald Rumsfeld has used the phrase to describe changes in public opinion in Iraq. News references to tipping points were frequent around the time Saddam Hussein's statue in Baghdad was toppled. And a *New York Times Magazine* article described Christie Brinkley's naming of her daughter "Sailor" as the tipping point for offbeat names for children. The phrase dates back to Morton Grodzins, a political science professor at the University of Chicago who published an article in 1957 on the "tip point," describing how white residents would move out of neighborhoods en masse when black proportions in the neighborhood exceeded some critical point.

Schelling had read about tipping while at RAND and expanded it into a model, a subset of a larger model he studied: critical mass. Few game-theory models can be used to describe so great a diversity of conditions as the model for critical mass. Situations as varied as the success or failure of a school dance and race riots can be illustrated and better understood with the application of the critical-mass model. One characteristic of the model is that people have very different cross-over points. Another is that the process involves conscious decisions and anticipations.

The name of the model is derived from physics. Nuclear engineers explain atomic energy in the following general terms:

When radioactive decay occurs in a substance like uranium, neutrons are emitted. These neutrons fly into space, unless they hit other uranium nuclei before leaving the mass of material. If they do hit other nuclei, they cause them to decay. The collisions cause energy to be released, and more neutrons to fly into space—unless those neutrons hit other nuclei, in which case, more energy and more neutrons are released, and so on. If the amount of uranium is large, there is a greater likelihood that a neutron will collide with other nuclei. There must be enough uranium so that the released neutrons cause an equal or greater number of additional neutrons to be released. This constitutes a "critical mass" of uranium, meaning that the process has crossed the critical point where it becomes a self-sustaining reaction. Any smaller amount will result in the chain reaction fizzling out. A larger amount (each neutron producing more than one neutron on the average) creates an explosive chain reaction.

The difference between achieving or failing to achieve critical mass in an atomic reaction is obvious—it determines whether the bomb explodes, or whether the plant produces electric power. "Critical mass" then, in physics, is variously used to specify the amount or rate of something required to create a self-sustaining reaction or process. When that amount is present, or when the process has reached a self-sustaining rate, the reaction has "gone critical."

The "somethings" described in critical-mass terms need not be limited to numbers of atomic particles or amounts of energy. In social sciences, critical numbers may be less specific than in physical sciences, but no less valid as a determining factor. Social scientists use critical mass to analyze a wide range of situations and behaviors. A common element among these is that they usually revolve around the relationship between the number of people who are either behaving a certain way or are expected to behave a certain way, and the degree to which that number encourages others to behave the same way.

"Critical numbers" often vary from one person to another: For each person, there may be a number or ratio of people making a related decision on a topic that is "enough" to compel him or her to make the same decision. This is most evident when there are binary choices, which makes the model applicable to questions centered on race.

For example, the following situation might take place in two different cities with different customs and standards of legal enforcement: Many pedestrians are waiting to cross a street and there is no traffic coming, but the traffic signal says "Don't Walk." In the first city, a few people become fed up with waiting and begin to cross the street. This is all that several others have been waiting for, and they follow. Although they wouldn't have jaywalked if they had been the only pedestrians, there are now "enough" people crossing the street to convince more people to follow the others.

With almost everyone else crossing the street, even the final die-hards join in and disregard the "Don't Walk" sign. This entire process may take only a few seconds, and the people involved are not likely to be counting the exact numbers of people who leave ahead of them. In the second city, where conditions are different, a few people become fed up with waiting and begin to cross the street. This is "enough" to encourage several others to follow. The rest are equally interested in getting across the street, but they don't anticipate that others are going to cross against the light. They wait for the light to change to "Walk."

In the first city, critical mass was achieved immediately. A self-sustaining chain reaction was set in motion with the first violation of the "Don't Walk" sign. In the second city, critical mass was never achieved. The crossover point of "enough" people was only reached for those who either disregarded or were unaware of the local laws and customs.

Schelling noted that it is important to consider what isn't known from such critical-mass examples as the jaywalking scenarios. We don't know how close the first example came to failing to achieve critical mass, or how close the second example came to achieving it. Perhaps in the second example, if just one more person decided there were enough people jaywalking for him to join in, that would have made the total large enough for others to feel the same way, which would have made the total enough for others to follow along, and so on in a chain reaction. Critical mass may have been only one person away.

The lesson of critical mass was similar to the lesson of Schelling's games. End results, or macrobehavior, can't necessarily be presumed to describe micromotives.[105] The fact that something fails doesn't tell us how close it was to success. Likewise, the fact that something succeeds doesn't tell us how close it came to failure. People often make judgments about success or failure of movements in social science, or the public appeal of organizations, by looking at final outcomes. These outcomes are then viewed as an expression of the "general will." Critical-mass models point out the dangers of reading too much into final tallies without careful analysis of the process and procedures that led to them.

A dramatic example of the achievement of critical mass on a political level that related to Schelling's work can be seen in the collapse of communism in Eastern Europe in the late 1980s and early 1990s. Schelling had tried to help the world survive to see it happen—but the change was nearly unimaginable right up to the time it took place. Brief sparks of independence were brutally crushed in Hungary in 1956 and in Czechoslovakia in 1968, and the Soviet Union seemed to have an oppressive, iron grip on the region. Somehow the Polish union, *Solidarity*, managed to maintain its precarious opposition to the government beginning in the early 1980s; but all in all, Eastern Europe appeared solidly communist.

Fateful change began in 1985, when Mikhail Gorbachev became leader of the Soviet Union's Politburo. Gorbachev's policies of *perestroika* and *glasnost* initiated stunning freedoms and reforms. By 1989, the Soviets participated in their first openly contested elections since 1917, and soon the momentum for democracy was unstoppable. The loosening of oppressive control brought rivalries, tensions, and complaints to the surface in the 15 Soviet Republics. In late 1989, Lithuania became the first satellite state to declare itself an independent country. Others soon followed, as economic difficulties overwhelmed the ability of the largest state, Russia, to prevent the union's deterioration.

Meanwhile, the tide of Gorbachev's repudiation of communism and encouragement of reform was unleashing democratic forces in Eastern Europe. In 1989, to the continual shock of outside observers, revolutions overthrew the communist regimes in Poland, Hungary, East Germany, Bulgaria, Czechoslovakia, and Romania. By 1990, the Cold War that had molded international relations and held the world hostage to nuclear destruction was over. In 1991, the Warsaw Pact, the communist block's rival alliance to NATO, was dissolved.

How could such an incredible change in the world's basic alignment of political power take place in such a short time? The critical-mass model provides an answer. In hindsight, we can see there were many discontented people in the communist-block countries, but that these people were afraid to challenge their governments because they didn't expect others to demonstrate the same defiance. With the new openness of *glasnost*, the degree of discontent became more visible, and people who would have otherwise remained silent were willing to speak out.

Argument about where the credit goes for initiating the change is common, but Schelling comes down firmly. "Gorbachev is my hero," he says. "He explicitly let loose of all the satellites and allowed the collapse of the Soviet Union . . . The guy certainly presided over the dissolution of the Soviet Empire."

Schelling developed a method for diagramming critical mass by plotting curves, where "actual" and "expected" numbers of whatever was being analyzed were represented on different axes. The "tipping point" and possible equilibrium points where the situation could resolve itself become easily seen. The entry of appropriate data on the graph is essential, but as a guiding model, it offers considerable insight into how change takes place or fails. The tipping diagram is an especially useful model for looking at cases involving racial tipping, which is how it had started out and why Schelling studied it. With Schelling's model the process of movement was apparent as was the danger of its acceleration.

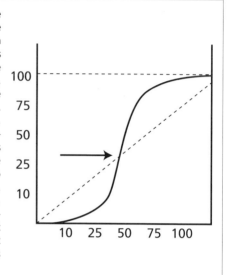

This situation could be jaywalking, the outbreak of racial rioting, the collapse of communism, or the change of a neighborhood. The horizontal X axis shows the number or percent of people expected to do it or participate in it, and the vertical Y axis shows the amount or percent actually doing so. The arrow points to the tipping point, where the event becomes self-sustaining, as actual exceeds expected, always encouraging more to join in until the ones whose views are least subject to outside influence are all that remain. The tip could go in either direction, though, and preventing it from crossing above the 45° angle can alter what follows considerably. If it tipped, it achieved equilibrium when there was 100-percent participation.

Schelling's tipping model was especially appropriate as a warning for sudden changes involving race, as it was easily visualized and understood, and forces propelling the changes were exposed. Individual expectations were the driving force, and when they were being met, the reaction continued, but created changing situations. Tipping had been applied to observations concerning the effect often caused when a few members of a minority moved into a neighborhood with a formerly homogeneous population. Some of the formerly homogenous population decided to leave or showed signs of leaving. Their departure left openings, so more members of the minority could enter. The increase of the new residents induced more of the old to leave, and so forth in this process. Some of the departures might have been motivated by the minority entrants who already arrived, some by the belief that the process, once started, would continue, and some by the fear that they might soon be selling their houses in panic.

In the 1960s, this model came to be applied to many areas in which the presence of racial minorities became the stimulus and white departure became the phenomenon. The phenomenon was repeated in school districts, occupations, clubs, fraternities, medical schools and colleges, public beaches, restaurants, nightclubs, public parks, and more. Complementary to the process of "tipping out" was the process of "tipping in." Not only was the departure of the white population induced by the appearance of minorities, but minorities themselves would be more attracted the larger the minority colony and the faster its growth, with some minimum size required to get a self-sustaining influx started. For both "tipping in" and "tipping out," part of the process may involve expectations. People did not wait until the "alien" colony exceeded their toleration before departing, nor did minority entrants wait until comfortable numbers had been achieved, as long as they could foresee with confidence that their numbers were increasing.

The point Schelling's segregation-integration games had made was also made by his tipping model: Micromotives could lead to macrobehavior that may or may not reflect the intent of those involved. The model showed that there were critical points at which small changes in behavior might lead to largely different results. Understanding that possibility, and being aware of how to control those points, was a matter of considerable public-policy significance.

In looking at how populations mix and group themselves, Schelling went beyond segregation and integration. He analyzed what was happening within discrete variables, what sorts of discrimination took place within the single groups themselves. Groucho Marx once said, "I would never join a club that would have me as a member," and while most people wouldn't go to this extreme, they did have preferences, or practical reasons, for attempting to limit the people with whom they associate.

Schelling's modeling of these various populations indicated the same thing about individual motive and group results as his segregation-integration models: that the movement of anyone affected the position of all the others. Often, the movement produced becomes self-sustaining, by continually changing some average or other factor to a level unacceptable to another group of people, whose movement creates a situation that is unacceptable to another group, and so on. Or it may entice a group of people, whose presence entices more people, etc.

Given these known individual motives, even if a situation is created that comes as close as possible to satisfying all those involved, the people involved will, in many cases, unravel that situation in a manner that is to their own detriment. No problem was more exposed by this than race relations. The movement of populations, Schelling had demonstrated, could lead to segregation even where attitudes of tolerance were commonplace.

CHAPTER 17

SINGAPORE

The dangers of racial situations unraveling contrary to the desires of the citizens involved are very real and can raise difficult social and political issues. What if a society has goals that are generally accepted by its population, but the effect of allowing the members of that society freedom of choice is to undermine the very goals those citizens support? Would such a society be better off sacrificing some freedom of choice and delegating more authority to those in leadership positions, if those leaders could prevent the unraveling of desired outcomes? Or do the dangers of possible misuse of governmental authority outweigh the possible benefits of strong governmental action? The questions are old ones, but one place where an efficient balance has been struck is Singapore.

A small island nation in Southeast Asia, Singapore sits between its large Islamic neighbors, Indonesia and Malaysia. The country of 4.5 million people is known for its organization, its efficiency, and its lack of corruption. It is an ethnically diverse society, with a population that is 77 percent Chinese, 14 percent Malay, and 8 percent Indian, along with a sprinkling of Eurasians and others, practicing Buddhism, Taoism, Islam, Christianity, and Hinduism.

On July 21, 1964, ethnic violence labeled "race riots" occurred between Chinese and Malays, leaving 23 dead and hundreds injured; violence broke out again on September 3, when another 13 were killed and more than 100 injured. "Racial harmony" has been a government goal ever since. Since its independence in 1965, Singapore has been dominated by one political party, the People's Action Party (PAP), with its course charted to a considerable degree by the remarkable Lee Kuan Yew, prime minister from 1959–1990 and currently "minister mentor." Lee saw Singapore grow from an island with few natural resources and massive unemployment into a model of prosperity, Asia's second-richest country on a per-capita basis. In Southeast Asia, where ethnic and religious violence is endemic, Singapore now exists in a stable, peaceful environment. Singapore's success is not a matter of chance. Raj Vasil, author of *Asianising Singapore*, says, "Today's multi-racial Singapore stands as the most monumental achievement of the ruling party, the PAP. Without this critical achievement, none of the other components of the Singapore success story would have been possible."[106]

A part of this success was that Singapore's leaders recognized the dangers Schelling's models exposed and were in a position to act to counter the "tipping" and "dynamics of motion" effects he discussed as forces that could threaten delicate racial relations. Singapore had sent students to study at Harvard under Schelling and his colleagues. Lee Kuan Yew described Schelling's influence on the country's public policy:

> For many years we have sent promising public officers to the MPA program at the Kennedy School, where they attended courses on public policy and economic behavior by Schelling and his colleagues. Three became Ministers . . . They found Schelling's perspectives and techniques insightful and practical in solving real life policy issues. So they invited Schelling to visit Singapore, to expose more Singaporeans, especially our public officers, to him and his ideas.
>
> Our approach to policy-making is a pragmatic one. To achieve economic and social objectives, we seek to use market forces rather than buck them. We look for solutions that work, not elegant theoretical constructs. But our conclusions often tallied with ideas that Schelling had analyzed and taught about. One example is our policy to maintain racially integrated housing estates, to prevent the "tipping" phenomenon that would quickly lead to total segregation of different ethnic groups.[107]

One of the three Singapore ministers who studied under Schelling at Harvard's Kennedy School was Lee Kuan Yew's son, Lee Hsien Loong. Paging through Schelling's latest book, *Micromotives and Macrobehavior,* had convinced him to enroll in the class "Conflict, Cooperation, and Strategy" when he first arrived at Harvard in 1979. Schelling's course addressed one issue of concern to Singapore, and of special interest to Lee Hsien Loong: segregation. He later followed in his father's footsteps, becoming prime minister of Singapore in 2004. And how did Schelling's views affect Singapore policy? Lee recalls: "There was some influence. We had been watching the problem for some years and eventually decided to do something about it . . . Schelling had analyzed this and we were therefore very conscious, that beyond a certain point, it changes very fast . . . That gave us some impetus to move faster than we might otherwise have done. But, we looked at it and I think, on our own, would have probably acted on it too, but maybe more slowly."[108]

The Singapore approach was to control the movement of population groups through public housing: 86 percent of Singapore's residents live in housing built by the government's Housing Development Board. To prevent segregation and encourage ethnic harmony, the HDB adopted an "Ethnic Integration Policy" prohibiting the sale and resale of public housing that would alter the ethnic composition of apartment blocks or neighborhoods beyond set levels. By law, there could be no free movement to alter racial composition or to "tip" neighborhoods from one race to another. With such a large share of the country's population in public housing, the policy prevented unforeseen motives from emerging. In a society with racial harmony as a goal—a goal that the citizens' behavior might unintentionally undermine—Singapore's housing policy prevented the development of segregated neighborhoods.

In a country where students observe "Racial Harmony Day" every year in school, all the while living in a region of the world rampant with threats of extremism and violence, Singapore may be seeing the expression of the individual motives of more of its people being realized by restrictive policies. Such sacrifice of individual choice to the government that results in greater achievement of individual goals will always raise questions and is perhaps something that would work only in limited instances or scale. But Schelling pursued problems with relentless reasoning and encouraged his students to do the same, and a logical solution for Singapore emerged. Lee Hsien Loong recalls studying with Schelling: "It's quite a remarkable experience. It's not new things, but a certain way of looking at problems and analyzing them and thinking through; whose incentives are which way and what the outcomes will be. And very often counter-intuitive, and very difficult to persuade people that it's correct."[109]

Racial tipping wasn't the only area where the influence of Schelling's thinking was to be seen in Singapore. Lee Kuan Yew noted, "Another is rationing of road space by the price mechanism." Prime Minister Lee adds, "Well, I suppose we could have worked something out, but maybe not quite so systematically." In Schelling's course at Harvard, they had discussed congestion models—the best known being "the commons," a model of a multiperson prisoner's dilemma, where cooperation best serves the common good but where there is no incentive for the individual to cooperate.

The model of the commons applies to many situations. For example, everyone might agree that, at crowded intersections where there are no traffic lights, having cars enter in a staggered, every-other manner would result in a relatively smooth flow of traffic. What actually occurs is that individual drivers aren't willing to be the "other" who waits. Congestion occurs at more than just intersections, but on the roads, as the younger Lee explained: "When you are driving down the road, you are really imposing a cost on everyone else. There is an externality; you're slowing down everybody else's flow, and time is money. Charge not just for space used, but for how much you slow others."

The plans Singapore adopted to deal with traffic congestion included "certificates of entitlement," where the right to buy a car is sold, and road pricing, in which those who use the roads are charged when they use them. The road-pricing policy requires every vehicle to be outfitted with a special dashboard device that can be read when the vehicle passes under gantries on the roads. As the vehicle passes, a fee is automatically deducted from a card the driver has inserted into the device. Singapore's government had the authority to impose the new policy, but the prime minister notes that it wasn't that autocratic: "Academically the principle is quite straightforward . . . but getting it done is an awful lot of tinkering and presentation and packaging." When one sees the traffic in Jakarta or Bangkok or other large cities in the vicinity of Singapore, the relative success of Singapore's traffic policies is apparent.

The awareness of interactive decision-making and government intervention in affecting outcomes had successes in Singapore. Schelling's influence helped encourage the process. Lee Kuan Yew adds, "Understanding the motives and incentives of the players, and how individual decisions add up to an overall outcome which we may or may not want—what Schelling called micromotives and macrobehavior—is invaluable in coming up with good policies."[110]

CHAPTER 18

MADMAN THEORY

Schelling's influence in bringing about cooperation in arms-control agreement was where his work as a strategist helped reduce tensions and create a more stable peace through finding the superpowers' common interests. Some say his successful work in this area was contradicted by his influence in a different direction: the effort to bring about peace by bringing a successful conclusion to a war, creating peace with military force. The Cold War was involved in both, and such a contradiction could exist in the role played by civilian strategists whose work reached those in the upper levels of government. As negotiations on the treaties with Russia progressed, the war in Vietnam continued. A strategy known as "the madman theory," which has been attributed to Schelling, was playing a part in the ongoing bombing campaign against the North. Schelling vehemently rejects having the term associated with him. As may have happened in the Berlin "take out a Russian city" proposal, however, others may have seen tactics in his presentation of analysis and explanations and in his examples—tactics which they thought fit to apply, their resulting strategies eventually becoming considered his. From the 1960s into the 21st century, many considered the madman theory a Schelling strategy.

A 1995 study conducted by the Defense Department's Strategic Command, "Essentials of Post-Cold War Deterrence," looked at strategies for dealing with states that could represent a threat to the United States. Obtained under the Freedom of Information Act in 1998, the study was reported on by the news network CNN.[111] The study concluded that the United States should maintain an "irrational and vindictive" quality in its threat of nuclear retaliation to intimidate possible threats by such nations as Iraq and Libya. If some elements of the U.S. government appear to be out of control, that could be beneficial. The ambiguity of possible U.S. action would more effectively deter chemical or biological attacks. The idea, it said, dated back to the 1960s and Schelling, and the Defense Department report cited his words: "It is not a universal advantage in situations of conflict to be inalienably and manifestly rational in decisions and motivation." The CNN story said, "[Shelling's ideas] were later adopted by Henry Kissinger and President Nixon in coercive air raids on North Vietnam as a way of forcing Hanoi to the bargaining table in the late stages of the Vietnam War."

Schelling responds, "That was no idea of mine. I had pointed out that a madman might make a threat that was credible on account of his madness. I had even suggested that Khrushchev's banging his shoe on a desk at the United Nations was intended to have such an effect, but I never anywhere suggested that the United States should engage in such tactic . . . Khrushchev may have needed a shortcut to deterrence, but the American government ought to be by nature and rich enough to arrange a persuasive sequence of threatened responses that are not wholly a matter of guessing a President's temper . . . I have often used recent examples to illustrate some point or tactic: mention does not mean approval." He points to his discussion of the topic in his 1966 book *Arms and Influence*:

> In the preface to that book I said, "I have often used recent examples to illustrate some point or tactic; mention does not mean approval, even where a policy was successful. The several pages examining the 1964 bombing in the Gulf of Tonkin do not mean that I approve of it (though in fact, I do); the several pages on coercive aspects of the bombing of North Vietnam in 1965 do not mean I approve of it (and, in fact, I am not sure yet); the several pages on the tactic of cultivating irrationality at the highest level of government, to make otherwise incredible threats sound credible, do not mean that I approve of it (and, in fact, I do not)." Incidentally, that successful "madman" is not bluffing, unless he's only pretending to be mad.[112]

The final sentence is typical Schelling: Even when answering a question about what has become a criticism of his past work, he still finds it important to clarify the concept.

"Mention does not mean approval," as Schelling put it; but in the mention there can be seen suggestion, and some would consider suggestion to be advice, or even suggested strategy. It was still considered a Schelling strategy, and one relevant to a different era, in Jonathan Schell's May 2003 article in *The Nation*, "Letter from Ground Zero: Madmen."[113] Schell begins by saying that during the Cold War, when deterrence was achieved by "mutually assured destruction," the question became: Why should either side believe the other's threats, and not do as it pleased? The answer, Schell writes, was what Schelling called a "slippery slope." If you didn't appear to your foe to be completely stable, "They'd think that you might plunge into the abyss in spite of yourself." The article continues: "Another idea, also pioneered by Schelling and others was the deliberate cultivation of a reputation of irrationality. Schelling called this the policy of 'rational irrationality.'" Like the Defense Department study, Schell says Nixon was one who adopted the strategy and called it the "madman theory."

Schell brings his article into the 21st century with the story of North Korea, which he says has "rediscovered the madman with a vengeance." North Korea's threat of using nuclear arms against the United States or its allies escalates the dangers of a war that could turn into the total destruction of the nation. No small nation, even one armed with a small nuclear arsenal, would challenge the United States. Only a madman would. Yet North Korea's leader, Kim Jong Il, appears to be capable of and displays such lunacy. He acts dangerously. "And yet it's also true those acts display shades of Thomas Schelling—'rational irrationality'" in deterring the United States.

The "madman theory" is Schelling's, not because he presented it as such or because he advocated it, but because of its association with him. The idea is nothing new, and he only used it as part of a discussion. His being credited with it as a strategy used in Vietnam, and the extensive damage and loss of life it led to in an unsuccessful attempt to bring the North Vietnamese to the bargaining table, is both inaccurate and unfair. Schelling's final words rejecting his responsibility for use of the "madman theory" in Vietnam make it apparent that he is correct in saying he suggested no such policy, and they indicate the strength and burden of his writing:

> If I analyzed Hitler's behavior toward Austria in 1938, or terrorists' extortionate threats, or spousal abuse, and concluded that sometimes threats are credible, and effective, because someone appears irrationally bent on some kind of vengeance, or is too crazy to realize what he's threatening, or if I point out that someone is immune to your threat if he doesn't understand your language, I'd be trying to help people understand something significantly important. These are things one has to know in order to deal with, or anticipate, bargaining tactics or bargaining realities. I even quoted the Honorable Mountstuart Elphinstone on a tribe in India that guaranteed various arrangements by threatening to kill themselves or their own children if an agreement were violated. 'If he is not attended to, he proceeds to gash his limbs with a dagger, which, if all other means fail, he will plunge into his heart; or he will first strike off the head of his child; or . . .' It is important to understand these tactics and these situations. If some senior government official thinks that's the way to win a war in Southeast Asia, he's pretty stupid, and I don't think he can be excused by saying it works for crazy people.[114]

The final two sentences contain a crucial dilemma of Schelling's work: "It is important to understand these tactics and these situations," and "If some senior government official thinks that's the way to win a war . . ."

Since his emergence as a Cold War strategist, Schelling saw his role as helping people "understand . . . tactics and . . . situations." He sought to reduce the complexities of the logic of international conflict and develop its terminology, so that policy decisions would be made on a more rational basis. With the 1960 publication of *The Strategy of Conflict*, he began having an influence on policy analysis unsurpassed in the world of civilian consultants. His influence reached high into government circles, with his discussions of how important it was to "understand these tactics and these situations" often providing definition.

Yet while he clarified strategy and made it more understandable by citing historical examples and hypothetical situations, something very serious could happen "[i]f some senior government official thinks that's the way to win a war . . ." The examples he used in his writing made his ideas clear, but suggestions could be found in the analysis. If a tactic had been used successfully before in some historical situation or on some more minor scale, perhaps it could be used successfully in a nuclear confrontation. Even if an example was clearly used to show the faulty reasoning behind some tactical approach, perhaps it would be advantageous if minor modifications to that approach were made or it were more fully developed.

While Schelling never advocated the "madman theory," or intended to see such a policy applied in the bombing of North Vietnam, there can be no doubt that people claim the strategy originated in his writing. It has been said that the launching of a sustained bombing campaign against North Vietnam was an expression of his views on inflicting pain, which became official U.S. policy. He never suggested dropping an atomic bomb on a Russian city as a response to a Soviet invasion of Berlin, but such an idea could have been extracted from certain discussions in his writing.

A similar issue is raised by ideas presented in his 1961 paper on brinkmanship, "Nuclear Strategy in the Berlin Crisis." Kennedy's National Security Advisor McGeorge Bundy's personal notes say the paper influenced the president. When Schelling wrote the paper, he wasn't writing to convince Kennedy to take the United States to the brink of nuclear war over Berlin—although it could have sounded like he was. He was writing to help Kennedy "understand these tactics and these situations."

The dilemma of Schelling's work is that the very strength of his presentation—his ability to analyze strategy and make complex ideas accessible—could become its danger, when such easily understood presentation is seen as advocacy or promoted unintended policy. Schelling shrugs it all off comfortably: "I don't think I was ever frightened at the thought that I may be wrong."[115]

Looking back at all the problems and possibilities for disaster that might have arisen from his giving advice and from people reading his works during the most dangerous years the world has ever faced, Schelling is not concerned about having written what he wrote or said what he said. It was something that had to be done, regardless of the dangers, and someone had to do it. There was no way of doing it with guarantees that everything was going to work out well, regardless of what was at stake—no way of knowing how his thoughts would be applied. When asked about the stress of his responsibility for presenting ideas and giving advice that others would interpret, and that such interpretations might point people anywhere from nuclear stability and safety to greater aggression and possible nuclear holocaust, he replies somewhat dismissively, "Well, I don't know. There are all kinds of people, whether they're in genetic research or whatever, who say 'I've just discovered something that is potentially very beneficial, but in the wrong hands could be misused. I think I'll go to my grave with the secret.'"[116]

Schelling's words did have important consequences, which raises questions of roles and responsibilities. He was among the elite group in the background, the Cold War's civilian strategists existing in the shadows, whispering in the ears of the decision-makers. Public figures had control, and although the strategic thinkers had influence, the general population barely knew they existed. The public held the elected and appointed officials responsible for decisions; they were the visible symbols of choice. The leaders looked to strategists for advice and for a basic understanding and explanation of the ideas and situations, the general and specific strategies, to guide them in their decision-making. The advice strategic thinkers gave, the words they wrote and spoke, provided the frames of reference for and pointed the direction to the specific decisions that emerged. The same words could become public policy. This nearly unknown group of strategists had a fundamental impact on society and choices made that involved survival. Yet this select few were democratically responsible to no one, though their ideas affected the world.

A common view is that the strategist or policy analyst avoids responsibility, because he takes no positions and avoids involvement in value judgments. He is assigned topics to consider and ideas to develop after political leaders have already arrived at basic policy decisions. His role is to provide objective analysis and determine outcomes of policy options, or to offer strategies and their likely outcomes. Choices have nothing to do with him. The question of him framing the views of decision-makers rarely comes up, because he is normally just developing options for dealing with decisions that have already been made. This view applies less to the elite strategists at Schelling's level, whose work formed the foundations for the approaches taken in decision-making. Avoidance of individual bias is basic at that level, and nothing characterizes Schelling more.

The elite Cold War strategists weren't held accountable to others, but to themselves. This position created a duty for them to hold themselves responsible for their own words and advice, since they understood the meanings better than others. They had a duty as scholars to provide accurate and unbiased data—data about what "is," not what "ought to be." They had a responsibility for being aware of how words work, how their words might affect those who had the power, who pushed the buttons.

No matter how accurate the strategist's advice or analysis, he still ran the risk of being viewed at a later time as immoral or a fool. His words could be misinterpreted or misused, as happened with Schelling. Mistakes could be made, regardless of the intent of his advice. In retrospect, the advisor may appear to have been on the wrong side in history, as U.S. interests changed. He may have done or written something that was helpful to people who were later considered villainous or dangerous, friends or allies who later became despots or even enemies. His work might have aided causes that, as time passed, were judged as misguided.

Strategists must be aware of the affects their words could have on the real world. Glenn Loury, a policy advisor and friend of Schelling's, describes the burden of the shadow role: "We can make mistakes and those mistakes can be profoundly costly to ordinary people. We march them off to war, we impoverish them, because we have some grand idea about how the world should be, or whatever it might be."[117]

Political economist Richard Zeckhauser, another of Schelling's long-time Harvard colleagues and a frequent strategic advisor, gives his view, and his caution: "Your obligation is to give the best advice you can, and to make your biases clear so that the person can interpret that. For example if asked to give view on what to do about genocide, you might say I'm a Jew, or I come from Eastern Europe, or I was in the Army Air Force and did a strategic bombing survey in World War II, so I may be overinfluenced by that."[118]

When a strategist offers specific advice, it is important for him to know whether the values held by those he is advising are similar to his own. Even objective advice reflects the advisor's values, and to assist in the making of a more effective decision that produces more efficient policy, when that policy is contrary to one's own personal values, is morally repugnant. The question is whether a strategist or policy analyst should be willing to offer his objective skills and avoid subjective involvement when the topic is something he feels strongly about, something he feels is wrong. Civilian advisors don't always get to choose the issues and facts they work with, and policies are often predetermined. The view of Schelling and most others is that his role is to provide analysis, not subjective judgment. It might be easy enough to say he should excuse himself from the situation, and one option is just to say "no." A strategist giving advice based on his own value system is unlikely to carry much weight. Francis Bator recalls that the more effective method is to say something like, "Given this value system or set of priorities, this would be best. I think otherwise and here are the arguments." At that point, make your argument and try to give a menu of alternatives. As for presidents, he adds, choices are always very hard.

An analyst's decision to take a public stand against policy because of his own personal values can only be made in special circumstances, where feelings are unambiguous and strong and effective options are limited. The strategist's role isn't policy maker, even though he must carefully consider the impact of his words and advice. Schelling's deviation from his objective role came with the invasion of Cambodia, when he and other Harvard professors, most of whom had held government advisory positions, made a public stand and spoke to the press opposing the Nixon administration. He took a stand on an issue that he felt required public confrontation. It was not a challenge to the system, but it was very out of character for Schelling—and his decision was a costly one. Schelling's influence in Washington was reduced significantly. Although he wasn't working as an advisor at the time, some in the intellectual community thought his actions and those of his group were inappropriate and unfair. It was a time when a political stance forced by his views on an issue, rather than his experience as a policy analyst, dictated his actions. His associates at RAND never seriously challenged his motives, and he remained a RAND consultant and visiting instructor into the next millennium.

To take the challenge farther (as Daniel Ellsberg did by releasing what came to be known as the Pentagon Papers in 1971) and override public accountability with personal opinion requires conviction and moral certitude that must rank the issue and public welfare involved beyond the structure of the government in which it operates. That is a major decision for an individual to make—trusting his personal values above society's system. But morality can require action when it sees immorality, and the policy analyst may be in the position to know and see what others don't. Making a public stand rather than refusing to participate as a policy advisor can be where ethics trump duty and the tradition of objective analysis.[119]

Schelling's work generally avoided specific recommendations. The elite advisors at his level, those with the privilege of influence and access to people in power, were aware of the importance of their views. Conceptual writing like Schelling's was open to a wider range of interpretations and applications than the specific work of most of the other 1960s strategists. His detached approach allowed him to base his thinking on the general ideas underlying the major theme of deterrence, rather than specific consequences his work might have in the immediate future. The policies that emerged from Schelling's work came both from people reading what he had written and listening to advice he gave. He explains: "I was trying to formulate principles that people might understand. I felt completely responsible for anything I wrote. I don't feel responsible for any bad judgment of people who might have read a book of mine. I thought, and still think, that people are likely to make better decisions if they understand things than if they don't."[120] Looking back at the advice he gave during the Cold War years, he doesn't worry about the advice itself and doubts he could have been misinterpreted.

Other strategists do not accept his belief that he hasn't or couldn't have been misunderstood, and his failure to bridge the gap between the abstract and practical policy is sometimes pointed to as the reason. Mort Halperin, his friend and coauthor, said, "Ideas are his strength and his weakness is the failure to spell out the policies to accompany them."[121] Ellsberg suggested that the reason Schelling devoted little attention to practical policy was that he approaches issues as problems first and presents general questions and solutions. Policy is only considered later. There are others who disagree with the view that he is only interested in the abstract and think it appears that way because he frequently has counterintuitive or off-the-wall ideas about important problems.

A difficulty with being misunderstood is that Schelling's ideas could become someone else's ideas. That's where responsibility for ideas becomes less clear. Schelling willingly accepts responsibility for anything he wrote at that time, for the actual words he used. It isn't possible to exert complete control over what happens to one's ideas, and Schelling can't be held accountable for all misinterpretations that may have occurred. What some suggest is that if he had been more operational in the presentations of his thoughts—if he had described how his ideas should be put into practice—there may have been less likelihood of his ideas being taken in ways other than those he had intended.

A 1998 RAND document held that Schelling's work raised questions without providing the answers.[122] It says that when he wrote and spoke about the possibilities that remained if things went wrong, Schelling discussed what could be done, if nuclear war took place, to limit the scope of war. He talked about war as cooperative as well as competitive, where through signals and tacit communication it would be possible to limit damages, to save cities, to avoid the use of certain weapons. Those were ideas that provoked new analysis and led to new formations of policy. They were also ideas that left unanswered questions. With war involving cooperation, how could there be a victor? How could the war be concluded when the sides were cooperating to avoid doing too much damage to each other?

There were also questions of practical application. What kind of military force would have been required to establish meaningful tacit communication with the Soviets in wartime for the sides to cooperate and accomplish all he proposed? What effect would that force have on deterrence in peacetime? In rebuttal, Schelling cites Korea as an example of a war that was both cooperative and competitive: The war was concluded by cooperation when both sought to avoid further damage.

The observation that Schelling the strategist focused too much on ideas while spending too little time on details, that he has been too much of a theorist while failing to describe how his ideas could be put into practice, may have some validity, in that the details might have helped keep some of his ideas, his occasional policy suggestions, closer to their original form. The better evaluation comes from friend and former colleague Francis Bator, who says it's "a bum rap."[123] An economist, Bator sees Schelling's situation as a question of economic efficiency: It's a matter of comparative advantage. Schelling's time could be used in one of two ways, on theory or application, while someone else's could be used doing just the same, and to use it in one would be to take it away from the other. It's like having a lawyer and a typist, and the lawyer does the typing . . . or like having Einstein do gardening rather than a gardener. For Schelling to spend his time working out practical details would mean taking him away from developing new ideas, something he did like very few other people could. As a strategist, concentrating on ideas was what he did best, so it was the best use of his time.

Schelling's approach was to avoid imposing his personal value judgments on situations and to find objective justification for what he did or said, not his subjective sense of what would be right. His topics in the 1960s didn't run the risk of being a personal point of view forced on a wider public. Preventing nuclear holocaust wasn't a controversial issue. It was only on the approach of how it could be achieved that there was less agreement. As a policy analyst dealing with monumental issues, he was attempting to do what could be done to play a valuable role without entering the subjective world of final decisions. Knowingly cautious, and distanced from the burden of public responsibility, the strategists would have accomplished little had focused on all imaginable outcomes of their words. When "thinking about the unthinkable," the possible outcomes included the all-too-obvious, and it was necessary to cover topics and arrive at understanding that could lead to policies without delay. It was the success of the greatest strategic thinkers to develop the grand strategies, and Schelling became the civilian leader in the field. But leaving implementation of policies to chance and ignoring the possible outcomes of implementation would have been turning a blind eye. It was Schelling's view that his role wasn't to present the specific policies to deter disaster, as much as it was to help prepare those who would have to make the real decisions understand the options available and the effects of what they might do if they were faced with the threat of nuclear war. That was his role as a strategist in his writing and his games: He prepared others to understand and be ready to act.

The Cold War strategists did have some responsibility for the outcome of their advice, and the interpretations given to the words they wrote. The degree to which they were responsible was defined by the impact those words were likely to have on those in public decision-making positions, and the strategists' awareness of their own influence. Schelling had an important role, and that role gave him responsibility, as he knowingly influenced those who held the power in their hands.

The strategists could not escape from responsibility by answering to no one and existing anonymously in the Harvard–MIT ivory towers or the RAND citadel. Their influence was felt in very human terms, although their names were rarely attached to the consequences of their actions. They couldn't be held completely accountable for all interpretations that came from what they said, but they were responsible for foreseeing dangers in ambiguity and in not having presented explanations that allowed decisions to be made with awareness of the full range of likely consequences; they were responsible for having avoided presenting interpretations that included possible negative outcomes. That was a burden that came with the privilege of being in the highest echelon of civilian advisors. Schelling is aware of the part he played: "For a person outside the government, I was probably as influential as anybody else. Maybe more than most."[124]

CHAPTER 19

CONCLUDING VIETNAM

By 1968, it was time to get out of Vietnam. LBJ's decision not to run made it easier—for a new president could do so without humiliation—but the months leading up to the presidential elections were marked by turmoil and tragedy. The Democratic National Convention went through periods of anarchy as crowds chanted "the whole world's watching," and U.S. athletes displayed black militancy at the Olympics in Mexico City. The musical *Hair* captured the generation gap by celebrating long hair, drugs, and nudity. Two of America's heroes, Martin Luther King Jr. and Robert Kennedy, were assassinated, and public opinion turned more and more against the war. That autumn brought Richard Nixon to power in a close election, and Henry Kissinger, Schelling's old friend and colleague, was in the White House as national security advisor. The new president faced challenges from all sides, but Vietnam remained the first concern.

When Nixon came to the White House in 1969, the Soviets had invaded Czechoslovakia. All negotiations for abandoning Anti-Ballistic Missile development, so promising under Johnson and McNamara, fell through. Eventually, with the encouragement of his Harvard friends, Kissinger persuaded Nixon to go ahead with it. By the time Kissinger took his post in the White House, he was resolved to resurrect the ABM Treaty. It would take him a considerable period of delicate negotiations, and the treaty was still years off.

Anti-war protests became more widespread, and the Center for International Affairs was raided by the activist group Students for a Democratic Society. Founded as an organization to work for a "participatory democracy," SDS became more and more of a bold anti-war protest group as the 1960s progressed. A faction of it, The Weathermen, splintered off to become more radical and violent in their protests, promoting revolutionary activity. During the SDS break-in at the center, someone spray-painted "death to Sally Cox" on the wall for unknown reasons. (Sally Cox, secretary to the center's director, Bob Bowie, was the daughter of Archibald Cox, who later became the Watergate special prosecutor investigating President Nixon, and whom Nixon fired.) Not long after the initial raid, the SDS returned to the center—this time with more than vandalism as their goal. A bomb exploded in the building at 2:00 A.M. No one was hurt, but the damage was extensive. Detectives and a bomb squad examined the scene and concluded the bomb had been put in a desk drawer.

Schelling's concerns were not only for his personal safety and that of safety of his colleagues. The timing of the bombing indicated an intent to avoid casualties. He realized, however, that he had two safes for classified documents, and after the SDS raid he was required to report the violation of his office space to the FBI. One safe contained RAND documents and was classified "Secret." He was still doing consulting work for RAND, and they sent him studies of weapon systems for review. The other safe, rated "Top Secret," was for work from the Institute for Defense Analyses, a think tank that did work for the Department of Defense. The RAND materials came through the mail, and he would call for a courier when the projects were ready to be returned. The Defense Department work was always "top secret," and sometimes came strapped to the wrist of a naval officer.

Schelling decided to get rid of his safes, and the issue of the security of safes containing secret documents was of enough concern that the president of the university appointed a committee, which included Schelling, to discuss campus security. The sit-ins, violence, and activism inspired by the anti-war movement had created a need for new procedures. Activism at Harvard had included a bomb threat, and Nathan Glazer, who later became Schelling's colleague, recalls the comment Schelling made at the time: "Anyone with a handful of dimes can close down any institution."[125]

By this time, the anti-war movement had grown stronger and more widespread. In October 1969, a national Vietnam moratorium day was held, where 50,000 protesters filed past the White House carrying lighted candles, while another 100,000 came together on Boston Common. Nixon's vice president, Spiro Agnew, blamed the media—the "nattering nabobs of negativism"—for their defeatist attitude and biased reporting. Casualties continued to mount and, by the end of the year, Vietnam had become the longest war in the nation's history. In November, 250,000 marched in a peaceful rally from the Capitol to the Washington Monument, while 200,000 rallied in San Francisco's Golden Gate Park.

On April 30, 1970, President Nixon announced that American forces had entered Cambodia to stop the flow of supplies from North Vietnam to the South. His action was taken without consulting Congress. The announcement would mark a dramatic change in America's already uncertain view of its participation in the war. There were sympathy strikes for peace at 451 colleges, and there was a great deal of agitation on the Harvard campus. The president's war-policy approval rating dropped from 65 percent to 48 percent, and at a Kent State University protest, National Guardsmen killed four unarmed students.

It was the invasion of Cambodia that made Schelling and a number of his colleagues believe that Nixon had no intention of getting out of Vietnam, and that Kissinger supported his actions. They did not believe the reason given: that a huge underground intelligence complex existed just over the Cambodian border and that it needed to be neutralized. They thought this expansion of the war suggested that the administration was going far beyond the rational conduct of what could be in the nation's interest, and that the government was conducting the war for reasons that couldn't be supported. They had all been Kissinger's colleagues, and they decided to confront him to express their concerns.

On Friday May 8, 1970, Schelling (who had been Kissinger's closest Harvard colleague) took 12 other Harvard faculty members, old friends of Kissinger's and most of whom had been government advisors, to tell him they had finally given up on the administration. Schelling was chosen to head the delegation, which included Paul Doty, who had advised Kissinger on SALT; Adam Yarmolinsky, Eisenhower's science advisor; social relations professor Seymour Martin Lipset; Michel Waltzer, a government professor who taught on just and unjust wars; Richard Neustadt, who taught on the powers of the presidency; Francis Bator, from the Johnson administration; and Ernest May, a history professor who was Harvard dean.

Schelling called his friend Rem Robinson, a naval officer assigned to Kissinger's staff and said they would like to come and talk to Kissinger. To Schelling's embarrassment, they were invited to lunch. He thought it might not be appropriate to come down for a lunch gathering when the purpose was a confrontation to announce that the intellectual community was there to "break relations" with him and the president. Yet they all assembled in the White House for a steak luncheon, with Kissinger unaware of the reason for their visit.

Speaking for the group, Schelling informed Kissinger that they were really there to tell him they were disgusted with the Nixon administration's conduct of the war in Southeast Asia and that they were so disaffected, they were withdrawing any intellectual support that they, as the academic community, might have given. He said that he would like each person to take five minutes to say exactly what he thought. The viewpoints varied greatly, but all were harshly critical. As they went around the room, Kissinger sank deeper and deeper into his chair, and his face grew ashen. He finally said, "Give me 60 days, and I assure you, you'll change your mind."[126]

Following the meeting, they went out and were greeted by the press. Sixty days later, Schelling polled the group to see whether anyone had changed his mind. None had. He wrote to Kissinger, telling him, "You told us to wait 60 days and we did, and none of us changed our view."

Kissinger later wrote of the meeting and expressed disappointment and indignation: "Most had been my close colleagues and friends . . . they were there to confront me . . . These were the leaders of their fields; men who had been my friends, academicians . . . That they disagreed with our decision was understandable . . . But the lack of compassion, the overweening righteousness, the refusal to offer an alternative, reinforced two convictions: that for internal peace of our own country the war had to be ended, but that also in doing so on terms compatible with any international responsibility we would get no help from those with whom I had spent my professional life." The meeting, he said, completed his "transition from the academic world to the world of affairs."[127]

Michael Kinsley, editor of Harvard's *Crimson*, accompanied the professors to the White House meeting:

> The climax was a slow, pause-punctuated lecture by Schelling, who had been closest to Kissinger of them all. 'As we see it,' the economics professor said, 'there are two possibilities: either the President didn't understand when he went into Cambodia that he was invading a sovereign country, or he did understand. We don't know which is scarier.'
>
> Schelling saw the invasion as a moral issue. Even if it accomplished some of America's objectives, it was wrong to inflict a war on a sovereign and innocent bystander nation. 'Whether or not it succeeds on its own terms,' Schelling argued, 'it shouldn't have been done.' But for Kissinger, no moral issue was involved in the invasion; the U.S. gets its forces safely out of Vietnam. There was no way their two minds could meet in rational discourse. Kissinger asked his former colleagues if he could answer them off the record. No, said Schelling, this was a confrontation and not a discussion. In that case, Kissinger said, he could not go into details of the administration strategy. All he would say was that 'the President has not lost sight of his original objective or gone off his timetable for withdrawal.'
>
> These were Kissinger's old friends, but they left embittered . . .[128]

The day after the meeting Francis Bator received a telephone call from a *Times* of London correspondent he knew. The correspondent had it "on good authority" that the group had threatened Kissinger during the luncheon meeting that unless they saw a change in policy, Kissinger's Harvard job (he was officially on leave of absence) would no longer be there for him. The "good authority" was Katherine Graham, owner of *The Washington Post*. No such threat was made. Bator believes Kissinger lied to Graham.[129]

The bitterness that resulted from that meeting didn't vanish. Schelling would not see Kissinger again for several years, and Kissinger refused to ever set foot on the Harvard campus again. Schelling had lost his audience in the executive branch, his access to high-level influence.

For Schelling, this was a new experience: He had taken a public stand on an issue. Kinsley described it as having been on a "moral" basis, and it appeared that way to Kissinger. What it had been was a stand against what Schelling saw as "bad policy" on an important issue. It wasn't something he had done before; it wasn't something often done by strategic thinkers, the rational analysts responsible for providing insight and understanding. Final policy decisions were for the public figures. This time things had gone too far. Schelling was not acting in an official position as a government strategist at the time of the confrontation, but he was always a strategist, and he and his colleagues were often in the service of the government. The government knew him as a strategist, and he had burned bridges by taking a stand.

Over the years, other events related to Vietnam took place beyond public view, events seemingly unrelated to Schelling but where his influence played a role. It was a role he couldn't have known about at the time, but the country would be rocked by the convergence of the careers of three men: Daniel Ellsberg, Mort Halperin, and John McNaughton. They were Schelling's friends, and he had helped bring them together—not by design, but by coincidence.[130]

Schelling recommended all three for the positions that eventually brought them to Washington. They worked in seemingly unrelated positions, but their paths intertwined, and the mixture was volatile.

In 1957, Schelling had recommended Daniel Ellsberg for a position with the RAND Corporation. In 1960, Schelling brought Mort Halperin from Yale to the Center for International Affairs at Harvard. When Richard Nixon took office, Kissinger asked Schelling for staff recommendations. Schelling recommended Halperin, who became a National Security Council staff member. Unlike Ellsberg and Halperin, John McNaughton wasn't a strategist, and he moved into the administration after Schelling recommended him for a job in the Department of Defense.

Paul Nitze, Kennedy's assistant secretary of defense, asked Schelling to become deputy assistant secretary for arms control, but Schelling turned him down. Instead he recommended his friend McNaughton, a Harvard law professor who was looking for something new. Nitze offered McNaughton the job for a year, and Robert McNamara was so impressed with McNaughton, he asked him to stay on.

The connections between the three men began in 1964, when McNaughton was assistant secretary of defense and Ellsberg began one year as his special assistant. As McNaughton's assistant, Ellsberg had access to classified Defense Department documents and read those that would be included in the Pentagon Papers. McNaughton had the original access to the classified government information and conversations and, when Ellsberg was his aide, he had the opportunity to see the deceit that characterized U.S. policy and to begin reading the documents that would become evidence for the world to see.

At the White House, in an effort to ensure itself of staff solidarity, officials launched an ill-fated wiretapping campaign of people of whom it was suspicious. FBI Director J. Edgar Hoover and Attorney General John Mitchell were among those who questioned Halperin's loyalty to the government. The campaign began on May 9, 1969, with what would be a 21-month tap of Halperin's home phone, three days before the attorney general granted the FBI the authority.

With the White House wiretaps on Halperin, his association with Ellsberg was soon discovered, and he became a source of increasing concern and suspicion to the administration. With their growing contacts and passing of information, Ellsberg was drawn more to make the decision to go public in a way that wasn't available to Halperin. On June 13, 1971, the New York Times began to publish the Pentagon Papers after Ellsberg made them available.

Awareness of America's long and secret involvement and governmental dishonesty had become public record. For many, it added more fuel to the anti-war movement. The evidence of The Plumbers, the secret unit to "plug leaks," against Ellsberg presented at the Watergate hearings was a factor in two of the three impeachment articles adopted against President Nixon that led to his resignation.

Ellsberg's decision to release the Pentagon Papers has always been controversial and cost him the friendships and respect of many former RAND colleagues. There are those who say it was ego rather than conscience that motivated him, or that he violated some code of honor or great trust bestowed on the elite advisors in the world of the strategist. They have had little to do with him since. When Ellsberg attempted to visit RAND in 1997, he was told by the organization's president that he was not welcome.

Yet others who stood by him. One RAND compatriot who never deserted Ellsberg was Tom Schelling. The gratitude is evident in the inscription Ellsberg wrote to Schelling for his 80th birthday.[131]

To my teacher and friend Tom Schelling
The most brilliantly original and creative mind I've ever encountered,
from whom I've learned more than from any other.
For a lifetime of treasured friendship . . .

Daniel Ellsberg

CHAPTER 20

SELF-COMMAND

In the early 1970s, the theme of "self-command" took Schelling's work in new directions. It was to be a form of game theory, but one in which both players were the same person. Schelling's idea grew out of a conversation with the dean of Harvard's School of Public Health. At the time, bypass surgery was new, and the dean thought there should be some process established for evaluating new surgical techniques to determine what was most successful. Schelling recalls, "We had a big conference on coronary bypass surgery. I was sitting beside him at lunch and I said, 'I don't mind having a lot of ham for lunch, but to roll it up and stuff it with mayonnaise seems to be going a little far.' "[132] He thought it seemed reasonable that, at a conference on heart conditions, one could control the impulse to eat both ham and mayonnaise. His reaction prompted Schelling to mention that control of conditions might make the impulses people would like to avoid easier to control.

The conversation moved on to the question of smoking, and Schelling wondered whether there might not be better circumstances that would make it easier for people to help themselves quit. The dean told him a National Committee on Substance Abuse was being formed that needed an economist. Schelling volunteered, becoming the committee's only "amateur." The other members included psychologists, sociologists, lawyers . . . all people who dealt with some aspect of addiction. The common view on the committee was that addicts couldn't help themselves, and they needed to get into some kind of treatment. Schelling was less sure, offering as examples that heroin users shouldn't listen to music they associate with drug use, that many who quit smoking relapse when drinking. The committee got tired of him talking, and suggested he write up a paper on substance abuse and how people can try to cope with their own behavior.

Schelling's article, titled "No Thyself," was published in the journal *The Public Interest*.[133] Schelling offered practical advice for people dealing with uncontrollable behavior—wear mittens to bed to stop oneself from scratching bites or hives in the night, for example—and concentrated on non-clinical arrangements or rational choices to control undesired future behavior (such as addiction, but not limited to it). He pointed out that shame is a deterrent of unwanted behavior and suggested making legal arrangements that would encourage one to keep a commitment to one's self: such as swearing an oath to maintain desired behavior and posting a reward for evidence leading to your own conviction for violating the oath. The principal point was that the "you" of the present and the "you" of the future weren't the same—and that one could act to control unwanted behavior by the future self.

Schelling used smoking to illustrate a rational approach to controlling undesired behavior. He told the story of a man trying to quit the habit. For the first two months, the man had an extremely difficult time, battling constant cravings for a cigarette; but in the past few weeks, things were better. The man was starting to feel optimistic he was going to make it and really quit for good. One day, a friend stopped by after work and left an open pack of cigarettes on the coffee table. The man noticed the pack shortly after his friend left, but it was too late to catch him. Since the two were getting together the next morning, the man put the pack in his jacket pocket and hung the jacket in the closet. He sat down in front of the TV to have a before-dinner drink and watch the news; then, shortly after settling in, got up and walked to the closet to find his jacket. He took the pack of cigarettes out of his pocket, looked at them for a bit, then walked to the toilet, and dumped them in. One flush—then he returned to his drink and the television.

Schelling's example illustrated someone coping rationally with an anticipated departure from rationality. The man thought he might commit the irrational act of smoking after making the serious and rational effort to quit. Since he anticipated that the temptation would be too great, and that the irrational urge to smoke would overcome him, the rational thing was to empty the pack into the toilet, flush it, and remove the opportunity for temptation.

To illustrate how this can become strategy, Schelling asked: What if the man himself had never smoked, but it was his wife who was trying to quit? Suppose she'd been having a rough time, but she was holding on and succeeding, and then the man's friend stopped by, leaving his cigarettes behind? If his wife was out, the man would certainly dispose of the cigarettes before she came home. Schelling said that a key to success in situations of coping rationally with lapses from rationality is to treat one's future self—the one not trusted to behave—as if it were "another self" or, as he sometimes put it, as "another's self." This was a new application of the same strategies Schelling had presented in his game-theory work.

Dealing with the later untrustworthy self requires creativity and planning, but it can be done. Arrange penalties and make commitments to hold yourself to if you smoke, overeat, drink, or commit whatever the act is that you are trying to avoid. One suggested commitment is to make a large donation to a political candidate you despise; write a check to the Republican/Democratic Party or whomever you find most offensive, and arrange for it to be out of your control that the check is sent in your name if you fail. Disable yourself: Throw your keys in the darkness if driving after drinking too much is likely to be a problem.

Schelling once mentioned how a college student who didn't trust himself to stay in and study on the weekend for an important exam could put his keys in the mail to himself on Friday, so they'd be delivered to him on Monday. If you overeat and can't resist the food you see, commit yourself by ordering lunch in advance. Reschedule: Do your shopping before breakfast if you spend too much time and money. If you're trying to loose weight and don't trust yourself, use a buddy system: Exercise together, order each other's meals.

Presenting the American Economic Association's 1983 Richard T. Ely Lecture, Schelling raised a new issue about self-command. He began the lecture with the example of a woman who had decided to give birth without taking anything for pain. She instructed the doctor not to have gas available for pain, since she knew she would use it if it were available to her. The delivery was very painful, and she told the doctor to give her gas for relief. In such a situation, a conflict exists between the two "selves." Schelling asked which "self" has priority: the one who gave the original instructions or the one demanding the painkiller?

It is as though the person is two different people, a first person who knew what she wanted and a second person who couldn't do what the first person wanted. In this case, denying the painkiller could raise legal questions about which "self" is the real person. Schelling's message was still that the "self" who knows there may be a problem controlling what it may do at a later time can anticipate those temptations and take steps to prevent the later "self" from doing what it hopes to avoid.

Schelling's interest in self control made him the appropriate person for the position he held his last six years at Harvard: director of the Institute for the Study of Smoking Behavior and Policy. It had taken him three times to successfully quit smoking himself, so he was aware of the challenges.

While Schelling worked to help individuals exert greater self-control over their own lives, the American public was attempting to exert control over the direction of foreign policy in Vietnam. Extricating the United

States from Vietnam was a complicated process, as troop withdrawals were coupled with the mining of Haiphong Harbor and increased bombing raids against the North. In 1972, public opinion was decidedly against the war, and the Democrats nominated the outspokenly anti-war George McGovern of South Dakota to run against Richard Nixon. Nixon's landslide 521–17 victory was tainted by the break-in at the Democratic National Committee headquarters at the Watergate Office Building in Washington.

At Harvard, Derek Bok had become president, and it was, he said, "an ugly, unpleasant time."[134] The radical Students for a Democratic Society held a convention on campus the first year he was there. Trust between the faculty and students had shattered. Just as he'd always avoided the Cold War fears gripping the nation, concentrating on his work instead, Schelling continued during these turbulent times to focus on his students, his research, and his writing.

CHAPTER 21

GLOBAL WARMING

The end in Vietnam came when Richard Nixon resigned the presidency in 1974 and was replaced by Gerald Ford. The Americans evacuated, as Saigon fell to the communists in 1975. It was the end of an era. How bad the news was in Southeast Asia wasn't known, and an event took place that went unnoticed by many, pushed from the front pages by the story of the presidency and Vietnam. The Cambodian invasion Schelling and his colleagues had made a stand against had truly mattered. The U.S. raids had been one of the factors that contributed to the destabilization of the Cambodian government, and the Khmer Rouge, led by Pol Pot, came to power. The Khmer Rouge would kill millions of its own people before being driven out in 1979.

It had been 30 years since the beginning of the Cold War. The Cold War rivalry had eased and the world had become a safer place since 1953, when the Russians caught up with the Americans by testing their hydrogen bomb, and the *Bulletin of the Atomic Scientists* had set the clock at two minutes to midnight. The Vietnam protest days were a thing of the past, and things were calming down. Schelling had been a part of it all since 1948, and while it wasn't all over yet, his Cold War role was fading now that the nuclear showdown had eased.

Events outside Harvard and Vietnam would soon demand the nation's attention. In October 1973, a war broke out in the Middle East. During the Yom Kippur Arab-Israeli War, Israel's superior military power dominated the field of action. The Organization of Petroleum Exporting Countries, or OPEC, initiated a boycott of oil that demonstrated their power to the rest of the world. The resulting U.S. oil shortage was accompanied by lower speed limits, license-plate-number gas rationing, and an increased demand for fuel-efficient Japanese cars. Reliance on Middle East oil raised questions about the viability of other energy forms.

When the energy crisis of 1973–74 hit, Schelling had already begun to develop an interest in energy policy. He was still interested in nuclear policy, but from another perspective. He had spent the years since 1957 as a nuclear strategist, working to help keep the Cold War from spiraling out of control, to help see that through mistakes, miscommunication, or accident, nuclear war didn't result and end in unthinkable tragedy. Nuclear war between the great powers seemed considerably less likely, and his new interest in nuclear policy was about a new danger: nuclear proliferation.

In the early '70s, the Committee for Economic Development asked him to do several studies, one on nuclear proliferation. He found that the Shah of Iran was planning on having 18 reactors and getting bomb material out of them, and that Egypt also wanted reactors. Nuclear proliferation was expected to be a byproduct of nuclear power reactors, and his transition to energy interests was taking place during the energy crisis of 1973–'74.

In 1977, Schelling was part of a group of 20 nuclear engineers, academics, chemists, and economists who gathered to study nuclear energy on a Ford Foundation grant. The result of their two-year study was a 400-page report that found nuclear energy produces no carbon dioxide emission and results in no greenhouse warming. Out of the 400 pages, two were devoted to carbon dioxide emission and greenhouse warming. Two years later, he was part of another study that involved 20 people from the academic world, business, and scientific laboratories. Their 600-page report, "Energy: The Next Twenty Years," included 10 pages scattered through it that mentioned "the greenhouse" topic.

His real awareness of the global warming issue began with a phone call from National Academy of Sciences senior officer, Bob White. White invited him to chair a committee to advise the White House on the "carbon dioxide issue." President Jimmy Carter, who had been elected in 1976, was going to a summit meeting with Chancellor of West Germany, Helmut Schmidt, in Venice, and Schmidt had put on the agenda "the carbon dioxide issue." The White House didn't know what to do. Carter's science advisor, Frank Press, asked the National Academy of Sciences to do a quick study and tell them how to handle this item. Not sure how to deal with it, the academy chose Schelling to provide an answer. When White called him and asked him to chair a committee. Schelling said, "I don't know a damn thing about the subject." White showed up in Cambridge with John Perry, an expert. They explained the topic to Schelling, saying it was part science, part diplomacy, and part policy judgment—he was the right man and he could learn the science.

They gathered a committee, and Perry and Schelling wrote a report recommending that the best thing to do with that agenda item was to get it off. They weren't ready for it. Carter took the advice. After Carter lost his bid for reelection in 1980, Press became president of the National Academy of Sciences. A Synthetic Fuels Bill passed the Senate, and it included a requirement for a carbon dioxide study to be done by the National Academy of Sciences. Press asked Schelling to be a part of the study, and he wrote the Policy and Welfare Implications chapter in the final report. Schelling's work was well received, and he became in demand for conferences on the greenhouse effect. He was one of the first economists in America to get drawn into the greenhouse climate change issue.[135] He had learned the science and unlike most others who understood the science, he understood the economic and policy topics that accompanied the issues.

Beginning in the late 1970s, his primary subject for research and writing was greenhouse effect and global warming, as it became a widespread concern in America. Unlike nuclear war, opinion was not unanimous on the dangers posed. While he was among the first to be aware of the possible dangers global warming presents, he was not an alarmist. He felt that it wasn't enough to say that global warming was a problem and people should stop making it worse, and to just talk about how bad things could get. His views didn't always make him popular with those who shared his awareness of the process that was taking place. Some thought he wasn't showing sufficient respect for the frightening possibilities, or as many believed, certainties of disaster that lay ahead.

As with nuclear deterrence, Schelling raised questions. If it is such a problem, whose problem is it? If things can be done about it, who should pay for them? If part of the problem comes from poor countries, why should they be concerned enough to use their resources preventing it, when it might hurt the fragile economies they already have? Was there technology that could make the whole problem go away? Even if the problem was as bad as some people thought, what about people living on the fringes today, where starvation and disease claim untold lives daily: should our resources go to saving them now rather than being concerned about generations of the future? How would you tell those people that?

He was more specific in his policy advice on global warming and related problems than he usually had been in his work on nuclear deterrence. Schelling was the first person to speak consistently about geoengineering solutions to environmental problems. Geoengineering, which he described as, "not a well-defined concept, but it involves tampering with the environment,"[136] has been somewhat controversial. He says that in the future there will be benign, economically effective direct intervention in the radiation balance and there will be safe, convenient, economical alternatives to carbon fuels. One could put things in the stratosphere to screen out one half-percent of the sunlight and that would block the greenhouse effect. Sulfur would work, as could be seen from observing the effects of volcanoes. Carbon black would work and commercial airlines could tune their engines to blow it out in their exhaust. Schelling said, "The amount we'd have to keep out is so small that even the astronomical observatories wouldn't know the difference. It would be nothing like a hazy day." Using giant Mylar balloons to act as huge mirrors reflecting light back to earth, covering polar ice caps with carbon black to raise the levels of the seas— there were a variety of ways to interfere with the environment to make it suit the needs of the future.

While raising questions about the global warming phenomenon and looking at solutions for the future, Schelling also tried looking backward. It was an approach he sometimes used to help avoid making assumptions and to promote imaginative thought. He said that since global warming wasn't expected to be a serious problem for another 75 years, it would be interesting to put oneself back 75 years and to consider what people living then would have anticipated would be the leading environmental problem in the present day. His answer was mud, as it was a time of narrow tires and muddy roads. His point was that it was important not to imagine climate change superimposed on today's world. In places where people are under-nourished, sanitation is poor, and water is impure, climate change might not be as disastrous as it appears if those conditions were improved.

Schelling also questioned the view that concern for the climate of future generations be valued at the expense of the present. Of greater concern, he felt, was the immediate need for sanitation, health care, education, and mosquito abatement in the developing world. Malaria and dengue fever could be dealt with, and there could be great relief in present day suffering.

In 1997, the Conference on Climate Change met in Kyoto, Japan. Many issues were on the agenda, but the central one was carbon dioxide. Schelling had written a paper before that conference briefly summarizing how interest in the issue of the affects of carbon dioxide and about the greenhouse effect had grown over the previous 20 years, and how the severity of the problem remained an uncertainty. He made his point that he thought the impact on the developed countries was likely to be very small, while the developing countries were vulnerable. He added, "But even they should be much less vulnerable fifty years from now when climate change may begin to make itself felt; their own development is probably their best defense against the vagaries of climate."[137]

Though his proposed solutions were sometimes controversial, his ideas and position were clear. He considered global warming a real problem, something that would have to be addressed and cooperatively controlled. His views weren't ambiguous, or alarmist. He saw it as a complex problem, and he was presenting ideas and questions to get others to see what issues needed to be resolved. Former colleague Charles Hitch said it was Schelling's special ability "to transform unfocused discussions into focused ones, directed toward answering what he has identified as the right question."[138]

With Schelling's method of raising questions and presenting unpopular solutions, the strategic thinker's dilemma that had been apparent during his Cold War years reappeared. It was like the Cold War, in that he provided analysis to promote greater understanding, but couldn't control how his words were used. But it was different, in that he took more of a stance and offered solutions like geoengineering. He promoted policy. His words were sometimes taken in directions other than where he had intended them to go, or was aware they would head. In this case it was not interpretation or application; it was exploitation and intentional misuse. He still couldn't control what became of what he said.

Schelling's words were used to support the oil industry and business in their rejection of concern over global warming and their attack on the Kyoto Protocol. For 20 years, he had known that the carbon emissions the Protocol sought to limit were at the heart of the problem the world was coming to realize it faced. Schelling's views were sometimes used to contradict his own beliefs.

In 1995, he was quoted as supporting testimony before the House of Representatives Science Committee Subcommittee on Energy and Environment. The argument made was that, "If warming occurs, it is more likely to bring net benefits than losses to Americans and most of the world."[139] For support, Schelling was cited as concluding that the impact on the developed world would be negligible. In 1998, after the Kyoto Conference, it was the chief operating officer of the American Petroleum Institute that testified before the House Reform and Oversight Committee on National Economic Growth, Natural Resources and Regulatory Affairs. "Distinguished professor" Schelling's views were used to argue that the language in the Kyoto Protocol permitting emissions trading presented an unworkable system.[140]

Schelling was again quoted in testimony before a House of Representatives committee hearing on the Kyoto Protocol, which placed voluntary limits on carbon dioxide emissions, a position he favored. The Small Business Survival Committee said in prepared testimony, "Thomas C. Schelling, a Distinguished Professor of Economics and Public Affairs at the University of Maryland, and a believer in the woes of global warming, acknowledged the following: 'Any cost of mitigating climate change during the coming decades will surely be borne by the high-income countries.' Therefore, problems of the Kyoto Protocol are two-fold. First, 'developing' countries are not required to reduce their 'greenhouse-gas' emissions, and therefore, businesses in those nations will avoid the draconian costs heaped onto the backs of U.S. firms. These 'Third World' companies will possess cost advantages in international markets, hurting U.S. exports, as well as advantages in U.S. markets themselves, cutting consumption of domestically produced goods and services by U.S. consumers." They went on to say that Schelling offered a declaration "that could only be made by a cloistered ideologue," in saying slowing global warming would cost the relatively low price of a few trillion dollars.[141]

Schelling's views sparked some controversy in 2006, when an op-ed piece he wrote, titled "It's Getting Warmer," appeared in the February 23 issue of *The Wall Street Journal*. In the article, he said that while "global warming" had been going on for more than a decade and it had been the hottest decade on record worldwide, whether this was a result of the "greenhouse effect" was less certain. Regarding the question of whether it could be some natural, not man-made, climactic change, Schelling said: The Intergovernmental Panel on Climate Change, which he described as "a cautious body not disposed toward outright conclusions," had noted human influence. "Something is going on," he said. But just what is less clear, as he stated when he asked and answered the question: "The popular guessing game—do we see a greenhouse 'signature,' can we identify a clear 'signal' in the 'noise'?—is probably premature." He mentioned that history of sudden changes in global atmospheric temperature have happened in other times, and random or random-seeming influences such as El Niño continue to take place, while volcanic emissions can cause climate change. There are man-made influences besides greenhouse gases, including aerosols of dust and sulfur emissions and "heat islands" produced by urbanization. He mentioned how oceans act as a huge "cooling reservoir" that delays atmospheric warming, since the specific heat of water is great relative to air. The question this raised for Schelling was not "whether we can discern a signal in the noise, but discern a signal among other signals . . . Greenhouse warming is not clearly established by the temperature record nor is it in any way ruled out. We may see the greenhouse signal clearly in another decade or two. Meanwhile we have to rely on what science can tell us."

The earth's greenhouse gasses allow for an atmosphere with a wide range of temperature. Earth is unique in our solar system for its temperature range, and greenhouse gases are to be thanked. Venus has so *much* greenhouse atmosphere that water couldn't exist as liquid, but only could be vapor and Mars so *little* that water couldn't exist as liquid but only could be ice. That carbon dioxide molecules absorb infrared radiation has been known for a century. The earth's atmosphere is transparent to most solar radiation; but as the earth, warmed by daylight sun, radiates energy back into space it does so in the infrared part of the spectrum, and the carbon dioxide absorbs some of it and gets warm. Schelling notes that citrus growers in California and Florida make use of this phenomenon and use smudge pots (ceramic tubes of burning crude oil) on clear, still nights to produce a blanket of carbon dioxide that captures some of the heat radiating from the ground and keeps fruit from freezing.

Carbon dioxide is only one of the gases that have that property, the most important being water vapor, and it should be a part of the estimated enhancement of temperature. He doesn't reject the concerns people express about the greenhouse effect. In fact, he says, "I find the case for prospective greenhouse warming to be almost beyond doubt." The questions aren't about the realities but the magnitude and speed. "Rarely is there such scientific consensus as there is on whether the greenhouse effect is real, even though it cannot yet be incontrovertibly detected in the climate record."

What he believes is there are many unanswered questions. "The uncertainties are daunting: The best the IPCC can do is give us a range of possible warmings for any given increase in carbon dioxide concentration. And the upper bound of that range has been, for two decades, three times the lower bound—an enormous range of uncertainty. On top of that are the uncertainties of what the change in temperature will do to climates around the world. And on top of that are the uncertainties of what those climate changes may do to the worlds we live in, and what people will be able to do to adapt successfully to what change is allowed to occur."

His conclusion is very far from panic:

"I'd buy insurance. I'd do it prudently, and without great alarm. Yet!"

The article drew a range of responses. There were heated objections in letters to the *Journal*'s editor, including one who felt it was inconsistent, saying, "Schelling . . . states that 'greenhouse warming is not clearly established by the temperature record.'" Later he says, 'I find the case for prospective greenhouse warming to be almost beyond doubt.'" Another writer said, "He reaches his position by the selective exclusion of inconvenient facts." The nephew of his old colleague, the great nuclear strategist, Albert Wohlstetter took a different view, calling the article "an eloquent case . . . a thoughtful one that merits a read."

Another environmental topic Schelling's looked at was the recycling movement in the 1990s. While it was not an issue of interest comparable to global warming, it was another where his distinctive analysis came into play. It included encouraging thrift with the greater use of leftovers, more careful planning of meals, and improvement of skills of purchasing to find items less likely to be thrown out. He considered the waste in not using the often ignored half-used containers in the backs of cupboards and refrigerators, not discarding safe perishables, or failing to eat oversized portions in restaurants.

Schelling thought it was valuable to include people's social values and their willingness to change their personal behavior as factors in the struggle to reduce the tremendous waste taking place. He was skeptical about how successful relying on the thrift of consumers would be on its own. It was a question of economic analysis, and markets would induce consumers to convert. His observation was supported when coffee prices had gone up suddenly in 1955, coffee sales were cut in half. With only half the coffee available, coffee consumption went down by only one-fourth. People were apparently more careful and brewed less often and in smaller pots, only as much as they needed, wasting less.

It was Schelling making observations in a different way about a problem that had seemed to have an obvious solution. The obvious solution involved guilt and calls for personal choice and sacrifice. It was guilt that was difficult to avoid. Schelling's economic realities presented a way of seeing things that didn't make the issue a cause, where there were good guys and bad guys, but offered an understanding of the forces at work.

CHAPTER 22

MODELS IN GAME THEORY

In 1978 Schelling's *Micromotives and Macrobehavior* was released. The book often applies game theory as it offers ideas that help make behavior easier to understand and frequently easier to predict. It presented situations where individuals' decisions lead to results that are exactly opposite of their intent. It describes what he calls "musical chairs," situations where the outcome will be the same in the aggregate, regardless of what choices individuals make. Segregation and integration are discussed and analyzed, and the forces at work behind changing patterns of the mixing and sorting of not only race, but also age, sex, and income.

He spent considerable time presenting models,[142] which are the social studies constructs that demonstrate the basic features of many situations in society in an easily understood way. Models may help make aggregate behavior easier to predict and to encourage or prevent. People often look at the combined outcome of individual decisions. In some cases it may be possible to view a group of people as approaching being a "collective individual." One could then interpret the results of the individual decisions that members of the group make as an expression of a commonly held sentiment. For example, at a high school football or basketball game, it is likely that the spectators attending the game from each of the schools involved have, for the most part, decided which team they hope will win. They want the school they attend to win.

But often, as Schelling demonstrated with his models on segregation, individuals make decisions in response to the environment they perceive, and by doing so, change that environment in a manner that affects decisions made by others, whose decisions then affect others, and so on. And often these decisions are made not on the environment an individual currently perceives, but the one he anticipates will be created by the decisions of others. In these cases, looking at the results of interactive decision-making may lead to incorrect assumptions about the intentions and desires of the people involved. The systematic results of this sort of individual decision-making may not be easily predictable or understood. This is true even when the characteristics and motivation of the population involved are

175

known. In selected cases behavior models can be especially useful. Without them, knowledge of individual behavior will not, by itself, lead to rational predictions of aggregate outcomes. In addition, the study of aggregate outcomes may only allow for logical deduction about individual motives with the help of a mediating model. Individuals' preferences, and the results produced by the interaction of their decision-making based on those preferences, are not necessarily consistent.

An example of such a model is the thermostat. The thermostat's function is to turn the furnace on or off when the temperature of a room reaches a certain temperature. If the temperature drops, the thermostat signals the furnace to turn on, and the furnace heats water, taking time as the temperature continues to drop. The hot water circulates through radiators, heating the air, taking more time before bringing the temperature up. Once the temperature is up, the thermostat turns the furnace off, but the radiators are still hot, heating the air. The temperature continues to rise. Eventually it drops and the thermometer turns on the furnace again, which begins heating water as the temperature in the room continues to drop.

The thermostat is a model of many behavior patterns that occur in cycles where there is a lag time between when a need for a solution to a situation is known (when the thermostat turns on the furnace) and by the time the need has been met, there has been met or in the rush to meet the need, too much has been produced or done (the temperature continues to rise after the thermostat shuts down the furnace). This can be seen in individual as well as aggregate situations. A child can eat chocolate until he feels he has had enough, which is usually when he has had too much. On a larger scale, after *Sputnik* went up, the thermostat clicked on. There was a rush in the United States to produce more scientists, and top students were channeled into science and engineering. It took time, and by the time these students were out of school, the demand wasn't as great, and people weren't walking away from the jobs they had. There were shortages of people in other careers.

"Lemons" was another model presented. The "lemons" upon which this model is based are not fruit, but poor-quality used cars. When someone sells a used car, it is likely that he knows whether or not it is a lemon. The buyer, however, only knows the average value of that year's model of car. The average price for used cars is based on the overall distribution of "lemons," average cars, and better-than-average cars. Therefore, the average price for a used car is a high price for a "lemon," but a low price for a good used car. Owners of better-quality used cars are reluctant to sell them at a price based on an average, so better cars appear less frequently on the market.

The result of this is that the percent of "lemons" on the market increases. Cars that had been the average cars at first have become better-than-average cars in the new market. This is because the new market is based on the average frequency of "lemons" in a market that no longer includes the best used cars. These cars begin to vanish from the market, since the new average price undervalues them. This process is continuous, and, if left to go unchecked, can completely eliminate a market.

George Akerlof, the originator of this model, generalized it further. He presents it as a model of markets in which there is unequal, or "asymmetrical" information between two parties. An example is life insurance. An insurance company has a great deal of general statistical information to use when it sets its rates for an individual's policy. This information is derived from experience and study of probable life expectancy. The individual, however, may well know things that make the company statistics inaccurate. The company bases its rates on the premise that some people are going to die soon and their beneficiaries will collect more than the insured contributed, but others are going to live long enough to pay in more than the company will pay out. For those who are not likely to survive to the company's break-even point, the insurance is a good deal. Some people may know this. Perhaps all their ancestors died young from heart disease, or perhaps they are contemplating suicide in some easily disguisable form. On the other hand, there are likely to be some people with a high probability of surviving well beyond normal life expectancy. People in this category may find themselves unwilling to pay an insurance premium based on a range of life expectancies from short to long. If they decide not to "subsidize" the poorer insurance risks and quit buying insurance, then the life expectancy of the remaining pool of customers will go down. When the life expectancy goes down, the insurance rates go up. As the rates go up, another group of people is put into the position of subsidizing the remaining group. They may then drop out of the insurance plans, leaving a group with an even shorter life expectancy, forcing the insurance company to raise rates even higher. The market in this scenario is doomed to collapse, as it moves in the direction of only retaining the worst insurance risks, and charging rates that could only be afforded by those who have no need for insurance.

The implications of this model are that there are certain sorts of markets that society values that are subject to self destruction through asymmetrical information. Some sort of regulation or supervision may be required in these cases.

A better known model was "the commons," first proposed by Garrett Hardin in his 1968 essay "The Tragedy of the Commons" and based on the observations of characteristics of common pasture in England and Colonial New England. Common land was village property that was available for unrestricted use by both the villagers and their animals.

In general, Hardin's observation was that as more animals were put on the common land to graze, there was less grass available for each animal, so the animals produced less milk and meat. However, as long as there was any profit to be made by grazing one's animals on the common, the villagers would be encouraged to do so. Even if individuals realized that the total amount of meat or milk the grazing animals produce might be higher if all the villagers restricted their use of the commons, there is no motivation for an individual to act on his own to do so.

The commons model is a metaphor for situations in which people harm each other by pursuing their own interests, and would be better off if they could be restrained, but no one gains individually by self-restraint. It is a multiperson Prisoner's Dilemma. The use of natural resources is often an example of the commons problem. All oil companies are aware that there are limits to the amount of oil available, but much of it is in common pools in which many companies have wells. For one company to slow down or stop drilling accomplishes little, other than increase the amount of oil being pumped out by its rival companies. Killing of whales in the open sea is another illustration. We may applaud a nation that signs an agreement to renounce the killing of whales, but this only leaves more whales available to those countries who still hunt them. Those countries will gain whatever commercial benefits there are that draw people to whale hunting, and the whales will be equally dead. This model also influenced Singapore's decisions on road pricing policy.

Overcrowded highways at rush hour, when traffic barely moves, present another variation of the commons. The frustrated drivers would be better off under a system that would stagger the demand for use of the road, or with strict car-pooling requirements. However, as long as these don't exist, the individual gains little by making sacrifices on his own.

Many forms of congestion fall under the general model of the commons. These have two distinguishing features. First, only those who use the common are affected by the way it is used, and they are affected in proportion to how much they use it. Second, the costs of using or overusing the common are in the same "currency" as the benefits.

These features can be illustrated by using an example from the common that is the namesake for the model. Suppose a village has a common that is used for grazing dairy cattle. Milk is the villagers' sole product. If only a few cattle have the entire common to themselves, they will produce

1000 quarts of milk per year. As the number of cows increases, the amount of grass they would each have to eat would decrease, leading to a decline in the milk production of each cow. Assume the following linear decline:

Cows	Quarts/Cow/Year	Total Milk Production
1	1000	1000
100	900	90,000
200	800	160,000
300	700	210,000
400	600	240,000
500	500	250,000
600	400	240,000
700	300	210,000
800	200	160,000
900	100	90,000

If we look at this in view of the economic concept of utility, the village would be best off slaughtering any cattle in excess of 500. Any cows beyond that number result in a decline in total milk production. However, if we look at it from the point of view of an individual villager who owns cattle, the result is different. Even if there are already 800 cows on the common, a villager with 10 cows is paying nothing for the common, and stands to lose 2000 quarts of milk if he voluntarily takes his cattle off. If for some reason he took them off anyway, the community would gain more than 2000 quarts overall, because the common would be slightly less crowded, and the remaining cows would be slightly more productive.

The Dollar Auction is a very effective model of escalation. It provided a good model for how the United States got so entrenched in Vietnam without an easy exit strategy. The game is simple. A dollar is offered for auction to be sold to the highest bidder. The single condition is that both the highest bidder and the second highest bidder have to pay the amount of their final bids (for example, if the highest bid ended up being $.25, and the second highest bid was $.20, the highest bidder would pay the auctioneer $.25 for the dollar, and the second highest bidder would pay the auctioneer $.20 and receive nothing). The surprisingly consistent, and seemingly illogical result of this game is that the dollar will be sold for more than a dollar, and the second bidder will pay over a dollar for nothing. Typically, the Dollar Auction proceeds as follows: Someone makes a small opening bid, which is quickly raised by other small amounts. At this stage it is likely that the participants are just taking part in a spirit of fun or in the hope of getting a cheap dollar, and are not attempting to foresee the consequences of the bidding.

For illustrative purposes, say the opening bid is $.10 by bidder A. Bidder B raises it to $.15, followed by a bid of $.20 by bidder C: A ups it to $.25, B to $.30, C to $.35. At this point it may still appear that the auctioneer was foolish to offer to sell the dollar, but the participants are beginning to realize they stand to lose money if they are not the winners in the bidding. Perhaps A, being the low bidder at this point, will drop out, since it will cost him nothing. This leaves B bidding against C. B could also drop out at this point, but it would cost him $.30, while upping the bid only $.05 might get him the dollar. So B raises the bid, thus putting C in the same situation at a more costly level (C would lose $.35 by dropping out). An interesting point, and one important to the auctioneer, occurs when one bidder reaches $.50. If the other raises the bid, the auctioneer is guaranteed a profit.

The trap in the Dollar Auction is that each participant has more and more to lose by not raising the stakes. Once the price reaches a dollar, a bidder finds himself in the awkward position of being forced to bid more than a dollar to avoid losing all the money he has bid so far. The same is true for the other bidder. By this time, both bidders are going to lose money, and it becomes a question of how much. While results vary widely, the dollar is likely to be sold for four or five dollars, or a total combined value of eight to ten dollars, as long as no cooperation between bidders enters in. The Dollar Auction effectively demonstrates how easily escalation can take us beyond our original idea of what we are risking.

The Dollar Auction has a number of significant characteristics. It is based on the problem of how to deal with "sunk costs." A sunk cost is an investment that can't be retrieved. In this game it's the money one has already bid. He will either spend that money buying the dollar if he is top bidder, or paying for nothing if he isn't.

The difficult question with sunk costs, as the Dollar Auction illustrates, is knowing when to press forward and when to give up. When an oil company makes a large investment doing geological studies and procuring drilling rights, and begins the gamble of drilling where it thinks oil should be found, its wells may come empty. The expense has been great and the company is tying up valuable resources. On the other hand, the rewards might be spectacular, if oil is finally located—maybe it's just a little deeper, or a mile away in another direction. How much longer should the company keep searching, once they have made the great initial investment that brought them this far? The Dollar Auction is very effective for understanding how situations like commitment of troops can get out of control.

CHAPTER 23

THE JOHN F. KENNEDY SCHOOL
OF GOVERNMENT

As Schelling's interests were evolving, he was taking part in the creation of a new institution at Harvard, the John F. Kennedy School of Government. The Kennedy School was to become Schelling's academic home. It became a professional school for public administration that combined the academic study of government with the world of practical politics, and emphasized methods for making progress through the political process. The origins of the school dated back to 1936, when a wealthy businessman who had been active in the Roosevelt administration, Lucius Littauer, made a gift for the founding of the Harvard University's Graduate School of Public Administration. The school became a midcareer master's degree program for government leaders and civil servants from third world countries, known as Mason Fellows, and Littauer left money for fellowships. Persuading Harvard that it needed something more was not an easy task. Derek Bok, who was President of Harvard University at the time, was convinced by Schelling and several of his colleagues, among them Dick Neustadt, Don Price, Fred Mosteller, and Howard Raiffa, to make establishing a new institution a priority. Harvard needed a school to bring an academic foundation to the practical world of public policy decision-making and to educate people in the profession of policy making.

In 1969 a small group of faculty members, including Schelling, Bator, Raiffa, Neustadt, and Graham Allison, helped design a curriculum and recruit a faculty to teach at the school, expanding the course offerings. Schelling had to quit his association with the Center for International Affairs to be a part of it. They developed a curriculum, the Master in Public Policy program, and started taking students. Former Harvard President Derek Bok recalls Schelling's roll in the process. "I remember him chiefly as one of the handful of faculty members who really founded the Kennedy School and devoted tremendous efforts to ensuring its success. Without the interest of Tom and a few others, such as Dick Neustadt, Don Price, Fred Mosteller, Howard Raiffa, etc., I never would have decided to make the building of the School a priority. It was their presence and dedication that made it seem conceivable to create an entirely new professional school for professional service; without them, the effort couldn't possibly have succeeded."[143] David T. Ellwood, current Dean of the Kennedy School, commented on Schelling's role in the creation of the institution when he spoke of the Nobel Prize award: "It should come as no surprise that such an exceptional scholar who had a profound influence on policy would be one of the founders of the modern Kennedy School. Tom's vision and inspiration are a central part of who we are and what we aspire to be, and we could not be more pleased to see him receive this well-deserved recognition."[144]

Harvard was interested in establishing a memorial to John Kennedy. To bring practical politics and the academic study of government closer together, the Institute of Politics was established. The Master in Public Policy program and the Institute of Politics program were combined and with the cooperation of friends and members of the Kennedy family, the school of public policy was renamed the John F. Kennedy School of Government and dedicated in 1978. At the same time, the school was relocated in its own new building. Schelling became the Lucius N. Littauer Professor of Political Economy.

One of its early professors describes the school in its early years as a very self-conscious institution where "There was a lot of time spent contemplating our navel."[145] There was uncertainty about just what the school was supposed to be, where it was going; it was very aware of its pioneering role in its field. There were other schools of public policy, but the Kennedy School was something new. A considerable amount of concern existed about the school's standing in comparison with other schools at Harvard, especially in Arts and Sciences. The Kennedy School wanted members of the Economics or Government Departments on their committees, but it wasn't the other way around. There were exceptions like Schelling and others who had reputations in their disciplines. It could be frenetic, going in too many directions at once. It wasn't integrated into the university as well as its Princeton counterpart, the Woodrow Wilson School of Public and International Affairs. There was always something going on, people were always coming in. The Kennedy School in those first years was very extravaganza, and extremely energetic.

As the school grew it acquired an exceptionally capable and experienced faculty. There was a combination of people who were thinking on extremely high levels who had to solve problems on a daily basis. The executive programs brought scholars together with practical people. It was a good combination of challenging, motivated, and diverse people. The mature school was a comfortable home for practical academics.

Schelling was in his element and was surrounded by like-minded scholars. He was very comfortable at the School, and enjoyed the interchange of ideas that was continually taking place. His intuitive approach was recognized and appreciated. Herman "Dutch" Leonard, a professor of public administration, arrived at the school in 1979. He recalls hearing a story about Schelling from those early years of the school.

"The story is that there was a faculty committee to study the 'Harvard faculty parking problem.' It has been said that there are three relevant groups and interests around a university: sex for the undergraduates, football for the alumni, and parking for the faculty. My experience is that that is roughly right. You can imagine what the 'parking problem' looks like at Harvard. Harvard has a higher concentration of prima donnas than any other place on the planet. The faculty parking problem is not that we have too many parking places to distribute—it is, roughly, that no matter how you distribute the parking places, (a) there will not be enough; and (b) [far worse] you will be implicitly or explicitly announcing some form of hierarchy among the eminent—which, of course, is anathema. So what to do?

"The story goes that Tom was unable to attend the first meeting of the committee, so the chairman told him that the first meeting was for brainstorming alternative methods of distribution, and that the committee would meet and come up with some ideas and make a list, and that Tom could think on his own about alternatives and that if he had thought of any that weren't on the committee's list, he could add them at the second meeting. So it came to pass that the committee had thought of half a dozen materially different alternatives—and, when Tom came to the second meeting, he had a list that included all six of the committee's alternatives, plus another dozen materially different new ones."[146]

Schelling taught a course based on his experiences as much as his studies, "Conflict, Cooperation, and Strategy." The course was problem-based, and involved bargaining theory, game theory, and other topics that applied to rational strategic decision-making. It was a course he had been teaching, and would continue to modify and teach, for his entire career, his signature course.

Along with offering "Conflict, Cooperation, and Strategy," Schelling taught other courses in the early years of the school. One offering when the school originally opened was a course on microeconomic analysis and public policy taught jointly by Schelling and Bator, who took turns presenting and were never in the same room at the same time. In the 1980s, Schelling paired with the black professor Glenn Loury to teach "Public Policies in Divided Societies." It began by dealing with Afro-American issues, then quickly expanded to divided society issues in general, including Northern Ireland, the Middle East, castes in India, and the Native American populations of Central and South America. The two disagreed on policy. Contrary to student expectations when the topic was discussed in class, Schelling favored affirmative action, while Loury was opposed.

Loury was a conservative black political activist, and recognized as such. Schelling's analysis of conditions presented insights that could have led to specific policies. As with nuclear strategy, he concerned himself with the underlying concepts. He maintained his usual strategist's posture of clarifying the situation and leaving policy decisions to others. He used his tipping models to show how communities could "tip" from integrated to segregated, how racially integrated neighborhoods' futures could be determined by peoples' expectations of what they had wanted to avoid happening. He never proposed to Loury the idea of advocating or promoting any policy that would encourage white movement into integrated areas to prevent the exodus that would result in neighborhood tipping.

On the days Schelling taught "Conflict, Cooperation, and Strategy," before class he would head from his office upstairs to the cafeteria on the main floor at noon to get his lunch, then return to his office to get his notes together before class. Lunch usually included a sandwich and a beer. A beer: "It made him human," is how one of his teaching assistants put it. He smiled a lot during class and enjoyed challenging his students to think, to share his joy in solving problems.

The Singapore government ministers were among the many students Schelling taught and influenced. He also taught a number of his future colleagues and associates at Harvard and RAND. Those whose careers were at Harvard included Harvey Feinberg, provost of the university; and Dutch Leonard, MaryJo Bane, and David Ellwood of the Kennedy School. Bob Klitgaard became dean of the RAND Graduate School of Policy Studies.

Another of his students was future Nobel laureate Michael Spence. In his autobiography for his Nobel Prize, Spence wrote about the teachers who had influenced him the most and said, "Thomas Schelling, as all who studied with him knew, had an extraordinarily original mind. Unique in our experience was his capacity to analyze using carefully constructed analogies, with just the right number of similarities and differences . . . I think I tended more to being just fascinated by how markets and mechanisms like them worked. A great deal of that interest and motivation came from hours spent with Tom Schelling. It could be tipping points, focal points, sorting out congestion . . . Schelling's curiosity seemed endless and his capacity to shed light remarkable." When Schelling was Spence's advisor and Spence turned in the first draft of his doctoral thesis, Schelling told him to rewrite it because he thought it contained something good, but he wasn't sure, because Spence "had done such a good job of concealing it."[147]

These students had seen the rational, imaginative Schelling everyone knew. Another of his early students, Richard Zeckhauser, had seen him the same way, but caught a glimpse of something else. When he was a graduate student, he invited Schelling over to his shabby basement apartment, and his roommate and few others were there. Schelling spent the whole evening talking about his love of children. He recalls Schelling saying, "You're waiting for your child to be born, then your child is born. Somebody comes out you've obviously never seen before, you don't know whether it's going to be a boy or girl, then you fall in love."[148] It was the sort of thing Schelling rarely did, be so open and vulnerable.

His secretary at the Kennedy School, Connie Higgins, rarely saw the emotional side. He was always even-tempered, and in the 25 years she knew him, she heard him let loose only one time. She liked working for him and their relationship was relaxed. He respected her, and didn't act like some of the "hot shot" arrogant younger faculty.[149]

Schelling was shown considerable respect by his colleagues. One day in an international relations class following a speech given the evening before at the Kennedy School Forum by an especially erudite speaker, a young instructor said to his class that he had had a difficult time following the presenter's ideas, even understanding the vocabulary. He had been beginning to become embarrassed, until he saw Tom Schelling, and noted that even he was looking around.

Dutch Leonard observed that, "It was widely said, and it was true, that once you had thought about a problem long and hard, and had come up with three or more creative possible solutions to it, then it was time to take Tom to lunch; and he would come up with another half-dozen ideas you hadn't thought of."[150]

At school faculty meetings Schelling was taken seriously and there was some deference to him. The close connection between his mind and his tongue sometimes caused him to run away with his own thoughts, and his ideas would take on a momentum of their own. It could make a tedious meeting fascinating, but he would leave looking sheepish afterward, and there were times when he couldn't stop his mind from taking over even at short meetings with tight agendas. Often he spoke to reformulate points or to stimulate ideas, rather than to state his views. There were some younger faculty who were reluctant to speak after him. It was a collegial atmosphere, but as the institution grew, the atmosphere wasn't always unified.

A tension began to develop over an ideological difference between two groups. The question that brought about the division concerned the proper role of the policy analyst. Schelling's view was the same as it had been since the Cold War, and there were other economists in the school who generally agreed. They believed that the approach to policy analysis was to begin by rationally analyzing situations, seeking to understand how things work and what outcomes would be. His idea had been to "solve the puzzle first." Policy was something that came after understanding. Throughout his career Schelling had fought against the idea of beginning with outcomes, what he saw as looking at problems backward, and had believed that strategic analysis was required in advance to understand situations before developing public policy.

A group headed by Steve Kelman and future Secretary of Labor, Robert Reich, held a different view. This group cared about policy management as well as public policy analysis. Their main argument was that values couldn't be separated from public policy, and the antiseptic and purely analytical approach of Schelling's group was incomplete. Policy analysis, the Reich group felt, was to be used in determining a successful path to the goal one hoped to achieve. They believed it was necessary to acknowledge and identify openly what one was trying to achieve or affirm when carrying out a policy.

The conflicting definitions of what role an analyst should assume presented a thorny issue. The Kennedy School faculty members who advocated policy management were interested in formulating original policy based on values they held. The question this raised was a serious one, because once they entered the world of "my value, what I feel, how the world should be a better place," they could make mistakes, and those mistakes could be profoundly costly to ordinary people. They could argue the opposite, and say how profoundly beneficial, but there was influence with no responsibility, as they were the analysts, not the public officials. Schelling believed there must be an objective justification for what analysts do, not a subjective sense of what would be right.

There was one meeting in particular where the differences were made clear. Reich and some others were presenting papers. Reich's paper was a challenge to cost-benefit analysis, and he used a story about building a bridge from the mainland to an island to make his point. He said one might find that cost-benefit analysis led to the conclusion that the bridge to the island should not be built, because when all the calculations were done, the cost of the bridge exceeded the expected benefits from traffic back and forth. But the analysis, Reich went on, was faulty. He said that once that bridge was built, the islanders and mainlanders, instead of being separate people with nothing to do with each other, would be integrated. The forecast use of the bridge was based on surveys and demand analysis prior to its building, and would give an inaccurate measure of the bridge's true benefit. The mainlanders and the islanders would be different people after that bridge was built, they'd be a different community. And if you believe in community, you should build the bridge, no matter what cost-benefit analysis concluded.

A professor who attended the meeting remembers what came next. "I remember Tom going apoplectic. I mean, he was animated and vituperative in his rejection, and he used the word 'fascistic.' He said something like, 'If you think like that, you can get any conclusion you like. You start out thinking the world would be a better place with the island and the mainland connected. You ignore the evidence on the expressed demand of the people who were there, saying they'll be different people after the fact. Well, who are you? You just overruled those people in the interest of some vision. Well, that's a way of thinking about acting publicly that can justify anything.'"[151]

CHAPTER 24

LIFE CHANGES

The changing and continuing charac- ter of Schelling's work was apparent in his 1984 book *Choice and Consequence*. The book addressed a variety of topics that require choice and have consequences, including self-command, game theory, and arms control. Without pass-

Schelling in center with sons, left to right, Daniel, Robert, Tommy, Andrew.

ing value judgments, it also presented choices as economic questions, such as whether the poor should have the right to fly in second-class airplanes and waive the safety regulations. Is the "pricelessness" of human life that requires such attention to air safety really a program for the rich by the rich, one that requires others to accept the value they place on life?

Schelling's family life changed along with his professional life. His boys grew up and went their own ways. Andrew had developed an interest in Sanskrit and Sanskrit poetry while attending the University of California at Santa Cruz and turned it into a career. He began translating poems for publication and writing poetry of his own. He eventually settled in Boul- der, Colorado, where he taught at the alternative Zen-based school, Naropa University. Young Tom was the first of the boys to marry and give Schelling a grandchild. He made a career of building maintenance.

Daniel decided to study ethnomusicology and went to Harvard, where he was required to take a science course. He chose geology, and discovered his true interest. After earning his PhD, he accepted a position at the Uni- versity of Utah in their soft mineral research center, doing mineral explo- ration for governments around the world. Robert's interest in art and sculpture showed up early, and he attended woodworking school in an old warehouse in rural Massachusetts. He later moved to California, where he did an apprenticeship, learning to do finishing stages of bronze sculpture, then began doing his own abstract bronze work. Back in Massachusetts he leased space with other artists to put on rotating shows to sell their work.

As his sons were growing up and moving off on their own, Schelling's marriage was failing, and some of his friends could see the signs. Corinne was an excellent cook, and the Schellings hosted occasional dinner parties. The gatherings were always wonderful intellectual occasions, but some got the feeling Tom was never really happy about them, that he was in Corinne's domain, adopting his wife's mode of behavior. He was happy to have friends there and enjoyed the discussions, but there was no sense of fun. After 40 years, he and Corinne were no longer right for each other. Tom made up his mind to bring it to a conclusion.

The time had come . . . He was going to marry his longtime secretary and friend, Alice Coleman. He went to his close friends at the Kennedy School to tell them about his decision. Francis Bator recalls that Schelling came to his office and closed the door, then said, "I want to tell you about something. You're the first person I wanted to tell." Bator was a friend of all three—Tom, Corinne, and Alice. Richard Zeckhauser remembers the day he heard the news. He was in his office on the telephone talking to the refrigerator repairman about a missed appointment, when Schelling knocked on the door. He waved for Schelling to come in, gesturing for him not to speak. After hanging up, Zeckhauser apologized, then Schelling said he had some news: He and Corinne were getting divorced. Zeckhauser was embarrassed and had started saying he was "so sorry" and offering similar other condolences when Schelling said, "There's a woman I've known for 25 years," adding, "You know her." Utterly confused, Zeckhauser was trying to think of people they'd known that many years when Schelling said "Alice Coleman" and described his feelings for her. Divorce proceedings were initiated in 1989, but it was a long process. Tom and Alice made their breaks and moved in together, but nothing could be finalized.

As the 1989–1990 school year drew to a close, Schelling ended his career at Harvard. He was nearing 70, Harvard's mandatory retirement age. Robert Putnam became dean of the Kennedy School Schelling's final year there and was not happy to see him leave. He recalls, "Tom was easily the most senior figure here, the 'go-to guy' in tough situations, to use American sports jargon. This was true of purely intellectual issues, of course, but it was also true of personal and collegial matters. For someone of extraordinary intellectual power and productivity in a profession that is notoriously competitive and impersonal, Tom was amazingly and refreshingly concerned about his colleagues' personal needs."[152]

It might have been time to move on, he thought, as younger academics were joining the faculty, and he wanted to keep working full time. There could have eventually been a less comfortable relationship between Schelling and the dean if he had stayed. Putnam only stayed a year, and the old-timers, Richard Neustadt, Bator, and Schelling had been called on for advice by Derek Bok as he sought a replacement. Bator and Schelling wanted Al Carnesale. Joseph Nye was also on the list, and was aware of their preferences, that both were less interested in him. Several years later he became the dean. Nye and Schelling had both been at Harvard for years and respected each other, so the preference for Carnesale might not have been a factor. Still, things were changing at the school and working in a new environment wasn't an unpleasant prospect.

While he could have remained at Harvard in some emeritus or part-time position, Schelling wasn't ready to slow down, and there were schools that saw Harvard's mandatory-retirement policy as a way to latch on to highly qualified and recognized older faculty. Schelling received offers from both the University of California at Los Angeles and UC Irvine, followed by an offer from the University of Maryland in College Park.

A former colleague, Michael Nacht, was dean of the School of Public Affairs at Maryland, and the chairman of the Economics Department there had been Schelling's teaching assistant in the 1960s. Alice's elderly father lived in New York, so Maryland would be much closer to him than California. Schelling found Washington professionally interesting, so he accepted the Maryland position. At his new school he would continue teaching "Conflict, Cooperation, and Strategy" and offer a course in "applied economics." He could also continue with his academic research and writing.

He and Alice had married in 1991 and settled down in the Washington suburb of Bethesda, Maryland. They moved into a comfortable two-story brick home with a wooded backyard and gardens for Alice to tend. Schelling recalls, "My most serious regret is that Alice and I should have gotten divorced and married a few years earlier than we did."[153] It was soon apparent to his friends what a change the marriage made in Schelling, how much happier he became, how his intellectual qualities hadn't changed but his personality had. Daniel Ellsberg liked Corinne, but said that with her there was a tension. With Alice, Schelling was looser, more relaxed—just happier. In the words of Richard Zeckhauser, their relationship is "a remarkable thing to see."

Schelling led a busy professional life after leaving Harvard, both at the University of Maryland and beyond, and he was content. His ideas and insight remain in demand; he recently served on a National Academy of Sciences panel studying the threat of smallpox as a terrorist weapon. He pointed out that it had elements of "mutually assured destruction," since once released, it would be out of control and could return to destroy those who released it.

Tom and Alice Schelling at Nobel ceremony

He continued to publish, at times exhibiting the special Schelling genius and confidence that he had said things correctly which Mort Halperin had observed during their years together at Harvard. Siddharth Mohandas recalls one such occasion: "As an editor at *Foreign Affairs*, I had my own experience with Tom Schelling's mastery of strategy. He had submitted a piece to the magazine on handling global climate change and I was assigned to edit it. Like many of the draft articles *Foreign Affairs* receives, Schelling's article was filled with interesting insights but was somewhat technical in its expression of them. Accordingly, I edited the piece to excise it of jargon and to render the prose as accessible as possible to a general audience, without compromising the arguments it contained. I sent the piece back to Schelling explaining that this was standard practice at the magazine and that I would be happy to discuss any of the edits with him. I also mentioned that we were on a fairly tight production schedule and so I needed to hear from him in the next few days.

"Three days passed and I heard nothing. So I called and left a message at his office explaining that we were going to press in a week and that I needed to discuss the article with him. Two more days passed without a response, so I called and left another message. Another two days passed and, growing increasingly panicked, I called his home number and left a message with his wife. Finally, the next day I received a phone call from Schelling in which he flatly informed me, 'I didn't like your changes.' Moreover, he explained that we could pretty much take the article in its original form or withdraw it. With only a few days left to our press deadline, we were in no position to sub in another article. In the end, Schelling's article was published with only minor revisions.

"What made the situation hilarious in retrospect was that it dawned on me that Schelling had employed a gambit straight out of *The Strategy of Conflict*: cutting off communication to prevent further bargaining. ("An asymmetry in communications may well favor the one who is unavailable for the receipt of messages, for he cannot be deterred from his own commitment by the receipt of the other's," p. 26) Schelling had played me like a violin. All in all, the episode only increased my respect for the man: he practices what he preaches!"[154]

CHAPTER 25

TABOO

What's so astonishing about the last 60 years? What's the most important event that didn't happen? Sixty years, four months, day before yesterday, Hiroshima was bombed. Sixty years, four months ago tomorrow, Nagasaki was bombed. There has been no use of nuclear weapons in anger in warfare in over 60 years.

Nobody in 1945, 1950, 1955 or 1960 could ever possibly have had any confidence or any belief even that we would complete the century with no more use of nuclear weapons—even though nuclear weapons have been acquired by at least eight nations since then. In 1960, the renowned novelist C.P. Snow was quoted on the front page of the New York Times, and saying if the nuclear-armed powers do not drastically disarm promptly, intercontinental thermonuclear war within the decade is a mathematical certainty.

Well, that decade has been compounded four and a half times and no nuclear war. Is this a matter of good luck? Was it inevitable? Was it a result of wise policy or even unwise policy? How did it happen that we got through 60 years and no nuclear weapons used? There have been tens of thousands of nuclear weapons. Nuclear weapons have been stationed in Greece and Turkey during times of upheaval. Nuclear weapons have been carted around the United States in jeeps, not recently but back in the early days. Nuclear weapons didn't even have—U.S. nuclear weapons—didn't even have combination locks on them to keep a stolen weapon from being detonated. How did we go through 60 years?

∼

These were the introductory words to Schellings's address, "An Astonishing Sixty Years," delivered in Stockholm, Sweden, on December 8, 2005. The occasion was the Nobel Lecture, given two days before he received his award as Nobel Prize in Economics for 2005. He was speaking on a concept he had introduced 10 years earlier in a Distinguished Scholar-Teacher Lecture at the University of Maryland marking the 50th anniversary of the dropping of atomic bombs on Hiroshima and Nagasaki. The argument he had developed is that the world has become protected in part by what he described as a "taboo" on the use of nuclear weapons that has grown increasingly strong over the years; and while there is no way to be sure, there is reason to believe that as new countries acquire nuclear weapons, the taboo will continue to be respected. It is a topic he has written and spoken about often and that he sees as a source of some optimism for the future.

Webster's defines "taboo" a number of ways, among them, "banned as constituting a risk," "a prohibition imposed by social custom," and "banned on grounds of morality or taste." The word was introduced to the English-speaking world by the great English sea captain James Cook following a visit to Tonga in 1771. Cook noted that the Polynesians had a term to describe certain actions or possessions that were prohibited as violations of something sacred or as defiling, and the violations of the prohibitions would bring about some untold serious retribution. Those actions were so wrong that one didn't even consider doing them or possessing what was "taboo." Schelling's use of the word is closer to Cook's meaning. In his Nobel speech he said, "A taboo is not merely a prohibition, but it's a prohibition that people feel is somehow if not supernaturally at least enforceable by some kind of super human power."

He presents his case for the taboo with a discussion of its evolution, focusing on U.S. policy, then expanding to the wider world of the present. Nuclear weapons were an option five years after Hiroshima in the Korean War, first when North Korea had South Korean and American troops nearly forced off the peninsula and isolated in Pusan, where it appeared they would be unable to survive or be evacuated. British Prime Minister Clement Atlee flew to the United States to convince President Truman to refrain from using nuclear weapons, but MacArthur's Inchon landing turned the situation around and forced the North Koreans to retreat. A second possibility came in Korea when the United States made what Schelling describes as "what I think was the most unwise military decision that any American ever made," bringing China into the war by pushing too close to the Chinese border. Using nuclear weapons against battlefield targets or using them against targets in China were both options rejected by Truman.

When Eisenhower became president in 1953 and agreed with Secretary of State John Foster Dulles that the distinction between nuclear and non-nuclear weapons was false, a new chapter in international relations was opened. The issue of whether nuclear weapons were conventional took on new significance for Eisenhower during the escalation of tension between Taiwan and mainland China. The issue centered on two small islands, Quemoy and Matsu, that Taiwan controlled and China wanted.

The United States was bound by treaty to regard an attack on Taiwan as an attack on the United States. Chiang Kai-shek, in a move that invites game theorists' envy for its strategic use of "commitment," moved half of Taiwan's army to Quemoy without first notifying the United States. If China attacked the small island, it could wipe out half Taiwan's forces, leaving Taiwan incapable of defending itself. That raised the stakes from a squabble over the little island of Quemoy to the survival of Taiwan, to which the United States was committed. Eisenhower responded by sending nuclear artillery to Taiwan. The Chinese didn't challenge to see whether Eisenhower was bluffing. Eisenhower's comment at the time was that he could see no reason nuclear weapons shouldn't be used "exactly as you would use a bullet or anything else."

John F. Kennedy found nuclear weapons repulsive, especially after the Cuban crisis, and Lyndon Johnson said, early in his presidency, "Make no mistake, there is no such thing as a conventional nuclear weapon. For nineteen peril-filled years, no nation has loosed the atom against another. To do so now is a political decision of the highest order." The taboo was emerging. Schelling says, "I think Lyndon Johnson, in mentioning nineteen peril-filled years, felt that somehow incredibly, the world has survived nineteen years after Hiroshima and Nagasaki with no nuclear weapons used. And I think he took that as a powerful precedent or tradition that nuclear weapons were not to be used lightly, maybe not at all, except in the direst circumstances."

Schelling offers examples where nuclear weapons could have been used but weren't, as the taboo became well-established. In 1973, Israel had two Egyptian armies isolated in the desert where there were no civilians, and it was not certain Israel would be able to hold off their attack. The target seemed ideal, but the taboo had stretched to 28 years by then and Israel didn't violate it. Schelling offers a possibility for Prime Minister Golda Meir's restraint that twists the taboo slightly into something more calculating, when he adds, "I have a hunch she thought sooner or later, we're going to face enemies who have nuclear weapons, maybe in the long run the taboo is in our favor; maybe it would be wrong to break the taboo now because a generation from now who knows how many of our inimical neighbors will have acquired nuclear weapons? And if we break the taboo, they may not feel the taboo."

Richard Nixon not using nuclear weapons in Vietnam and Margaret Thatcher not considering their use while defending the Falkland Islands against Argentina are examples of the taboo in effect. The Soviet's failure to use nuclear power to stave off humiliation in Afghanistan is evidence that the taboo is real and not just a Western concept. The Soviets of the 1950s would have behaved differently, Schelling suspects, but the taboo against the use of nuclear weapons had become too strong 20 years later. He says, "Where nuclear proliferation begins to frighten us, the remarkable conformity of Soviet and Western ideology is a reassuring point of departure."

Having established the idea and historical background of the taboo, Schelling discusses issues related to it. One that goes back to a time when the taboo concept was only congealing relates to the years Schelling was most influential in policy. He thinks that partly because of Robert McNamara and because of the Cuban Missile Crisis, both Presidents Kennedy and Johnson didn't like nuclear weapons. They turned instead to building up non-nuclear defense capability.

At the time, Soviet policy was that any war in Europe would automatically go nuclear. In spite of that policy, the Soviets followed America's lead with a massive buildup of non-nuclear defense forces. It was the signaling and unspoken agreement Schelling so often spoke of, and it was serving to secure the taboo. He says, "I consider this—that is the Soviet tacit collaboration in what I would call an unacknowledged arms control understanding, namely, let's both sides build up conventional forces so if there is a war, it doesn't need to go nuclear—I consider that probably, next to the Anti-Ballistic Treaty, the most important arms control we ever had between East and West, but it was never acknowledged as arms control."

Schelling comments on the taboo and its relationship to Hiroshima by quoting Alvin Weinberg, who was in charge of the Oak Ridge National Laboratory when it was producing the uranium for one of the first two bombs. On the 40th anniversary of Hiroshima, Weinberg commented, "Are we witnessing a gradual sanctification of Hiroshima, that is the elevation of the Hiroshima event to the status of a profoundly mystical event?" He described the worldwide attention and emotional involvement the commemoration brought out. Schelling says the 50th anniversary wasn't quite the same, and of the 60th anniversary, "I don't see anything." He thinks it is because the memory was real to people on the 40th, but there are no longer so many people who know Hiroshima as a real event from their lifetimes.

That is what raises the question of whether the taboo will survive in a world where the use of the atom bomb fades into memory and nuclear proliferation alters the scene. He expresses optimism about India and Pakistan. They have had nuclear weapons for a decade and have been concerned with nuclear weapons policy much longer. Both have been active in arms-control conferences and in the literature. At his 2003 lecture when he received his honorary doctorate from Erasmus University Rotterdam,

Schelling said the world could expect the Indian and Pakistani leaders to be adequately in awe of the nuclear weapons they both possessed. This was the case because there were "two helpful possibilities. One is that they share the inhibition—appreciate the taboo . . . The other is that they will recognize, as the United States and the Soviet Union did, that the prospect of nuclear retaliation makes any initiation of nuclear war nearly unthinkable. The risk is that one or the other may confront the kind of military emergency that invites some limited experiment with the weapons, and there is no history to tell us, or them, what happens next."

Schelling isn't quite as optimistic about the emerging nuclear powers, but he isn't totally pessimistic either. He says he has "a strong hunch that Iran is going to get nuclear weapons, and North Korea is going to get nuclear weapons. And the question is will they be as awed by these 60 years without a nuclear event, will they be as awed as Alvin Weinberg was at the Biblical quality of the Hiroshima event? Will they feel the taboo—the one that John Foster Dulles wished to get rid of but couldn't because you can often get rid of a convention that's written on paper, you can burn the paper, but it's very hard to get rid of the convention that's in everybody's mind?"

There aren't indications North Koreans or Iranians have inculcated the taboo, and he cites Iran President Mahmoud Ahmadinejad's call to wipe Israel off the map as evidence. Schelling pointed out the MAD nature of the call, how it would be national suicide for Iran to consider the use of nuclear weapons against Israel. He believes it may be important to help them think in those terms: "I think we want the Iranians to learn to think in terms of deterrence. What else can Iran accomplish, except possibly the destruction of its own system, with a few nuclear warheads? Nuclear warheads should be too precious to give away or to sell, too precious to 'waste' killing people when they could, held in reserve, make the United States, or Russia, or any other nation, hesitant to consider military action. What nuclear weapons have been used for, effectively, for 60 years has not been on the battlefield nor on populations; they have been used for influence."

He also makes the point that if Iran develops nuclear weapons, the United States should assist the Iranians in making sure their weapons are secure in any time of disruption. With the uncertainty of riots in the streets or civil war, there must be safeguards on who gains access to and control of them.

Schelling makes a powerful, yet somewhat unsettling, point about getting Iran and North Korea to recognize the taboo when he says, "In all these 60 peril-filled years, nuclear weapons were used to deter enemies, not to destroy them. And I think we want the Iranians individually with North Koreans, to learn to think deterrence. Now that may not be comfortable for Americans because who are they going to deter? Us. We're going to be on the deterred end."

Deterrence, a favorite Schelling topic, had been relegated to a thing of the past in some people's minds since the end of the Cold War. He believes that's not the case, as new countries acquire nuclear weapons. He says: "The era of deterrence is still here because we're going to be deterred by the Iranians if they get nuclear weapons; we're going to be deterred by the North Koreans, if they get nuclear weapons. And it may well be that the North Koreans want nuclear weapons to make sure that the United States never participates in military aggression against North Korea. And I think if we can find any way to assure them that they don't have to worry about that, maybe they won't so badly need nuclear weapons."

Schelling also deals with the taboo and its meaningfulness in many people's nightmare scenario: terrorists acquiring nuclear weapons. "Terrorists can't be deterred anyway—we don't know what they value that we might threaten, or who or where it (what they value) is," he notes. Again he is not very "doomsday" and sees the taboo as offering an element of hope. While deterrence may continue as a dominant force prolonging the taboo between nation-states, the question becomes what reinforces the taboo with terrorists.

Nathan Gardels, editor of *New Perspectives Quarterly*, put the question to him in an interview shortly after the announcement of his being awarded the Nobel Prize: With the al-Qa'idas or Aum Shinrikyos, whom Gardels described as either nihilists or making their calculations in some metaphysical realm, was there anything to prevent them from ignoring the taboo and using nuclear weapons?

Schelling's response was, "I don't know if deterrence fits somehow into their metaphysics, but these groups are not likely to have much physical competence. Aum Shinrikyo did a lousy job of trying to poison people in the subway. They don't strike me as the kind of people who could put together a nuclear weapon if they had the fissile material. They might not be able to recognize if fissile material bought on the black market was really any good. Most terrorist groups would have a hard time finding people who actually have the technical competence in making a bomb who would be willing to devote themselves to doing so—going off into seclusion, leaving their jobs and families for long periods and risk, in the end, being vilified as the bomb builder. It is simply too hard to recruit topflight scientists, engineers and machinists needed to do the job. And if they were able to do that, they would have put together an intellectual team that would have a hard time submitting to terrorist goals. Once such a group managed to put together a bomb, they would likely find it too precious to use and instead try to leverage influence from its threatened use." They could use their weapons more effectively for influence than for pure destruction: "Even terrorists may consider destroying large numbers of people and structures less satisfying than keeping a major nation at bay." So he sees hope for the taboo surviving, but again with the unsettling condition that "we may have to get used to being influenced by people we don't like who have nuclear weapons."

For the taboo to continue, Schelling believes the United States must play a leading role and that it hasn't played that role ideally. He says that "a big issue for the United States government is whether it considers what Foster Dulles called the taboo to be in the American interest or not. America is rich in nuclear weapons and I imagine that somebody like the President of the United States or the Secretary of Defense feels that if we've got all of these nuclear weapons, we've invested so much in the nuclear weapons, we have so much intellectual experience in how to use nuclear weapons, it would be a shame to be unable to use them when it may appear to become necessary.

"I would somewhat prefer they think . . . we are so rich in people and structures and culture, that it would be a shame to have some of that destroyed by other people's nuclear weapons. And maybe it's in our interest, I hope they will think, to preserve this taboo, do what we can to maintain the notion that any nation that ever introduces nuclear weapons is likely to incur the hostility of the rest of the world, may even be denied sovereignty by the rest of the world."

The United States began to undermine to taboo to some degree when the Senate failed to ratify the Comprehensive Test Ban Treaty in 1999. The treaty would have made it illegal to test nuclear weapons of any size anywhere, whether underground on land, at sea, or in space. President Clinton signed the treaty, and on September 22, 1997, submitted it to the Senate. He asked for Senate approval in his State of the Union addresses in both 1998 and 1999, but Senator Jesse Helms, chairman of the Senate Foreign Relations Committee, described it as a low priority, that the treaty "from a non-proliferation standpoint, is scarcely more than a sham." The vote finally came in October 1999, and the treaty failed by a 48-51 vote.

Schelling considers this unfortunate: "I know of no argument in favor of the Comprehensive Test Ban Treaty, which the U. S. Senate rejected in 1999, more powerful than the potential of that treaty to enhance the nearly universal revulsion against nuclear weapons. The symbolic effect . . . should add enormously to the convention that nuclear weapons are not to be used and that any nation that does use nuclear weapons will be judged the violator of a hard-earned tradition of non-use. When the Treaty is again before the Senate, as I hope it will be, this major benefit should not go unrecognized." In his Nobel address he put it, "I think symbolically the treaty was going to be an act by 180 nations to say nuclear weapons are under a curse. We don't want them even tested. I think it was an opportunity for the U.S. Senate to participate in making nuclear weapons a pariah."

Schelling also faults the talk about nuclear weapons and their use that has emerged from the Bush administration as a U.S. practice that doesn't buttress the taboo. He suggested to the Nobel audience that the United States should "play down its interest in developing some new kinds of nuclear weapons. We hear about the Bush administration's interest in developing some nuclear weapons that can penetrate deep into the soil, where they might, if they explode, vaporize and destroy chemical weapons or biological weapons and so forth . . . And not talk about their freedom to use nuclear weapons whenever it becomes militarily expedient, because I think our strongest hope to avoid having nuclear weapons used against any of us, Swedes or Americans, is to have countries like North Korea or Iran know that Lyndon Johnson's 19 peril-filled years have become 60 years and maybe then 70 years, and any use of nuclear weapons will be severely castigated."

His taboo argument is comforting, as it holds out hope for a more peaceful world, especially to those who grew up during the Cold War. The "inevitability" of nuclear annihilation no longer hangs over the general public. Maryland professor George Quester, writing in *The Naval War College Review*, concluded that the chances are as high as three out of five that there will be no nuclear weapon used by the year 2045, marking a century without use. Yet he says that both ordinary citizens and analysts around the world find his estimate too optimistic.

The taboo raises questions and brings comments from a range of observers, which both challenge and reinforce Schelling's views. Observations fall at times into issues of the nature of the taboo itself. Is what Schelling describes really a taboo, and does a taboo on military weapons have historical precedents? Another category is the taboo in practical politics, and how it has affected the relationship between nuclear and non-nuclear powers. The question of what can be done to strengthen the taboo, and what is not being done, is also in the literature. Dealing with changing technologies and with difficult-to-deter adversaries, especially terrorists, and how the taboo is involved is another topic. Also discussed is whether the taboo can remain if a nuclear weapon is ever used.

The question of whether a taboo as described by Schelling is a reality was addressed by Verna Gehring of the Institute for Philosophy and Public Policy at the University of Maryland. Gehring makes a distinction between "local" and "universal" taboos, the latter being self-evident and not requiring individual consideration in making a decision. Incest is one such taboo, whereas local taboos are specific to a culture or place. Consideration of the action is part of the prohibition in the universal taboo.

After Hiroshima and Nagasaki came the birth of the nuclear taboo, but strategist Paul Nitze is cited as having argued that conventional weapons could achieve what nuclear weapons could, negating their necessity. Gehring states that, "If attitudes are measured by actions not words, then nuclear policy makers have no taboo on nuclear warfare." She goes on to describe the continued buildup of the American arsenal and various Defense Department plans over the years.

She also considers the use of nuclear weapons as symbols of status and as bargaining chips as contradictions of the taboo. In an unflattering evaluation of Schelling's perception of the congealed taboo, she comments, "Professor Schelling asks why we should not consider conventional the nuclear bomb of no greater ordinance than in current use . . . In this intuitive acceptance of nuclear weapons as 'unconventional' or 'different,' Professor Schelling looks for ethical justification from nuclear warfare, which would warrant his optimism for a continued ban." The issue she raises is that there are such powerful non-nuclear bombs for certain uses that could also be achieved by nuclear bombs of low yield, why continue to regard all nuclear bombs as special, as Schelling does.

Gehring notes that, in Polynesia, taboo had a second use that applies more appropriately to the nuclear taboo and may serve to encourage its survival. This was when things usually taboo were permitted in extraordinary circumstances if devoted to a special purpose: "There is good reason to believe that atomic weapons are taboo in this second sense. That is, some taboos restrict actions and objects for devoted use." Such words are quite an enabling step from Schelling's idea that, "A taboo is not merely a prohibition, but it's a prohibition that people feel is somehow if not supernaturally at least enforceable by some kind of super human power." It is somewhat of a slippery-slope definition.

The sort of taboo that allows "devoted use" might come into play if the leadership of al-Qa'ida or some other such group were located, buried deep in an underground bunker where they might be thought to possess a stockpile of biological weapons, or worse. Such a situation might lend legitimacy to the use of advanced deep-penetration nuclear warheads to be used to dig out and destroy the group and the threat. Following such an event, George Quester, whose experience includes teaching at the U.S. Naval Academy and the Department of Military Strategy, says the world would be "less likely to condemn, and more likely to applaud, the next use of nuclear weapons if it preempted and headed off a WMD attack against a major population center."

But breaking the 60-year taboo in such circumstances raises other questions. The frequently discussed use of weapons of mass destruction by terrorists has occurred less than the amount of words spoken about it might lead one to believe. There was anthrax in letters to public figures, the Aum Shinrikyo cult in Tokyo did use sarin gas. The distance from September 11 grows, and the next use of a weapon of mass destruction still looms in people's minds, even as some ask why an attack hasn't come. The CIA reports that analysis of an al-Qa'ida document recovered in Afghanistan in the summer of 2002 indicates the group has procedures for making mustard agent, as well as the deadly nerve agents, sarin, and VX. The Mayo Clinic says chemical weapons are "relatively easy to produce," including one of the most deadly of all, ricin, "a poison which is produced from castor bean plants relatively easily and inexpensively in great quantities." The plant is grown worldwide, and no antidote or vaccine for it is available.

D.A. Henderson of The Johns Hopkins University notes that the number of countries engaged in biological weapons experimentation has increased from four in the 1960s to 11 in the 1990s, and those organisms are now around. He adds ominously, "Recipes for making biological weapons are now available on the Internet, and even groups with modest finances and basic training in biology and engineering could develop, should they wish, an effective weapon at little cost." Anthrax, he cites as an example, "is easy to produce in large quantity."

With all this apparent opportunity, why haven't terrorists sought to make more use of weapons of mass destruction? It could be they've also been affected by a taboo. Perhaps they hope to become the government at some point and have been following certain social and cultural norms. Since governments haven't used chemical and biological weapons (or, when they did, their own people suffered horrifically), terrorists would not use them either, or so one theory goes. Perhaps using nuclear weapons in the "devoted use" circumstances described above (on the assumption that the enemy would do so, given the decline in confidence in accurate intelligence) would open the door to an era that couldn't be closed when no longer necessary.

A contrary view is that of Stuart Meyer of Northwestern University, who believes Schelling was incorrect in saying that terrorists can't be deterred. He uses conflict-theory references in saying he suspects Schelling would agree that a way to gain advantage in a "game" is to relax presumed constraints on one side. It is this that he says has "given Islamo-terrorism such power." Meyer supports as the game equalizer Representative Tom Tancredo's (R.-Colo.) suggestion that if a Western center is destroyed by Islamists, the centers of Islam in Mecca and Medina would be forfeited. Tancredo's suggestion of bombing the Muslim holy sites if Islamist terrorists attack the United States again earned him a considerably different response from *Esquire*, where he was named one of the recipients of the magazine's "2005 Dubious Achievements Awards." The heading for the Tancredo's "Achievement" read: "WELL, OUR NEXT THOUSAND YEARS ARE COMING TOGETHER QUITE NICELY."

The suggestion sounds like the surest way to guarantee that, should one more Osama get past the security barriers of the United States, there will be unlimited terrorists for the foreseeable future who would be bound by no taboo at all.

There have been other taboos. In World War II, chemical warfare was avoided, and there was an aversion to biological warfare. Naval forces have avoided confrontations on the high seas for much of the latter 20th century, except during the Falklands War. Nuclear proliferation is seen as something of a taboo. Violations of these taboos may be instructive, in that when they happened they didn't become widespread. What would follow a violation of the nuclear taboo is unknown, but the question is whether the taboo could be restored.

Other than not having a nuclear war, the taboo has had other effects. It has helped maintain a stable mutual deterrence between nuclear powers. Between nuclear and non-nuclear states there has been an erosion of deterrent power for nuclear states, as their threat or implied threat to use their weapons against a non-nuclear adversary has lost credibility. The nuclear taboo and the non-proliferation norm have been mutually reinforcing. An article in *The Naval War College Review* states, "The fact that nuclear weapons remained in the hands of a very small number of states in the 1940s and 1950s, combined with an emerging taboo, helped to prevent the normalization of nuclear arms. The stigmatization of nuclear weapons, in turn, facilitated creation of the nonproliferation norm by the mid-1960s."

Maintaining the taboo is a common concern. A worry for some in recent times has been that the United States appears to be attempting to shift the discourse on nuclear weapons; at times, policy appears to imply that the taboo doesn't apply to nuclear weapons themselves but rather to who has them. Jonathan Medalia, writing in *Arms Control Today,* describes the taboo on use of weapons as strong, but in danger for reasons touched on by Schelling. The day approaches when there will be no one alive who was a victim of Hiroshima and the after-affects, no one who will remember seeing the first photos of the victims. The numbers of those who remember the testing programs of the 1950s and 1960s is dwindling, and Medalia adds that with the ban on nuclear testing that made the weapons real, some of the horror has been lost.

In remarks to the Carnegie International Non-Proliferation Conference, Nina Tannenwald of Brown University's Watson Institute for International Studies adds that there is a lack of a widespread grassroots anti-nuclear movement today. She notes that there is really very little domestic cost to the administration for its failure to appreciate the taboo's importance and adopt new nuclear weapons policies.

In addition to their potential use by India, Pakistan, North Korea, Iran, and terrorists, some see threats to the taboo as having surfaced elsewhere. The U.S. interest in building new generations of nuclear weapons, the failure of the Non-Proliferation Treaty, and Russia's return to greater reliance on nuclear weapons all receive attention. Russia announced a new nuclear weapons doctrine at the beginning of 2000 that replaced the previous policy of nuclear arms use only "in case of a threat to the existence of the Russian Federation." The policy now authorizes use of nuclear weapons in war "if all other means of resolving the crisis have been exhausted."

How this threatens the taboo is described in a *Nuclear Press* story, where Schelling's *Arms and Influence* of 1966 was quoted to analyze Vladimir Putin's contemporary position: "If one is repeatedly challenged, or expected to be, by an opponent who wishes to impose dominance or to cause one's allies to abandon him in disgust, the choice is between an appreciable loss and a fairly aggressive response." The story continued: "Strategist Thomas Schelling could have been writing about Russia today. With NATO at its national borders, entangled in a counterinsurgency war in Chechnya which it probably cannot win, on the verge of economic, political and social collapse, Russia is itching to lash out at its enemies."

The relationship of the taboo to non-proliferation and the failures of the Non-Proliferation Treaty is another danger. The idea of nuclear weapons being taboo is basic to non-proliferation and essential to prohibiting their spread. If the spread can only be maintained by threat of force, the challenge is daunting. When nuclear weapons are believed to be truly illegitimate—an inhuman taboo—and that belief has become internalized, then non-proliferation is more hopeful.

The Non-Proliferation Treaty, took effect in 1970 and has 187 signatories, from the original nuclear powers all the way to The Vatican. The world's holdouts are India, Pakistan, Israel, Cuba, and North Korea, who withdrew in 2003. America's support has been central to its success, which has led to some concern in its 2006 dealings with India. Strobe Talbott of The Brookings Institution criticized a non-proliferation policy that "cuts extra slack for 'good' countries, like India, while cracking down on 'bad' ones—in other words, rogue states like North Korea and Iran." He observes there are many "good ones" that may be tempted to regard the treaty as an anachronism now that India has America's approval. "What both the Indian and American governments hailed as a breakthrough in relations between the two countries is a step toward a breakdown in the international non-proliferation regime," Talbot concludes. His views were echoed in editorial comment in United States and abroad.

For the taboo to survive, what has been suggested beyond Schelling's strong view that the United States ratify the Comprehensive Test Ban Treaty and avoid new roles for nuclear weapons in America's defensive posture? Tannenwald, among others, has suggested a declared "no-first use" policy as one step. Tannenwald says that policy-making on nuclear weapons must be democratized to encourage internalization of the taboo, and she suggests the creation of a government agency to show concern with control of the use of such weapons. She laments the demise of the Bureau of Arms Control, and asks, "Why not a Bureau of the Nuclear Taboo?" Questions should be posed publicly to policy makers whether the taboo is in the U.S. self-interest.

Another suggestion for maintaining the taboo is to refine its definition. In this view, there would be categories of violation should a nuclear device be used. One such proposal suggests that a "garbage bomb," a conventional attack on a nuclear power plant, be defined away as a non-violation of the taboo, keeping the taboo alive. With the use of nuclear weapons where there are few civilian casualties and targets are strictly military, the taboo might be restated as acceptable in certain instances (devoted uses), while other uses remain taboo. Where there is destructive nuclear escalation by a "rogue state," the world might be mobilized to punish that state. "The beneficial result might be a nuclear taboo renewed by experience rather than erased. It may be very important to seek to convey that the use of nuclear weapons did not reward the perpetrator," according to the Congressional Research Brief for Congress, "Nuclear Weapons: Comprehensive Test Ban Treaty."

With all the concerns and commentary, it remains clear that the nuclear taboo is one of the pillars of nuclear restraint. It is a glimmer of hope in a world where hope is often difficult to find. It looks for the civilizing element in us. Schelling's presentations of this very serious idea were never done before a more distinguished and intellectual audience than in Sweden in December 8, 2005. But even in his presentation as a new Nobel laureate, receiving the highest academic recognition possible, he was still Tom Schelling, with a twinkle in his eye and a serious message to convey—but delivering it with a very human touch. No erudite lecture for him, as he introduced the discussion of Soviet conventional arms build-up with the words, "Now the silly thing is," and described the U.S. Army's approach near the Chinese border during the Korean War with, "And you can't say, well, we crossed the Yellow and just marched 50 miles into China. What the hell is 50 miles?" His informality and the charm of his spontaneity only serve to strengthen his believability.

The taboo developed when Schelling was involved in his most important roles as a strategist. His deterrent strategies were basic to breathing life into the taboo and giving it time to grow, when the use of nuclear weapons was on everyone's mind. When asked what part he played in it, he is his usual modest self, saying, "I get a lot of satisfaction, but I don't think of myself as a particular hero. I think there were a lot of us who were thinking and writing along the same lines."[155] Those who were thinking along the same lines were the civilian strategists, the elite brotherhood of scholars who influenced policy-makers during history's most dangerous moments, when human survival was at stake.

When he reflects on how the struggle with Russian has gone, he says, "I think it went pretty well. We didn't have a war with them. After 1945 they didn't move anywhere in Europe. I think we may have exaggerated what they could do in places like Africa and Latin America. Compared to how bad things could have gone, things went pretty well."[156] Events like the Cuban Missile Crisis could have lead to something devastating and, "I think the danger of stumbling into a great big war was there up until the mid or late '70s."

Schelling has witnessed the worst of it, the time in America when people lived wrapped up in fear and anger. As others worried, he calmly thought about what needed to be done to keep it all from getting worse. His ability to retain a cool head and make rational decisions at a time when the nation faced real challenges, to see potential questions of survival as puzzles, was a great strength. He had a stoic attitude toward problem-solving that freed him look at questions of thermonuclear war in the same purely analytical fashion as he would look at any other logic problem. Thermonuclear war as a game, played rationally—it was humanity's best hope.

Schelling doesn't question what he did and thought during those dangerous years, nor has he had doubts: "Was I afraid I might be wrong and as a result, some big tragedy would happen? I don't remember being afraid I might be wrong. I don't really remember making recommendations, or implying in my writing things that then or now seem particularly dangerous to me. As I think back, I don't know where I was wrong. I think most of the things I said, if they were influential, it was because they were pretty self-evident, once they were pointed out."[157]

CHAPTER 26

RECOGNITION

In 1991, Schelling was elected president of the American Economics Association. It wasn't a position with great responsibilities, but it was recognition for lifetime achievement and a show of great respect from colleagues in his discipline.

Nineteen ninety-four was the fiftieth anniversary of the publication of *Theory of Games and Economic Behavior* by John von Neumann and Oskar Morgenstern, the book that represented the formal beginning of game theory, and it seemed a fitting year to recognize game theory's importance in the field of economics. While game theory was not traditional economics, the Nobel committee decided it was appropriate to award that year's prize to someone whose work had been in the field. They compiled a list of the leading candidates, ending up with five finalists. Lloyd Shapley's work concerned cooperative game theory, situations where players try to find a solution in their mutual interest. Reinhard Selten concentrated on non-cooperative games and had developed ways to distinguish between reasonable and unreasonable outcomes. John Harsanyi, who also focused on non-cooperative games, had developed ways for analyzing games of incomplete information. John Nash had developed the method for solving non-zero-sum games, or games in which the players' interests are not directly opposite.

The fifth finalist was Tom Schelling. In the theory of games, his most noted contribution was focal-point solutions—the tacit, cooperative efforts to solve problems—making him the only finalist other than Shapely who had concentrated on solutions to games of cooperation. The committee considered him primarily because it was their view that, more than anyone else, Schelling saw how game theory has applications across the spectrum of the social sciences. The committee decided the prize would only be given for theory that concentrated on non-cooperative games, thereby excluding Shapley and Schelling. On October 11, three Nobel Prizes in Economics were given, to John Nash, John Harsanyi, and Reinhard Selten.[158]

There were those both in and outside the academic community who felt Schelling had been unjustly overlooked. *The Washington Post* wrote:

"The task of integrating game theory into popular economics fell to Thomas Schelling, now a professor at the University of Maryland. Schelling found applications for game theory not only in arms control, but in designing environmental regulations, setting criminal penalties and reforming insurance markets—all areas in which the effectiveness of policies is determined in large part by how various parties react to them. Several economists said yesterday that Schelling's name was curiously omitted from the Nobel panel's laureate list."[159]

A stronger statement was made in *The Boston Globe*, in David Warsh's story, "A Phone That Didn't Ring":

> For most consumers of economic knowledge, the phone that didn't ring yesterday morning was perhaps more interesting than the three that did.
>
> Thomas Schelling, 73, didn't win the Nobel Award in Economics, although a sizeable segment of the American community would have preferred he share the honors with one man who did, John Nash of Princeton University. They supported Schelling not for proving any deep mathematical theorem but rather for showing how game theoretic considerations entered into the most mundane corners of everyday life, everything from the "intimate struggle for self-mastery" of the smoker trying to break the habit to the most terrifying considerations of nuclear strategy between superpowers . . .[160]

Schelling was not disappointed. He said, "When they did pick three game theorists, I did not really want to be picked as a game theorist. I consider myself a social scientist and I use a little game theory. If they had picked four instead, including me, I would have always had a hard time explaining what I was doing in that company."[161] He didn't consider himself a game theorist like the others. He said people just hear of him as a game theorist, so they call him one, but he rejects the characterization. It may be that he feels the description of himself as a game theorist inaccurately colors people's views of him, as he is a social scientist who uses game theory along with many other problem-solving skills.

Not considering Schelling a game theorist is no more accurate, though. He says that while some of what he does looks like game theory to people unfamiliar with game theory, much of his most important work is not. He offers as evidence the fact that some of his most important work contains no matrices. "An Essay on Bargaining" had no matrices, nor did his essay on focal points. Although some of his other work did include matrices, he says that his use of them to illustrate certain points doesn't change things: "That's like saying because I use an equal sign, I'm a mathematician."[162] Matrices are a common tool used in game theory, but they are only a tool, not a definition. Most of Schelling's most important work doesn't have a proper name. He refers to it as bargaining theory, though that isn't inclusive enough. Part of his objection can be explained by the fact that much of game theory has focused on zero-sum games, those in which the players' interests are in complete opposition.

Schelling's most productive work has been with cooperative games, games where players are attempting to coordinate their decisions to achieve mutually beneficial goals. Focal-point solutions are examples. Coordination achieved through vicarious thinking is a recurring theme in his work, from signaling during crises and warfare through arms control.

Despite his protests, there can be little doubt that Schelling is a game theorist. By the definition of vicarious problem-solving to optimize outcomes, his work has yielded many valuable insights. Daniel Ellsberg said, "It flatters the field of game theory to include him."[163] It would insult the field to ignore him. What best describes Schelling is both a game-theory user and theorist. He was the one who applied it and made it practical. He also used game theory to illustrate certain of his arguments and strategies and, as in "A Reorientation of Game Theory" in *The Strategy of Conflict,* expanded its theoretical boundaries.

Schelling's nuclear-strategy views received renewed attention in 2001, with the revival of the national debate over a space-based missile defense system. In May of that year, his opinions began showing up frequently. *Newsweek* carried a story on Schelling and his views, written by the editor of the magazine's international edition, Fareed Zakaria. Zakaria's article, "Don't Oversell Missile Defense," began with a recollection of a scene from the Woody Allen film *Annie Hall:* Diane Keaton and Allen are standing in line waiting for a movie behind an overbearing college teacher pontificating about the media guru Marshall McLuhan. Allen finally has too much and walks away—returning with Marshall McLuhan himself, who tells the arrogant professor "you know nothing of my work" and says that it's amazing he's allowed to teach anything.

Zakaria related this movie scene to Schelling, calling him "the Marshall McLuhan of this story, only smarter."[164] The point was that everyone was talking about the missile shield, or space-based missile defense system, as a form of deterrence, and speculating how it would work. It was time to pull out the real father of deterrent strategy and ask him.

Recognition of Schelling's work also came in the form of honorary degrees. He received an honorary doctorate in policy analysis from the

RAND Graduate School and a *doctorate honoris causa* from Erasmus University Rotterdam.

The crowning glory of Schelling's career came on October 10, 2005, when the Swedish Academy of Sciences announced its decision to award the Bank of Sweden Prize in Economic Sciences in Memory of Alfred Nobel—the Nobel Prize in Economics—to Robert Aumann and Thomas Schelling. The two would share the $1.3-million prize. Acknowledgment of the wide-ranging role Schelling has played in contemporary affairs had been formalized.

Aumann's work had been on "infinitely-repeated" games. He studied whether cooperation increased when games are continually repeated. His work has practical applications in explaining why some communities are more successful than others at managing common resources, price wars, and other multi-person problems.

The reception to Schelling winning the Nobel Prize was highly favorable in both the press and weblogs, the few exceptions coming from those who still consider him a "warmonger." University of Maryland Provost William W. Destler voiced a view common of many: "For us, it was never a question of whether Tom would win the Nobel Prize, it was just a matter of when." Typical was the comment of William C. Kirby, dean of the Faculty of Arts and Sciences at Harvard: "His acute understanding of game theory has propelled advances in the field and contributed to our hope for greater safety in the world. We congratulate him on this high honor."

David Henderson wrote in *Commentary*: "Mr. Schelling did it as a true social scientist, with spectacular results. His thinking led to important insights in areas ranging from nuclear war to figuring out meeting places to traffic jams to racial segregation. His specialty was understanding the behavior of real humans, and game theory was one of his tools. But it was just that—a tool."

Schelling thought the award was appropriately divided between a game-theory producer and a game-theory user. His own response to the announcement was a modest happiness: "I'm deeply honored by this recognition. I've been doing this for over 50 years and it's hard to find a shorthand way to describe my interests. But in my mind it all comes together, and what links this work is my fascination with how people react to and influence others—as individuals and as nations."

Following the announcement he was preoccupied, "on the phone, on email, on radio, entertaining TV crews in the living room, even entertaining some people from University of Maryland food service who brought me the Schelling Memorial Cake that they were introducing to their menu."[165] (Double-layer cinnamon-raisin bread, with creamy peanut butter and jelly on one layer, and chunky peanut butter with jelly on the other.) The cake may not be his lasting legacy. Perhaps the most flattering and insightful compliment was one that mentioned that the peace prize and the economics prize could have been awarded to one person, echoed somewhat in Steven Taylor of Troy University's weblog comment: "I would argue Schelling's theories have done more to promote peace than has the IAEA, this year's Peace Prize winner." A warm reception for the man who had said "peace was his profession."

So in December 2005, it was off to Sweden for the ceremonies. The prize itself was the culmination of a long selection process begun more than a year earlier, when the committee in charge decided on a prospective list of about 3,000 nominees, with the Royal Swedish Academy of Sciences responsible for the final choice after an arduous task of evaluating qualifications. Begun by dynamite's inventor Alfred Nobel with funds left in his will, the Nobel Prizes were first awarded in 1901 and, over the years, the recipients have included many of the great figures who have shaped our times. Along with economics, prizes are awarded in medicine, physics, chemistry, peace, and literature, and winners have included such figures as Albert Einstein, Alexander Fleming, Albert Schweitzer, Martin Luther King Jr., Marie Curie, the Dalai Lama, and Winston Churchill, to name but a few. It is an elite fraternity.

The week in Stockholm was filled with speeches by the laureates—Schelling's speech on the "nuclear taboo" among them—and social events, including a banquet at Stockholm's City Hall. "It has been exciting," Schelling said before the main awards ceremony began. "It has been an honor almost overwhelming."

The high point came at the Stockholm Concert Hall, where formal dress—tails for men and gowns for women—was expected. Outside, thousands of people crowded together in the cold Swedish air, hoping to catch a glimpse of the winners. Ninety people sat onstage, with King Carl XVI Gustaf in a tuxedo and his wife, Queen Silvia, in a blue gown and a crown.

Four people presented the accomplishments of the various winners. Schelling was introduced by Jorgen Weibull, a member of the Royal Swedish Academy of Sciences and chairman of the Economics Prize Committee. He spoke of Schelling's accomplishments, concluding: "It is an honor and a privilege to convey to you, on behalf of the Royal Swedish Academy of Sciences, our warmest congratulations." With that, Schelling walked to the center of the stage and shook hands with the king as he accepted the medal and certificate. He then bowed to the guests onstage and turned to the elegantly dressed audience of 1,600, who were giving him the customary standing ovation while trumpets echoed from one side of the stage to the other. It was recognition of a life spent in reflection, the moment his 84 years had been leading to, now arrived.

CHAPTER 27

POSTSCRIPT

Tom Schelling is a scholar who has spent much of his life in the secluded world of intellectuals. The ivory tower world is often characterized by the anti-intellectual general public as filled with impractical and out-of-touch professors who have their heads in the clouds and couldn't tell you the time of day. That wasn't true of Tom Schelling. His head was never in the clouds; he saw the clouds clearly, and they were mushroom-shaped. He knew the time of day, because it was on the Doomsday Clock.

The importance of the strategists' role is unquestionable—whispering in the ears of the decision-makers or writing the papers they would see, defining the situations and problems that exist, presenting options and ways for survival or exploitation, remaining rational in a world where other interests and fears often hold sway. The individual responsibility for the advice they gave is real, but there was ambiguity in how that responsibility could be assigned to them and difficulty in determining how successful, in the end, their advice really was.

What the great strategists like Schelling sought to accomplish with the Russians was achieved—the *Gotterdammerung*, the fiery twilight of the gods, never descended to destroy mankind. On the surface, they were successes. The people who took the strategists' advice appear to have been wise and to have chosen the correct policies. Yet as Schelling notes, "Whether it was successful, in that the Soviets had something in mind and we successfully deterred them from it, we really don't know."

Deterrence had worked. While specific examples, such as incidents like Berlin, can be cited, it is the overall check on the Soviets and their philosophy of expansion that makes it difficult to assess that period of history in any other way. From the beginning of the Cold War, the Soviets sought to add to the territory under their control, as well as to increase the number of adherents to their beliefs. The communists' spectacular success was in Asia, but they made far fewer inroads in the areas critical to the United States' sphere of influence. Although it would be impossible to sort out the degree to which the success of deterrence was a direct result of the civilian strategists' work, the use of their concepts and their impact as consultants were basic to the struggle. That can be said of Tom Schelling as much as it can be said of any of them.

Schelling's best-known strategic work had come in the Cold War years during the tense era of conflict between Russia and the United States. He has been described as the "father of deterrence strategy." America's strategy for survival during the years of threatened Soviet expansion was deterrence, and the acknowledgement of his role is good reason for him to feel pride and satisfaction.

Schelling the strategist has always been the public servant, but never a public figure. He has spent his adult life in the shadows, in the background. There are those who know him and realize the role he has played, but that number is small—a typical situation for the elite civilian strategists who helped shape American nuclear policy in the Cold War world. According to a RAND Corporation document, Schelling "established the basic conceptual structure of deterrence theory."[166] Until winning the Nobel Prize, however, Schelling hadn't received much recognition for this achievement outside an esoteric circle of academics and a small group of Washington insiders. The future Nobel laureate was just the friendly man people passed by, unaware of the magnitude of the impact of his ideas—a pleasant, trim figure wearing black pants and a white cotton shirt, driving his Honda Civic to his home in suburban D.C.

Tom Schelling the strategist did what needed to be done. Like many civilian nuclear strategists, he did some of his most important work in the secret think-tank world of RAND, where the separation of analysts from the public was intentional and successful. It was with these strategists that the boundaries between policy analyst, policy advisor, and policy maker were sometimes blurred. Schelling saw himself as an analyst, though the distinctions couldn't always be maintained. Putting so much decision-making influence into an isolated and unaccountable fraternity of scholars was a choice called for by the times. There were Schelling and his colleagues, the strategists who could meet the life-and-death Cold War challenges, and the burden was on them as scholars and as men of morals and courage.

Tom Schelling's definition of his role as a strategist was to identify and treat questions of policy as rational problems or puzzles to be solved. Once he had found the most reasonable solutions to the puzzles, he might consider ideas that would effectively apply practical policies to his solution. Always logical and imaginative, his innovative ideas frequently led others to consider new policies of their own. His honesty was that of a true scholar: Schelling always presented his ideas as they were, never tailoring them to suit a particular agenda. Rational thought without preconceived outcomes was a quality he considered essential in a strategist, whether addressing the issue of thermonuclear war, segregation, or global warming. Understanding mattered more than causes. There are those who considered his view too detached, too unfeeling, that Schelling was missing true commitment; Schelling himself believed that understanding was the key to any meaningful change, the starting point.

Schelling provided ideas and basic strategies, emphasizing forms of bargaining, frequently through signals, and often approaching problems with the use of game theory. Throughout the Cold War years, his purpose was consistent: He worked to prevent war, and if war were to happen, to make it less damaging. His strategic-bargaining methods continued to show up after the Cold War, in his view of self-control as a bargaining exercise between one's present and future self, for example.

As the years have passed, Tom's relationship with Alice has helped keep him young, and the twinkle in his eye radiates happiness. They exercise regularly, and Alice's hip replacement has not slowed her down. He moves with a spring in his step unusual for a man his age. The crew cut he's sported since the 1950s gives everything he does a more youthful look—an appearance only enhanced by his ever-present running shoes.

Schelling at the center of all 2005 Nobel Prize Winners assembled for a group photo. Left to right: John L. Hall, Robert J. Aumann, Roy J. Glauber, Richard R. Schrock, Thomas C. Schelling, Robert H. Grubbs, J. Robin Warren, Theodor W. Hänsch, Yves Chauvin, Barry J. Marshall, Mohamed ElBaradei, and Yukiya Amano, representing IAEA.

Schelling's was a long career, and in the spring of 2003 he retired from teaching. (He defines retirement as "being home for lunch with my wife.") The year Schelling was to leave Harvard, Paul Samuelson offered a fitting tribute: "In Japan Thomas Schelling would be named a national treasure. Age cannot slow down his creativity, nor custom stale his infinite variety."[167]

Schelling's influence carries on, and his methods don't change. Beginning with his interest in the Great Depression, Schelling has viewed society's problems, crises, and ills as puzzles. With a puzzle's solution comes understanding, and from understanding can come policy. Whether considering climate change, self-control, or even the fate of humanity in the nuclear confrontation of the Cold War, it has been the joy of thinking about things, about the effects of various decisions and how strategies work, that has motivated him and kept him going. Describing the quality that makes Schelling unique and his story compelling, friend and colleague Richard Zeckhauser said, "As much as any social scientist alive, Tom Schelling's work shows that ideas matter."

Thomas C. Schelling came to the aid of his country at a time when it was most necessary. There were heroes to rally around during those years when the struggle was the most difficult and the hours the most tense. There were also silent heroes in the shadows, their stories rarely told. The strategies that guided the struggle came from somewhere—the big themes didn't just appear. Deterrence, "mutually assured destruction," signaled communication, the hotline, arms control . . . these are the ideas Schelling's work and thought influenced. This is what Schelling, the great civilian strategist, achieved in the background, out of the public eye.

Now the public eye has discovered him, and the long overdue recognition is well-deserved. He is an American hero for our times.

Endnotes

1. The story of the *Vanguard* launch and a number of the other 1950s anecdotal events come from Eric F. Goldman, *The Crucial Decade and After, America 1945–60* (New York: Vantage Books-Random House, 1960).
2. Paul Samuelson letter to Richard Zeckhauser, 1989.
3. Thomas C. Schelling, *The Strategy of Conflict* (Cambridge, MA: Harvard Press, 1960).
4. The Royal Academy of Sciences Press Release: "The Bank of Sweden Prize in Economic Sciences in Memory of Alfred Nobel 2005." Online, October 10, 2005.
5. Edison quote, from Lewis D. Eigen and Jonathan P. Siegel, *The Macmillan Dictionary of Political Quotations* (New York: Macmillan Publishing, 1993), 16.
6. Thomas Schelling, interviewed by Robert Dodge, June 8, 2000.
7. Ibid.
8. Ibid.
9. Ibid.
10. Ibid.
11. Ibid.
12. Thomas Schelling, interviewed by Robert Dodge, June 22, 2000.
13. Ibid.
14. Thomas Schelling, interviewed by Robert Dodge, June 27, 2000.
15. Schelling described Fellner as one of the people who had been truly influential in his life; Thomas Schelling, interviewed by Robert Dodge, June 27, 2000.
16. Thomas Schelling, interviewed by Robert Dodge, July 2, 2002.
17. Thomas C. Schelling, "Raise Profits by Raising Wages?" *Econometrica*, July 1946.
18. James Tobin letter to Richard Zeckhauser, 1989.
19. The Marshall Plan had been organized after Secretary of State Marshall created a panel, the Policy Planning Staff, to analyze alternatives and prepare suggestions for dealing with poverty, and the resultant hunger and desperation that permeated Europe. George Keenan chaired the Policy Planning Staff and is often given nearly total credit for the creation of the Plan. Schelling disagrees with this evaluation, and said, "Well, he took a lot of credit for it. I think it's one of those things that had a lot of fathers." (Thomas Schelling, interviewed by Robert Dodge, June 9, 2000).

20. Peter Martin, *Questions of Evidence, the Twentieth Century World* (London: Century Hutchinson).

21. Thomas Schelling, interviewed by Robert Dodge, June 14, 2000.

22. References throughout to the changing time on the Doomsday Clock come from Mike Moore, "Midnight Never Came," *Education Foundation for Nuclear Science*, 1995. Online: www.thebulletin.org/article.php?art_ofn=nd95moore.

23. Thomas Schelling, interviewed by Robert Dodge, June 8, 2000.

24. ———, June 9, 2000.

25. Thomas C. Schelling, *National Income Behavior: An Introduction to Algebraic Analysis* (New York: McGraw-Hill, 1951).

26. Robert Solow's description of Schelling's writing comes from letter to Richard Zeckhauser, 1989.

27. *The Crucial Decade*, 137.

28. Thomas Schelling, interviewed by Robert Dodge, June 14, 2000.

29. Letter to Richard Zeckhauser for inclusion in "Distinguished Fellow: Reflections on Thomas Schelling," *Journal of Economic Perspectives* 3, no. 2 (September 1989), 153–164.

30. *The Strategy of Conflict*, 22.

31. Ibid., 48.

32. Thomas Schelling, interviewed by Robert Dodge, June 27, 2000.

33. Steven Pearlstein, *The Washington Post*, October 12, 1994, F01.

34. John von Neumann and Oskar Morgenstern, *Theory of Games and Economic Behavior* (Princeton: Princeton University Press, 1944).

35. Thomas Schelling, interviewed by Robert Dodge, June 14, 2000.

36. An interesting and quick look at statistics involving the U.S. nuclear program over the years is available online at http://www.cdi.org/nuclear/facts-at-a-glance.cfm

37. *The Strategy of Conflict*, 60.

38. Thomas Schelling, interviewed by Robert Dodge, June 23, 2000.

39. James Tobin letter to Zeckhauser.

40. Thomas Schelling, interviewed by Robert Dodge, June 8, 2000.

41. RAND's purpose, according to its incorporation, "50 Years of Service to the Nation." See online at www.rand.org/about/history.

42. Daniel Ellsberg interviewed by Robert Dodge, summer 2002.

43. Review of Kahn's *On Thermonuclear War* in Frankel, Benjamin, ed. *The Cold War, 1945–1991. Volume I, Leaders and Other Figures in the United States and Western Europe.* (Washington, D.C.: Gale Research, 1992).

44. Daniel Ellsberg, telephone interview with Robert Dodge, July 1, 2001.

45. Thomas Schelling, interviewed by Robert Dodge, June 9, 2000.

46. "Von Neumann: Architect of the Computer Age," *Financial Times*, December 24, 1999.

47. Robert Keohane, ed. *Neorealism and Its Critics.* (New York: Columbia University Press, 1986), 175.

48. For a similar Schelling discussion of the limitations on game theory, see *Choice and Consequence: Perspectives of an Errant Economist,* (Cambridge, MA: Harvard University Press, 2006), 214–215.

49. For a more complete discussion of the criticism of rational-choice theory, see Donald P. Green and Ian Shapiro, "Pathologies Revisited: Reflections On Our Critics" in *The Rational Choice Controversy,* Jeffrey Friedman, ed. (New Haven: Yale University Press, 1996).

50. *The Crucial Decade,* 311.

51. Thomas Schelling, interviewed by Robert Dodge, July 1, 2002. It was during this London summer that his writing began to exhibit his understanding and the refining of his ideas on game theory. He wrote an article, "The Strategy of Conflict: Prospectus for a Reorientation of Game Theory," that was published in *Journal of Conflict Resolution* 2, no. 3 (August 1958) and that was later included in *The Strategy of Conflict.*

52. Paul Samuelson letter to Richard Zeckhauser, 1989.

53. Malvina Reynolds, "RAND Hymn." Schroeder Music Company, 1961, recorded by Pete Seeger.

54. David Jardini, "Commemoration of 50th of Project RAND" (diss., Carnegie Mellon University University), 1996. Also see online at www.rand.org/publications/PAFbook.pdf.

55. Alain Enthoven's memories of Schelling at RAND: letter to Richard Zeckhauser, 1989.

56. *The Strategy of Conflict,* 207.

57. Ibid., 233.

58. Thomas Schelling, interviewed by Robert Dodge, June 17, 2000. He mentioned an idea similar to the Quaker proposal for the exchange of kindergarten-age students in *The Strategy of Conflict,* 136.

59. Peter George, *Red Alert* (New York: Rosetta Books, 1958).

60. Thomas C. Schelling, *International Economics* (Allen and Bacon: 1958).

61. Nobel Prize Committee 2005 Press announcement of October 10, 2005.

62. Antoine de Saint Exupery, *Terre des Hommes, III* (L'Avion: 1939), 60.

63. Observations on life at the center come from Morton Halperin, interview with Robert Dodge, Washington, D.C., June 26, 2002.

64. "Commemoration of 50th of Project RAND," 43.

65. Tyler Cowen, "Thomas Schelling, New Nobel Laureate," online at www.marginalrevolution.com/marginalrevolution/2005/10/schelling_and_a_1.html.

66. Pat Frank, *Alas, Babylon* (New York: HarperCollins, 1959).

67. Neville Shute, *On the Beach* (New York: Ballantine Books, 1957).

68. Since being awarded the Nobel Prize, recognition of Schelling's role in the development has reached public attention. Schelling published his hotline proposal, *World Politics* 23, no. 1 (October 1960): "two versatile, flexible, observation and communication forces." The hotline was to prove valuable in doing precisely what it had been intended for. Its use prevented possible mis-

understandings between the United States and the Soviet Union concerning U.S. fleet movements in the Mediterranean during the 1967 Arab–Israeli War, thereby avoiding a situation that could have become perilous. It has swung to something it wasn't, as in Kim Clark's "In Praise of Original Thought," in *US News and World Report*, October 24, 2005, where she writes, "Schelling applied abstract game theory to persuade John F. Kennedy to install a hotline to the Kremlin so that misunderstandings wouldn't set off a nuclear conflagration." Abstract game theory really wasn't involved. It was something that seemed painfully obvious.

69. Richard Reeves, *President Kennedy: Profile of Power* (New York: Simon & Schuster, 1993).

70. Ibid., 38.

71. "Game Theory Suggests Quick Action on Greenhouse Effect Is Remote," *The Washington Post*, June 13, 1990, b03.

72. Robert McNamara, et. al., *Argument Without End: in Search of Answers to the Vietnam Tragedy* (New York: Public Affairs, 1999), 169.

73. *The Strategy of Conflict*, 248.

74. Thomas C. Schelling, "Arms Control: Proposal for a Special Surveillance Force," *World Politics* 23, no. 1 (October 1960).

75. *President Kennedy*, 68.

76. Thomas Schelling, interviewed by Robert Dodge, June 17, 2000.

77. Bundy's notes say Schelling's paper made a big impression on the president: Reeves, Richard. *President Kennedy: Profile of Power*, 197. Further discussion of this influence is found in Ebrahim Afsah, "Creed, Cabal or Conspiracy— the Origins of the current Neo-Conservative Thinking in US Strategic Thinking," *German Law Journal*, online at www.germanlawjournal.com/article .php?id=312.

78. *President Kennedy*, 201.

79. Robert McNamara letter to Robert Dodge.

80. Arthur M. Schlesinger Jr., *Robert Kennedy and His Times*, (Boston: Houghton Mifflin, 1978), 504.

81. Ernest R. May and Philip D. Zelikow, eds. *The Kennedy Tapes: Inside the White House During the Cuban Missile Crisis* (Cambridge, MA: Harvard University Press, 1997). Citations used are: Hans S. Kroll, Lebenserinnerungen eines Botschafters Cologne: Kiepenheuer & Witsch, 1967, 524–527. *FRUS 1961–1963*, 6:57.

82. Thomas Schelling, interviewed by Robert Dodge, June 23, 2000.

83. Most of discussion of war games is from Thomas Schelling, interviewed by Robert Dodge, June 17, 2000.

84. "Well, how could we do it?" is obviously Schelling's recollection.

85. Thomas Schelling, interviewed by Robert Dodge, June 17, 2000.

86. Thomas C. Schelling and Morton H. Halperin, *Strategy and Arms Control* (New York: Twentieth Century Fund, 1961).

87. Information about Schelling's arms control ideas comes in part from Morton Halperin interview with Robert Dodge, Washington, D.C., June 26, 2002.
88. Thomas Schelling, interviewed by Robert Dodge, June 27, 2000.
89. Ibid.
90. Francis Bator, interviewed by Robert Dodge, Cambridge, MA, October 9, 2002.
91. Carnesale was a guest speaker for a course entitled, "International Relations" at John F. Kennedy School of Government in spring of 1990 when he made this comment. Schelling's importance to theory of negotiations behind successful efforts was reaffirmed by Carnesale during telephone interview with Robert Dodge on July 28, 2000.
92. Fred Kaplan, "All Pain, No Gain," posted online by Slate on October 11, 2005.
93. ———, *The Wizards of Armageddon* (Stanford, CA: Stanford University Press, 1983).
94. Thomas Schelling, interviewed by Robert Dodge, June 23, 2000.
95. ———, July 1, 2002.
96. David Warsh, "Game Theory Suggests Quick Action on Greenhouse Effect Is Remote," *The Washington Post*, June 13, 1990, B03.
97. Robert McNamara letter to Robert Dodge.
98. Thomas Schelling, interviewed by Robert Dodge, June 27, 2000.
99. *Argument Without End*, 170.
100. Joseph Nye email to Robert Dodge, June 6, 2001.
101. Thomas Schelling, interviewed by Robert Dodge, June 17, 2000.
102. Schelling's conclusions on organized crime were first published in Thomas C. Schelling, "What Is the Business of Organized Crime?" *Journal of Public Law* 20, no. 1 (1971).
103. Schelling's tipping models for racial segregation were first included in "Strategic Theory and Its Applications," *The American Economic Review* 59, no. 2 (May 1969).
104. Malcolm Gladwell, *The Tipping Point: How Little Things Can Make a Big Difference* (New York: Back Bay Books / Little, Brown and Company, 2002).
105. For a more in depth discussion of tipping, see Thomas C. Schelling, *Micromotives and Macrobehavior* (New York: W.W. Norton & Company, 1978).
106. Amb Mark Hong, "Singapore's Success in Creating Racial and Religious Harmony." Online at http://sam11.moe.gov.sg/racialharmony.
107. Lee Kwan Yew letter to Robert Dodge, August 28, 2000.
108. Lee Hsien Loong, interviewed by Robert Dodge, Singapore, August 29, 2000.
109. Ibid. (continuing Lee comments are from the same interview).
110. Lee Kwan Yew letter to Robert Dodge, August 28, 2000.
111. Defense Department study: "Pentagon study: 'Irrational' nuclear policy a deterrent." CNN News. Online, March 1, 1998.
112. Thomas Schelling email to Robert Dodge, May 2003.
113. Jonathan Schnell, "Letter from Ground Zero: Madmen." *The Nation*, May 2003.

114. Thomas Schelling email to Robert Dodge, May 2003.

115. Thomas Schelling, interviewed by Robert Dodge, June 23, 2000.

116. ———, June 27, 2000.

117. Glenn Loury, interviewed by Robert Dodge, Boston, July 23, 2002.

118. Richard Zeckhauser, interviewed by Robert Dodge, Cambridge, MA, July 19, 2002.

119. Ellsberg and morality discussion, based on interviews with Robert Dodge in 2001.

120. Thomas Schelling email to Robert Dodge, May 2003.

121. Morton Halperin interview with Robert Dodge, Washington, D.C., June 26, 2002.

122. The discussion of Schelling's work and questions it raises are included in the work of David Andrew May, "The RAND CORPORATION and the Dynamics of American Strategic Thought, 1946–1962" (diss. Emory University, 1998).

123. Francis Bator, interviewed by Robert Dodge, Cambridge, MA, October 9, 2002.

124. Thomas Schelling, interviewed by Robert Dodge, June 23, 2000.

125. Nathan Glazer letter to Richard Zeckhauser 1989.

126. This is Schelling's recollection of the encounter with Kissinger: Thomas Schelling, interviewed by Robert Dodge, June 20, 2000.

127. Henry Kissinger, *White House Years* (Boston: Little, Brown and Company, 1979), 555.

128. When the *Harvard Crimson* retold the story, they were closer to Schelling's account. Nathaniel L. Schwartz and Robert K. Silverman, "White House Whiz Kid: Kissinger Serves World But Still Leaves Harvard Behind." *Harvard Crimson,* June 5, 2000.

129. Francis Bator, interviewed by Robert Dodge, Cambridge, MA, October 9, 2002.

130. The story of McNaughton, Halperin, and Ellsberg comes from several sources. Seymour M. Hersh, "Kissinger and Nixon in the White House," *Atlantic Monthly,* May 1982, is thorough on Halperin and Ellsberg. The story of McNaughton's background comes from Morten Halperin and Schelling. Additional information comes from Daniel Ellsberg.

131. Daniel Ellsberg. Book inscription to Thomas Schelling in *Risk, Ambiguity and Decision* (New York: Garland Publishing, 2001).

132. Thomas Schelling, interviewed by Robert Dodge, June 23, 2000.

133. Thomas C. Shelling, "The Intimate Contest for Self-Control," *Public Interest,* September 1980.

134. Derek Bok, interviewed by Robert Dodge, Cambridge, MA, July 39, 2002.

135. A development of awareness of global warming issue traced in Thomas C. Schelling, "The Environmental Challenges of Power Generation." *Energy Journal* 19, no. 2, (1998).

136. Thomas Schelling, interviewed by Robert Dodge, June 21, 2000.
137. Thomas C. Schelling, "Some Economics of Global Warming," *The American Economic Review* 82, no. 1 (March 1992).
138. Charles Hitch letter to Richard Zeckhauser, 1989.
139. Thomas Moore Gale, "Prepared Statement of Thomas Gale Moore Senior Fellow, Hoover Institution Before the House Science Committee Subcommittee on Energy and Environment," November 16, 1995.
140. William O'Keefe, "Prepared Statement Before the House Government Reform and Oversight Committee National Economic Growth, Natural Resources and Regulatory Affairs," September 16, 1998.
141. Raymond J. Keating, "Prepared Statement by Raymond J. Keating Chief Economist for the Small Business Survival Committee Hearing on the Kyoto Protocol to the United Nations Framework Convention on Climate Change," June 4, 1998.
142. Schelling's use of models in social science can be seen in part as an outgrowth of the influence of the early years studying with William Fellner. For a more complete explanation of the models presented here, see Schelling's *Micromotives and Macrobehavior* (New York: W.W. Norton & Company, 1978).
143. Derek Bok email to Robert Dodge, June 8, 2001.
144. David Ellwood: Kennedy School News, online at ksg.harvard.edu/ksgnews.
145. Glenn Loury, interviewed by Robert Dodge, Boston, July 23, 2002.
146. Herman "Dutch" Leonard email to Robert Dodge, June 8, 2001.
147. Michael M. Spence, "Thomas Schelling," autobiography for the Nobel Foundation.
148. Richard Zeckhauser, interviewed by Robert Dodge, Cambridge, MA, June 29, 2002.
149. Connie Higgins, interviewed by Robert Dodge, Cambridge, MA, June 29, 2002.
150. Herman "Dutch" Leonard email to Robert Dodge, June 8, 2001.
151. Glenn Loury, interviewed by Robert Dodge, Boston, July 23, 2002.
152. Robert Putnam email to Robert Dodge, June 11, 2001.
153. Thomas Schelling, interviewed by Robert Dodge, July 20, 2000.
154. Siddharth Mohandas email to Robert Dodge, May 2006.
155. Thomas C. Schelling, interviewed by Robert Dodge, July 20, 2000.
156. ———, June 23, 2000.
157. ———, June 27, 2000.
158. Discussion of the 1994 Prize decision comes in part from Sylvia Nassar, *A Beautiful Mind* (New York: Simon & Schuster, 1998).
159. Steven Pearlstein, "3 Economists Win Nobel for Gauging Game Theory's Business Role," *The Washington Post,* October 12, 1994, F01.
160. David Warsh, "A Phone That Didn't Ring," *Boston Globe,* October 12, 1994.
161. Thomas Schelling, interviewed by Robert Dodge, June 27, 2002.

162. Ibid.
163. Daniel Ellsberg telephone interview with Robert Dodge, July 20, 2001.
164. Fareed Zakaria, "Don't Oversell Missile Defense," *Newsweek,* May 14, 2001, 34.
165. Thomas Schelling email to Robert Dodge, October 27, 2005.
166. "Commemoration of 50th Anniversary of Project RAND," 43.
167. Paul Samuelson letter to Richard Zeckhauser, 1989

Sources

This story comes primarily from the recollections of Tom Schelling. The ideas we discussed are not cited specifically. Quotes and quoted work from his written works are. The material comes from interviews that were done at Schelling's home in Bethesda, Maryland, on June 8, 9, 14, 17, 20, 21, 23, 27 of 2000; July 18, December 22, 27 of 2001; and July 2 of 2002.

Email exchanges and visits took place throughout and after up to the time of completion in 2006. Comments from his interviews are cited by date. Most general historical information is not included in the notes.

Interviews:

Francis Bator, John F. Kennedy School of Government, Harvard University; Deputy National Security Advisor to President Lyndon Johnson.

Derek Bok, John F. Kennedy School of Government, Harvard University; President, Harvard University 1971–1991.

Al Carnesale, Chancellor of UCLA, member of U.S. negotiating team for ABM Treaty and Strategic Arms Limitations Treaty (SALT I).

James Digby, senior staff member at RAND, where he has been since 1949.

Daniel Ellsberg (3), policy analyst who released Pentagon Papers.

Morton Halperin, Senior Staff of National Security Council in Nixon Administration, advisor in administrations of Presidents Lyndon Johnson and Bill Clinton.

Connie Higgins, Tom Schelling's secretary at Kennedy School at Harvard University

Lee Hsien Loong, Prime Minister of Singapore.

Glenn Loury, Professor of Economics, Boston University; formerly at John F. Kennedy School of Government, Harvard University.

Tom Schelling (12).

Richard Zeckhauser, Professor of Political Economy, John F. Kennedy School of Government, Harvard University.

Letters:

To Robert Dodge:

Lee Kuan Yew, Minister Mentor, 2004–present; Senior Minister of Singapore, 1990–2004; Prime Minister of Singapore 1959–1990

Robert McNamara, U.S. Secretary of Defense 1961–1968

To Richard Zeckhauser (courtesy of Richard Zeckhauser):

Alain Enthoven, Stanford Graduate School of Business, Economist with RAND, Deputy Assistant Secretary of Defense.

Nathan Glazer, Harvard Graduate School of Education.

Charles Lindblom, Professor of Economics and Political Science, Yale University; past President of American Political Science Association.

Paul Samuelson, Nobel Prize winner in Economics, 1970.

Robert Solow, Nobel Prize winner in Economics, 1987.

A. Michael Spence, Nobel Prize winner in Economics, 2001.

James Tobin, Nobel Prize winner in Economics, 1981.

Email:

Derek Bok, John F. Kennedy School of Government, Harvard University.

Donald Green, Professor of Political Science and Director of Institute for Social and Policy Studies, Yale University.

David M. Kennedy, Donald K. MacLachlan Professor of History at Stanford University, winner of the 2000 Pulitzer Prize in History for *Freedom from Fear.*

Herman "Dutch" Leonard, Professor of Public Management, John F. Kennedy School of Government, Harvard University.

Siddharth Mohandas, former Assistant Editor of *Foreign Affairs.*

Richard Neustadt, Professor of Government, John F. Kennedy School of Government, Harvard University; advisor to Truman, Kennedy, and Johnson administrations.

Joseph Nye, Dean of John F. Kennedy School of Government, Harvard University; Assistant Secretary of Defense, Chair of National Intelligence Council.

Robert Putnam, Professor of Public Policy, John F. Kennedy School of Government, Harvard University; Dean of John F. Kennedy School 1989–1991.

Thomas Schelling.

James Q. Wilson, Professor of Public Policy, Pepperdine University; formerly of Harvard; government advisor from the 1960s to the 1990s; Trustee of RAND.

Dissertations:

Ayson, Robert. *Thomas Schelling and the Concept of Stability.* Diss. King's College London, 1996.

Jardini, David. *Commemoration of 50th Anniversary of Project RAND.* Diss. Carnegie Mellon University University, 1996.

May, Andrew David. *The RAND CORPORATION and the Dynamics of American Strategic Thought, 1946–1962.* Diss. Emory University, 1998.

Books:

Bierman, Scott H. and Louis Fernandez. *Game Theory with Economic Applications.* Reading, MA: Addison-Wesley, 1998.

Chang, Lawrence, and Peter Kornbluh. *The Cuban Missile Crisis, 1962.* New York: New Press, 1992.

Craig, Campbell. *Destroying the Village: Eisenhower and Thermonuclear War; Epilogue: McNamara's Dialectic.* New York: Columbia University Press, 1998. Columbia International Affairs online.

Eaton, John, Milgate Murray, Peter Newman, eds. 1987. *The New Palgrave: Game Theory.* New York: W.W. Norton.

Frankel, Benjamin, ed. 1992. *The Cold War, 1945–1991.* Volumes 1–3. Washington, D.C.: Gale Research.

Friedman, Jeffrey, ed. 1996. *The Rational Choice Controversy.* New Haven: Yale University Press.

Gaddis, John Lewis. *Strategies of Containment.* Oxford: Oxford University Press, 1982.

Goldman, Eric F. *The Crucial Decade—And After, America, 1945–1960.* New York: Vantage Books-Random House, 1960.

Issacson, Walter. *Kissinger, A Biography.* New York: Touchtone, 1992.

Kaplan, Fred. *The Wizards of Armageddon.* New York: Simon & Schuster, 1983.

Keohane, Robert O., ed. 1986. *Neorealism and Its Critics.* New York: Columbia University Press.

Kissinger, Henry. *White House Years.* Boston: Little, Brown and Company, 1979.

Manchester, William. *The Glory and the Dream: a Narrative History of America, 1932–1972.* Toronto: Bantam Books, 1974.

May, Ernest R. and Philip D. Zelikow, eds. 1997. *The Kennedy Tapes: Inside the WhiteHouse During the Cuban Missile Crisis.* Cambridge, MA: Harvard University Press.

McNamara, Robert, et. al. *Argument Without End: in Search of Answers to the Vietnam Tragedy.* New York: Public Affairs, 1999.

Nassar, Sylvia. *A Beautiful Mind.* New York: Simon & Schuster, 1998.

Poundstone, William. *Prisoner's Dilemma.* New York: Doubleday, 1992.

Reeves, Richard. *President Kennedy: Profile of Power.* New York: Simon & Schuster, 1994.

Schelling, Thomas C. *Arms and Influence.* New Haven: Yale University Press, 1966.

———. *Choice and Consequence.* Cambridge, MA: Harvard University Press, 1984.

———. *Micromotives and Macrobehavior.* New York: W.W. Norton & Company, 1978.

———. and Morton H. Halperin. *Strategy and Arms Control.* New York: Twentieth Century Fund, 1961.

———. *The Strategy of Conflict*. 1960. Cambridge, MA: Harvard University Press, 1980.

Schlessinger, Arthur M. Jr. *Robert Kennedy and His Times*. Boston: Houghton Mifflin Company, 1978.

———. *A Thousand Days, John F. Kennedy in the White House*. Boston: Houghton-Mifflin, 1965.

Vasil, Raj. *Asianising Singapore*. Singapore, Institute of Southeast Asian Studies, 1995.

Zeckhauser, Richard, ed. 1993. *Strategy and Choice*. Cambridge, MA: MIT Press.

Congressional Testimony:

Gale, Thomas Moore. "Prepared Statement of Thomas Gale Moore Senior Fellow, Hoover Institution Before the House Science Committee Subcommittee on Energy and Environment." November 16, 1995.

O'Keefe, William. "Prepared Statement Before the House Government Reform and Oversight Committee National Economic Growth, Natural Resources and Regulatory Affairs." September 16, 1998.

Schelling, Thomas C. "Testimony to the Senate Subcommittee on Energy, Nuclear Proliferation, and Government Processes." July 3, 1981.

Addresses:

Schelling, Thomas C., "Self-Command in Practice, in Policy, and in a Theory of Rational Choice," *The American Economic Review* 74, no. 2 (May 1–11, 1984). (Richard T. Ely Lecture, 1984)

———. "Distinguished Scholar-Teacher Lecture." College Park, MD, University of Maryland. April 19, 1995

———. "An Astonishing Sixty Years." Nobel Lecture, Stockholm, Sweden. December 8, 2005.

Television:

"Conversation with Arjo Klammer," Featuring Thomas Schelling. Television video series. National Economics Club, May 23, 1996.

Friedberg, Erhard. Interview with Thomas Schelling. Public Television.

Note:

Ellsberg, Daniel. Book inscription to Thomas Schelling in *Risk, Ambiguity and Decision*, by Daniel Ellsberg. New York: Garland Publishing, 2001.

Other Writings:

"50 Facts about Nuclear War." The Brookings Institute. Online, June 25, 2006.

"50 Years of Service to the Nation." The RAND Corporation. Available online.

Associated Press, "Nobel Prize Co-Winner—Schelling," *New York Times*, October 10, 2005.

———. "Nobel Prize Winner Urges Deterrence." *New York Times*, October 10, 2005.

"The Bank of Sweden Prize in Economic Sciences in Memory of Alfred Nobel." Nobel Prize Organization, 2005. Available online.

Chandler, Clay. "The 60-Watt Mind-Set Human Factors Hold Off Energy Efficiency." *The Washington Post*, A01, November 14, 1997.

Cooler, Kenneth J. "Nuclear Dilemmas India New Power Raises Crucial Questions." *The Washington Post*, A01, May 25, 1998.

Cowen, Tyler. "Thomas Schelling, New Nobel Laureate: Note my biases, Schelling was my Harvard mentor." Available online.

"Dubious Achievement Awards," *Esquire*, February 2006.

Finnon, Dominique, "Discussion of Thomas Schelling's Paper 'The Environmental Challenges of Power Generation,'" *Energy Journal* 19, no. 2 (1998).

Galbraith, James K., "Did the U.S. Military Plan a Nuclear Strike for 1963?" *The American Prospect*. Available online.

Gehring, Verna, "The Nuclear Taboo," *Institute for Philosophy and Public Policy*. College Park: University of Maryland. Available online.

Green, Donald P. and Ian Shapiro. "Pathologies Revisited: Reflections On Our Critics" in *The Rational Choice Controversy*, Jeffrey Friedman, ed. New Haven: Yale University Press, 1996.

Hersh, Seymour M., "Kissinger and Nixon in the White House," *Atlantic Monthly*, May 1982.

Henderson, D.A., "Bioterrorism as a Public Health Threat," *Emerging Infectious Diseases* 4, no. 3 (July–September 1998).

Henderson, Nell. "Retired U-Md Wins Nobel." *The Washington Post*, A01, October 11.

Ignatius, David. "Madman's Bluff: Why Deterrence Still Works," *The Washington Post*, C01, May 10, 1992.

"Kennedy School Luminary Wins Nobel Prize," *Harvard University Gazette*, October 13, 2005.

Launius, Roger D. "Sputnik and the Origins of the Space Age," NASA History Homepage. Available online.

Medalia, Jonathan. "Nuclear Weapons: Comprehensive Test Ban Treaty," Congressional Research Study. Available online 2005.

Meyerson, Roger B., "Nash Equilibrium and the History of Economic Theory," *Journal of Economic Literature* 36:1067–1082 (1999). Available online.

More, Mike, "Midnight Never Came: For Nearly Five Decades the Bulletin Clock has Told the World What Time it Is," *Education Foundation for Nuclear Science*, 1995. The History of the Doomsday Clock, available online.

Nacht, Michael, "Teaching Our Future Policy Makers," letter to the editor, *The Washington Post*, A10, July 8, 1991.

Passell, Peter. "Here's Food for Thought; Cutting Waste Can Be a Waste." *New York Times*, September 21, 1997.

———. "Global Warming: How Fast to Cut Back? Two Views; Until Payoff Is Clear, Haste Means Big Waste." *New York Times*, December 1, 1997

Pearlstein, Steven. "3 Economists Win Nobel for Gauging Game Theory's Business Role." *The Washington Post*, F01, October 12, 1994

"Pentagon study: 'Irrational' nuclear policy a deterrent." *CNN News*. Available online, March 1, 1998.

Richissin, Todd. "Nobel Winner Savors Honor." *Baltimore Sun*, December 11, 2005.

Quester, George H., "If the Nuclear Taboo Gets Broken," *Naval War College Review* 58, no. 2 (Spring 2005): 71–91.

Raiffa, Howard. "Distinguished Fellow: Reflections on Thomas Schelling." *Journal of Economic Perspectives*, Spring, 1989, 156.

Rowe, Peter. "2 Grads of SD Schools Share in Nobel Rarity." *San Diego Union Tribune*, October 15, 2005.

The Royal Academy of Sciences Press Release: "Nobel Prize Committee, he set forth: The Bank of Sweden Prize in Economic Sciences in Memory of Alfred Nobel 2005." Available online, October 10, 2005.

Sampson, Charles S., ed., LaFantasie, Glenn W., gen. ed. "Berlin Crisis, 1961–1962," *Foreign Relations of the United States, 1961–1963*, vol. 14, United States Government Printing Office, Washington, 1993.

Schelling, Thomas C., "Some Economics of Global Warming," *The American Economic Review*, March 1992: 1–14.

——— and William Fellner, "Establishing Credibility: Strategic Considerations in Defense of the Credibity Hypothesis." *The American Economic Review*, May 1982.

Schelling, Thomas C., "The Cost of Combating Global Warming: Facing the Tradeoffs." *Foreign Affairs*, 76, no. 6 (November–December, 1997).

———, "The Economic Diplomacy of Geoengineering," *Climate Change*, July 1996.

———, "How to 'No Thyself' All Year Round, Not Just New Year's; How to 'No Thyself' After New Year Is Over." Adapted from summer *Public Interest*, Sunday, Dec. 28, 1980: C1.

———, "What Do Economists Know?" *American Economist*, Spring 1995.

———, "Addictive Drugs: The Cigarette Experience." *Science*, 255, 5043 (Jan. 24, 1992): 430.

———. "It's Getting Warmer." *Wall Street Journal*, February 23, 2006.

———, "Self-Command in Practice, in Policy, and in a Theory of Rational Choice," *The American Economic Review*, May 1984.

————, "Arms Control: Proposal for a Special Surveillance Force," *World Politics*, October, 29, 1960: 11.

————, "Coping Rationally with Lapses from Rationality," *Eastern Economic Journal*, Summer, 1996.

————, "Vietnam: Reflections and Lessons," 4:2 *Asian Journal of Political Science*. Singapore: Times Academic Press, December, 1996, 103–107.

————, "Some Economics of Global Warming," *The American Economic Review* 82, no. 1 (March, 1992).

————, "Raise Profits by Raising Wages?" *Econometrica* 14, no. 3 (July 1946): 227–234.

————, "Strategic Theory and Its Applications," *The American Economic Review* 59, no. 2 (May 1969): 489–496.

————, "The Environmental Challenges of Power Generation," *Energy Journal*, 19, no. 2 (1998).

Schwartz, Nathaniel L. and Robert K. Silverman, "White House Whiz Kid: Kissinger Serves World But Still Leaves Harvard Behind." *Harvard Crimson*, June 5, 2000.

Spence, A. Michael, "Autobiography," *Prix Nobel. The Nobel Prizes 2001*, Editor Tore Frängsmyr, [Nobel Foundation], Stockholm, 2002.

Tannerwald, Nina, "Stigmatizing the Bomb: Origins of the Nuclear Taboo." *International Security* 29, no. 4 (Spring 2005).

Taylor, Steven, "Schelling Shares Nobel Prize." *PoliBlog* online, October 10, 2005.

"Terrorist CBRN: Material and Effects." CIA online.

Tesoro, Jose Manuel, "Icons of the Century: Ideas With Impact; Instant Industry," *Asiaweek*, December 10, 1999.

Tomes, R.R., "Nuclear Strategy, Deterrence, Compellence, and Risk Management Thomas Schelling Meets Joint Vision 2010." Presented for 65th Military Operations Research Symposium Marine Corps Combat Command. June 10–12, 1997.

Warsh, David. "Game Theory Suggests Quick Action on Greenhouse Effect Is Remote." *The Washington Post*, B03, June 13, 1990.

————. "Harvard's Advisors to the Soviets Have Problems of Their Own." *The Washington Post*, B03: June 19, 1991.

————. "A Phone That Didn't Ring." *Boston Globe*, October 12, 1994.

Wohlstetter, John C., "Global Warming: An Advocate Speaks, Calmly," *Letter From the Capitol*, February 27, 2006.

Zakaria, Fareed. "Misapprehensions About Missile." *The Washington Post*, A19, May 7, 2001.

INDEX